FRENCH LIT
AND ITS BAC

D0101797

5

The Late Nineteenth Century

WITHDRAWN

WITHDRAWN

FRENCH LITERATURE
AND ITS
BACKGROUND

EDITED BY

JOHN CRUICKSHANK

5

The Late Nineteenth Century

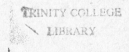
TRINITY COLLEGE
LIBRARY

OXFORD UNIVERSITY PRESS
LONDON   OXFORD   NEW YORK

Oxford University Press, Walton Street, Oxford OX2 6DP

OXFORD LONDON GLASGOW
NEW YORK TORONTO MELBOURNE WELLINGTON
KUALA LUMPUR SINGAPORE JAKARTA HONG KONG TOKYO
DELHI BOMBAY CALCUTTA MADRAS KARACHI
NAIROBI DAR ES SALAAM CAPE TOWN

ISBN 0 19 285033 4

© *Oxford University Press, 1969*

First published as an
Oxford University Press paperback by
Oxford University Press, London, 1969
Reprinted 1975, 1979

All rights reserved. No part of this publication may be reproduced, stored in a retrieval system, or transmitted, in any form or by any means, electronic, mechanical, photocopying, recording, or otherwise, without the prior permission of Oxford University Press

This book is sold subject to the condition that it shall not, by way of trade or otherwise, be lent, re-sold, hired out, or otherwise circulated without the publisher's prior consent in any form of binding or cover other than that in which it is published and without a similar condition including this condition being imposed on the subsequent purchaser

Printed in Great Britain
at the University Press, Oxford
by Eric Buckley
Printer to the University

Contents

Introduction

THIS is the fifth of six volumes appearing under the collective title *French Literature and its Background*. The previous volume in the series, *The Early Nineteenth Century*, dealt with various aspects of French Romanticism and ended with a chapter on Baudelaire. This fifth volume takes up the story from that point, covers the second half of the nineteenth century, and has a final chapter, 'Literature and Ideology', which includes a number of writers active up to the outbreak of the First World War. Some of these writers are discussed again, from a different point of view, in volume six.

As with the other volumes in the series, the aim here has been to investigate certain authors and themes in such a way as to raise questions and challenge assumptions, as well as to convey basic information. This approach is perhaps most noticeable in the chapters on Flaubert and on 'Realism and Reality in the Novel'. In a rather similar spirit, contributors have been left free to follow up their own particular interests and express their own judgements. Thus, for example, Maupassant receives an entire chapter as a short-story writer and Heredia is evaluated more highly as a poet than Leconte de Lisle. Varying critical methods have been adopted towards the different poets discussed. The chapter on Verlaine moves essentially from the particularity of certain key poems to wider considerations; the essay on Rimbaud goes in the reverse direction; the chapter entitled 'Symbolism and Mallarmé' uses both methods in varying degrees. While there are separate chapters on Flaubert, Verlaine, Rimbaud, Maupassant, and Zola, the 'history of ideas' background is also sketched in. Positivism, realism, nationalism, and the Catholic Revival are directly studied in Chapters 1, 3, and 11. Other aspects of the late-nineteenth-century intellectual background are dealt with more indirectly in the chapters on symbolist poetry and the nineteenth-century theatre.

A six-column 'Chronology' is a feature of each of these volumes. In the present case the Chronology again serves a variety of purposes. It enables the reader to relate major French literary works of the second half of the century to (mainly French) historical events, to literary works in English (including some of the better-known works of American literature), to the main European painters and composers of the period, to various works of criticism and aesthetic theory, and to influential European works of ideas from Spencer's *Social Statics* and Comte's *Système de politique positive* to Bergson's *Matière et mémoire* and Durkheim's *Le Suicide*.

JOHN CRUICKSHANK

University of Sussex
August 1968

1. Positivism and its Aftermath

THE period covered by this volume has often been described as 'the age of positivism', a time dominated by the ideas of scientific methodology, determinism, and materialism. Yet the reality was more complex and ambivalent; few periods saw greater intellectual turmoil than the later nineteenth century, or a more marked polarization of attitudes. It included both the most extreme development of positivism—in the 'scientism' of Taine, Berthelot, and others—and a widespread Catholic revival in thought and literature. The growth of agnostic and atheist *libre pensée* was balanced by renewed assertion of Catholic orthodoxy, highlighted in the declaration of papal infallibility. The upsurge of materialistic determinism went hand in hand with marked interest in magic, occultism, and a variety of theosophical and similar cults. In philosophy itself, the ideas of Comte, Littré, Taine, and Renan were opposed by Neo-Criticists like Renouvier and Cournot and Idealists such as Lachelier, Ravaisson, Boutroux, and Bergson. And in literature, Naturalism, pushed to its extreme in Zola's theory of the 'experimental novel', was coincident with Symbolism and its aspirations to the 'Idéal'. Science–religion; materialism–mysticism; anti-clericalism–papal authority; the literary cult of factual documentation–the poetic pursuit of the visionary and mysteriously suggestive: such antitheses, even within the outlook of individual writers, lent a richer interest to thought and literature alike during these years.

Intellectual conflict was fed by many factors. In the nineteenth century there was a marked expansion of professional philosophy, especially in the universities, and the resulting impetus given to academic history of philosophy revivified old arguments and created a breeding-ground for new ideas. Moreover, intellectuals disillusioned by such political events as the *coup d'état* of Louis-Napoléon joined to attack established ideas and sought an outlet in philosophical engagement for frustrated social idealism. The influence of foreign thinkers, mediated by historians of philosophy like Cousin and his Eclectic disciples,[1] added further fuel to the debate: Spinoza, Kant, Hegel, Schopenhauer; philological scholars like Creuzer, Burnouf, and Strauss; Feuerbach, Mill, Carlyle, Darwin, Spencer, Hartmann—the ideas of all these and others, if sometimes in rather garbled form, were invoked, discussed, attacked. Controversy was heightened too by the persisting conviction—questioned only by isolated thinkers such as Marx—that ideas govern history and that social order must wait on philosophical order, and at the same time by a quickening sense of the inadequacy of existing systems. After the mid-century the almost 'official' philosophy of Eclecticism came under constant attack, for example from Taine in 1857 in *Les Philosophes français du dix-neuvième siècle*. Above all, the decline of Christian faith continued, and the great questions of God, immortality, the soul, and the sanctity of moral values came increasingly under discussion. 'Ce n'est pas d'un raisonnement [Renan declared in *L'Avenir de la science*], mais de tout l'ensemble des sciences modernes que sort cet immense résultat: Il n'y a pas de surnaturel.' Such an assertion reflects both the clash of old and new creeds and the sense of dramatic conse-quence characteristic of intellectual discord at this time.

Renan invokes contemporary science to support his claim, and the nineteenth century was indeed a time of scientific advance out-shining even the age of Newton—not least in France, with Ampère in electrodynamics, Sadi Carnot in thermodynamics, Cuvier in palaeontology, Lamarck and Geoffroy Saint-Hilaire in zoology and the theory of evolution, and Claude Bernard and Pasteur in medical science, among many others. And whereas eighteenth-century science was familiar only to a minority, in the new age the power of science was evident to all in industrialization, railways, gas, and improved surgery. It was little wonder that the notion spread that scientific knowledge is alone reliable and that its advances can

[1] Royer-Collard (1763-1845), Cousin (1792-1867), and Jouffroy (1796-1842) are usually grouped as 'Eclectic' thinkers.

ensure material progress and human happiness. Victor Hugo reflects a widely shared confidence as he describes, in *Plein Ciel*, the advance of scientific progress—

> A l'avenir divin et pur, à la vertu,
>   A la science qu'on voit luire,
>   A la mort des fléaux, à l'oubli généreux,
> A l'abondance, au calme, au rire, à l'homme heureux . . .

—to a material utopia, and to a moral and social utopia also:

> Au droit, à la raison, à la fraternité . . .
> Au juste, au grand, au bon, au beau . . .

Other literary writers were hardly less impressed: Balzac studying the human 'species' produced by differing social environments; Stendhal—sharing the ideas of the Idéologues[1]—pursuing in a spirit of objective detachment 'son métier d'observateur du cœur humain' and seeking to present 'un grand nombre de petits faits vrais sur une passion, sur une situation de la vie'; Flaubert who, whatever his reservations about scientific progress, could still aspire 'à la majesté de la loi et à la précision de la science', could declare that 'le grand art est scientifique et impersonnel' and painstakingly document the fatal impact of character and milieu in the life of Emma Bovary; above all Zola, claiming that the experimental novel can demonstrate the determinism of heredity and environment and be as scientifically valid and enlightening as the work of psychologists and social scientists, that this new novel-form will be 'la littérature de notre âge scientifique'. And though the novel was most clearly affected, Hugo was not the only poet to draw inspiration from science—and even industry—as witness Louis Bouilhet, whose *Fossiles* (1854) was described by Flaubert as 'le seul poème scientifique de toute la littérature française qui soit cependant de la poésie', Laprade in *L'Âge nouveau* (1845), Sully Prudhomme, and Maxime du Camp, upbraiding his fellow poets in the preface to *Les Chants modernes* (1855): 'la science fait des prodiges, l'industrie accomplit des miracles, et nous restons impassibles, insensibles, méprisables. . . .'

---

[1] The 'Idéologues' include Destutt de Tracy (1754-1836), Cabanis (1757-1808), Maine de Biran (1766-1824), and Degérando (1772-1842).

mood of scientific confidence was transformed into an
l, aggressive system of ideas by the positivist philosophers.
ing the empiricism of the *philosophes* and Idéologues, they
asserted that our only knowledge must be based upon observation
and experimentation, that such alleged ways of knowing as intuition, divine revelation, *a priori* reasoning, and poetic or emotional
experience are invalid, and that therefore we can have no knowledge
about religious and metaphysical questions since all these refer to a
realm of 'ultimate realities', 'first and final causes', that can never
be observed. This approach—they went on to contend—should now
be applied to man and human society. In Taine's famous words:
'La science approche enfin, et approche de l'homme; . . . c'est à
l'âme qu'elle se prend, munie des instruments exacts et perçants
dont trois cents ans d'expérience ont prouvé la justesse et mesuré
la portée.'

Henri de Saint-Simon (1760-1825) gave a first, rather diffuse
expression of the positivist attitude—linked with a partial socialism.
Though sympathetic to the *philosophes* he felt they had been destructive rather than creative. What was now needed to re-establish social
harmony after the upheavals of the French Revolution was to undertake a scientific reorganization of society and (as a basis for this) to
replace the discredited outlook of Christianity by a new intellectual
synthesis. Scientists, and especially social scientists, should be
given far greater power in society; in economic affairs the managers
and workers should combine (against such parasites as kings,
aristocrats, and soldiers) to organize more efficient and progressive
methods of production and distribution of wealth; in religion we
should adopt a 'new Christianity', shorn of all unscientific super-
naturalism and based on love of our fellow men, especially of the
poorer classes. In these ways we can bring in the 'golden age' that
lies not in the past, in a Garden of Eden, or in a future life in heaven,
but in an imminent earthly future when social order and fraternity
shall become realities.

But positivism was stated in a more organized form by a one-
time disciple and secretary of Saint-Simon, Auguste Comte, probably the best-known French positivist of the whole century and
whose ideas influenced a diversity of thinkers (though probably less

than is sometimes alleged)—John Stuart Mill, Émile Littré, George Eliot, Harriet Martineau, and many others from England and Scandinavia to Brazil and North America.

In the opening 'leçon' of his greatest work, the *Cours de philosophie positive* (1830–42), Comte announces that he has discovered a 'great, fundamental law' concerning the development of the human mind over the centuries. According to this celebrated *loi des trois états* the human mind evolves from the theological state to the metaphysical state and, finally, to the scientific or positive state. In the theological state man seeks to know the first and final causes of the world and believes he can attain an 'absolute knowledge' of the ultimate reality of all that is. And in particular he attributes final causal power to one or more 'supernatural agents' whose intervention explains many of the events of the natural order. Thus, thunder is thought to be the outcome of the gods' anger; a plague is divine punishment for human sin. Within this stage in man's evolution there are subdivisions: man progresses from fetishism to polytheism and then to monotheism. But throughout it men's thoughts about the world and their own life and society are bounded by the theological attitude; the ruler within a society, the husband within the family, for example, are thought of as godlike, authoritarian figures. The second, metaphysical, state is a modification of the first. Men continue to seek for first causes and absolute knowledge, but now the 'supernatural agents' are replaced by 'abstract forces' such as 'Nature' that are alleged to be the ultimate causal factors behind all phenomena. The peculiar error of this stage, in Comte's view, is to attribute independent existence and power to our own abstract nouns. Gradually, however, in some areas of thought at least, men have advanced to the third—and final—state, *l'état positif*:

Enfin, dans l'état positif, l'esprit humain, reconnaissant l'impossibilité d'obtenir des notions absolues, renonce à chercher l'origine et la destination de l'univers et à connaître les causes intimes des phénomènes, pour s'attacher uniquement à découvrir, par l'usage bien combiné du raisonnement et de l'observation, leurs lois effectives, c'est-à-dire leurs relations invariables de succession et de similitude.

The law of gravitation is the prototype of the only knowledge we can attain; one can go no further than the causal explanations and predictions of phenomena which it allows and can say nothing, for instance, about such notions as 'weight' and 'attraction' in themselves.

Comte believed this new positive approach had progressively conquered in the natural sciences. Astrology had been replaced by astronomy, alchemy by chemistry, and so on. But the time had now come for this approach to be applied to man. This did not for him imply psychology based on introspection. Knowledge of man must be founded on a mixture of physiology and—a new science—sociology, 'la physique sociale'. To establish this one missing science is, he says in the *Cours*, 'le plus grand et le plus pressant besoin de notre intelligence' and 'le premier but de ce cours, son but spécial'. Sociology is still in its theologico-metaphysical infancy, and even a Jeremy Bentham is still trying to deduce a social science from an abstract notion like 'human nature'. Only by becoming truly positive will it be able (like other sciences) to predict future phenomena and thus allow us to modify society by scientific action. Comte grants in 1830 that sociology cannot 'immediately' attain the same 'degree of perfection' as the other sciences; later he will make far more confident and dogmatic claims. But he never doubted it could be scientific enough to achieve sweeping social improvements. 'Science, d'où prévoyance; prévoyance, d'où action': this was his motto from the second 'leçon' onwards.

And such was Comte's dominant preoccupation throughout the *Cours*, as in turn he offered an allegedly historical demonstration of the truth of the *loi des trois états*, as he discussed the methodology of the various sciences, trying to remove the theological and metaphysical elements still persisting in them, as he classified the sciences in their proper order, moving from the most simple to the most complex—mathematics, astronomy, physics, chemistry, biology, sociology—as, above all, he described the methods of social science. The basic method is observation, though he thinks it will be sterile unless one already has in mind some hypothesis one wishes to verify. But an equivalent of experimentation is also possible, for the sociologist (like a biologist studying a pathological case) can analyse those instances where the normal workings of society are disturbed, as in a condition of revolution. Comparison is a third important method—of human and animal societies and of coexisting human societies—but Comte stresses above all a new method, warmly welcomed by Mill and others: the historical method. By studying the history of societies up to the present, we can both verify the laws of social statics (what keeps a society relatively stable) and perceive the laws of social dynamics (what produces change, which tendencies are growing stronger and hence will become dominant in the future).

It was these ideas above all that led Littré to speak of the 'immense mental revolution' Comte achieved and led Mill to see him as 'one of the principal thinkers of the age', and that have earned him the status of a 'founder' of sociology. Yet Comte was too dogmatic and confident, too much in a hurry to obtain practical results and there- fore too uncritical a philosopher of scientific method: hence the strong criticisms to which his thought has been subjected even by admirers like Littré and Mill. As his thought developed, he became increasingly unfaithful to the strict positivist position, and that not only by his later elaboration of a new, positivistic religion centred upon worship of humanity. Even in the *Cours* itself he moves to 'scientism'—an exaggeration of the positivist outlook that greatly overrates both the potential range of science and the reliability, the certainty, of its conclusions. Comte, in fact, illustrates perhaps the most significant development in nineteenth-century positivist thought—the move towards an excessive confidence that science can solve all mysteries, answer all questions with complete assur- ance. Renan and Taine, amongst others, exemplified the same tendency.

Ernest Renan spent his youth in training for the priesthood, but was soon troubled by doubts as to the reality of the supernatural. A little later his study of biblical criticism and philology deepened his scepticism, and in 1845 he broke with the Church. But Renan was not primarily negative, and by 1848 he was composing *L'Avenir de la science* (not published until 1890 but written within four years of his break with Rome). This book is perhaps the most dithyrambic expression in the whole century of the high hopes that were fixed upon science—by which Renan means especially the science of *philologie*, the history of the human spirit over the ages. Whereas Comte was above all concerned with society and therefore tried first and foremost to make sociology scientific, Renan was still particularly concerned with religion and metaphysics. He therefore makes the audacious claim that science can provide a new religion. 'La science est donc une religion; ... la science seule peut résoudre à l'homme les éternels problèmes dont sa nature exige impérieuse-ment la solution.' To survey the development of the human mind, Renan argued, is to perceive that man has ceaselessly been evolving since primitive times towards ever greater self-awareness and self-control, towards an 'Ideal' of consciousness and perfection. The whole world-process is moving towards a goal which Hegel called the 'Absolute' but which Renan commonly calls 'God'. And the 'divine work of progress' is to bring 'God' into full existence: He exists now as an ideal; one day He will exist as a reality. This, in brief, is the centre of a 'religion of the Ideal' which Renan sur-rounded with many equivalents of the Catholic faith he had lost— the priesthood of scientists and philosophers, the hope of paradise on earth through science, and so on. And here, as with Comte, we see, first, a determined attempt to extend the scientific method to include the human sphere and, secondly, an even more ambitious and extreme form of scientism. Indeed, so great were Renan's pre-tensions that he himself began to doubt their validity in later life and seems to have ended in ironic scepticism.

The cult of science was embodied in an even more dedicated and hard-headed form by Hippolyte Taine. Having lost his Christian faith as a youth, he rapidly moved, under the influence of the Idéologues much more than of Comte, towards the positivist posi-tion. Taine's constant preoccupation was much less with sociology than with creating a more scientific psychology and history, and his approach is well stated in the famous *Introduction* to his *Histoire de la littérature anglaise* (1863-4). Here he claims that literary works can be scientifically explained and can reveal to us the great causal factors operating in history as a whole. Examination of literary 'documents' leads to deeper understanding of their author's psychology; this, complemented by study of his life and personality, allows us to discern the 'faculté-maîtresse'—the disposition of thought and feeling—which determines his work. And this, in turn, can then be 'explained' as the product of three causal facts, his 'race', 'milieu', and 'moment'—that is, roughly, his inherited personality, the social, political, and geographical background, and the historical situation in which he writes. Scientifically studied, a literary document can thus reveal to us 'la psychologie d'une âme, souvent celle d'un siècle, et parfois celle d'une race', and since all historical phenomena (of which literature is merely one particularly accessible example) are determined by the same 'forces primordiales', the scientist can move on to study their effects in the major areas of human civilization. *De l'intelligence* (1870) went even further: it attempted to do for a scientific psychology what Claude Bernard had achieved for a scientific physiology in his *Introduction à l'étude de la médecine expérimentale* (1865). In *De l'intelligence* Taine continually stresses the importance of factual documentation, experimentation, the search for causes, the principle of determinism, and the physiological basis of personality, and though he was angrily accused of materialism, this work helped to transform psychology from a merely speculative, introspective pursuit into a scientific discipline. A similar attitude animated his work as a historian in *Les Origines de la France contemporaine* (1875–93), to which he devoted the final years of his life, and he also affected contemporary literature, both by his writing, which included works of literary and art history and criticism, and by his personal impact on such friends as Flaubert and the Goncourts and admirers like Zola, Maupassant, and Bourget. He wrote: 'De tout petits faits bien choisis, importants, significatifs, amplement circonstanciés et minutieusement notés, voilà aujourd'hui la matière de toute science', and the Naturalists eagerly applied such a programme to the novel, accepting Taine's conviction that literature could contribute to the scientific understanding of human nature, revealing the physical, psychological, and social determinants of man's behaviour.

But Taine went a great deal further even than these claims for a scientific literary study, psychology, and history. Greatly impressed throughout his career by Spinoza and Hegel in particular, he also longed to achieve a synthetic explanation of the whole of life and the universe—to achieve a scientific metaphysics by means of a fusion of positivism (whose method gives certainty) and German idealism (which seeks the completeness of range that science at present lacks). He argues that by a process of successively repeated abstractions and verifications we can climb the pyramid of knowledge; we can move from the causes of particular phenomena to the causes of those causes, and ultimately grasp the supreme causes of universal life. And as he surveys 'l'unité de l'univers' and 'ces créatrices immortelles, seules stables à travers l'infinité du temps qui déploie et détruit leurs œuvres', he yields to an exalted pantheism in which Nature is deified and transformed into the ethical criterion for human life. His confidence in his 'method of abstraction' leads him even to assert that there are no limits to the scope of the scientific method, as in a famous passage in the *Histoire de la littérature anglaise*: 'Dans cet emploi de la science et dans cette conception des choses il y a un art, une morale, une politique, une religion nouvelles, et c'est notre affaire aujourd'hui de les chercher.' Well might J. S. Mill criticize this scientism for rejecting 'the inherent limitations of human experience'!

Comte, Renan, and Taine illustrated the widely ambitious hopes vested in science during this period, as did many others such as Berthelot who could even claim that 'le triomphe universel de la science arrivera à assurer aux hommes le maximum possible de bonheur et de moralité'. We have seen in each case that through science they sought to reach a new faith to replace the old Christian beliefs, whether Comte's 'religion of Humanity', Renan's 'religion of the Ideal', or Taine's pantheistic metaphysics. Divided between the strictly scientific outlook and something not unlike the religious aspirations they had begun by discounting, they ended by transforming science into a new St. Peter's key.

It was hardly surprising, however, that many of their contemporaries should have reacted against the positivists' dogmatic dismissal of the mysterious and spiritual in human life, against the moral and philosophical relativism embedded in their theory of knowledge, and against their tendencies to fatalism and materialism. The Neo-Criticist and Idealist philosophers argued that our behaviour cannot be shown to be wholly determined and thus reducible to invariable scientific laws, and insisted on the free creativity of the individual and therefore of society as a whole. They also challenged the positivists' interpretation of scientific method: far from giving certain knowledge, it can in principle give no more than useful hypotheses, having a greater or lesser degree of probability and being subject to constant revision. They rejected the exclusive equation of reality with the scientifically observable and condemned as undemonstrable the materialist as much as the fatalist view of man. They questioned, too, Comte's epistemological 'realism'—another source of his over-confidence—the belief that we perceive the world as it is, and argued that our personality is always active in our perceptions, that the world for us is in part at least our own 'representation'.

This 'idealist reaction' is widely illustrated in literature as well. Even a Parnassian like Leconte de Lisle was far from being the positivistic writer that has been sometimes alleged. Rejecting Du Camp's alliance of poetry and science, and Comte's didactic view of art, he seeks a poetic beauty '[qui] contient la vérité divine et humaine', perceived through 'la vision poétique', 'exprimant pour tous ce que chacun n'est apte à connaître que par elle'. The true poet 'voit du premier coup d'œil plus loin, plus haut, plus profondément que tous, parce qu'il contemple l'idéal à travers la beauté visible'. But the reaction was more marked in the succeeding literary generation: in the Catholic literary revival of the late nineteenth century exemplified in Huysmans, Bloy, Bourget, Jammes, and Claudel; in the theatre with the later plays of Dumas *fils* and still more with Maeterlinck, Villiers de l'Isle Adam, François de Curel, and others; in the rejection by some of the Naturalists themselves from about 1885 of Zola's preoccupation with material reality; in literary criticism with Brunetière and others; in most of the writers of the Symbolist tradition. Even the foreign writers most popular in France at this time were seen as idealists who offer arms against the *scientistes*—Carlyle; Tennyson (so much admired by Verlaine, Mallarmé, and other Symbolists); Ruskin; Russian novelists like Tolstoy; Wagner; and Hartmann and Schopenhauer.

Fully to explore and assess this movement of thought and feeling falls outside the scope of this chapter. Yet it is relevant to suggest, however briefly, that late-nineteenth-century French 'idealism' was as ambivalent as the scientism it opposed. Even the Catholic literary revival was philosophically less emphatic than one might suppose. Certain Catholics abandoned reason and intellectual argument—Bloy, the young Claudel, for example. What of those who did offer reasons for their conversion? Huysmans, for instance, describes in *En route* (1895) the factors which prepared him for divine grace. His family background left in him a taste for the rites and piety of Catholicism. Still more, disgust with life led him to a pessimism which only the Church, 'l'hôpital des âmes', could both explain and cure. Again, his love of artistic beauty was profoundly satisfied by the buildings and services of the Church. Yet—significantly—these reasons are non-philosophical, predominantly aesthetic and emotional. Others were drawn to Rome for primarily social reasons, fearful that moral and social order would crumble without the authority and objective standards of the Church and without the supernatural sanctions it can threaten. This was the emphasis placed by Paul Bourget, for example, both in his influential novel *Le Disciple* (1889) and elsewhere. But the intellectual arguments invoked in this novel, it can be suggested, did not really challenge either the validity of the scientific method or the positivist theory of knowledge in its proper form. At best Bourget made suggestive points against the over-confidence of *scientisme* by drawing attention to our feelings of moral right and wrong, of free-will and responsibility, and to the complexity of the human personality. And it is noteworthy that when Bourget later joined the Roman Church, his attitude remained utilitarian, pragmatic. Much the same was true of Brunetière, who defended Bourget in the *querelle du Disciple*. Convinced that Christianity was socially useful, he remained uncertain about its truth even as a Catholic, and the arguments he advanced were in the main philosophically negative: science cannot solve man's vital questions; biblical criticism has not established its charges against Catholic doctrine; the existence of an 'Unknowable' beyond the reach of science refutes the dogmatism of the atheist. To the end (and perhaps the same was true of Barrès also) Brunetière was a *croyant non-croyant*, and it is perhaps significant that one of his last lectures should have been called 'Les Difficultés de croire'.

The position of some late-nineteenth-century Symbolists was no less ambiguous. They, too, revolted against a deterministic, materialist view of man, and aspired (in Nerval's words) to 'forcer les portes mystiques . . . qui nous séparent du monde invisible', seeking a 'spiritual' reality beyond externals, using symbols and 'correspondances' and a mysterious, suggestive poetry in an effort to evoke the 'Idéal'. Rimbaud asserts that the poet can be 'un voyant', even the medium for a power speaking through him, that he can end as 'le suprême Savant'—'Car il arrive à l'Inconnu!' Yet he came to discount the 'folies' of this visionary phase, his 'saison en enfer', and, giving up poetry, spent his life in the world of practical affairs, even interested (so it would seem) by the notion of scientific progress. Mallarmé can speak of the poem as 'un instrument spirituel' and of 'la joie de contempler l'Éternité', and he once described himself as 'une aptitude qu'a l'univers spirituel à se voir et à se développer'. Yet it is doubtful how far he ever believed in a transcendental reality, and he ends, in the words of one critic, commenting on *Un Coup de dés* (1897), with the conclusion that 'we are all mortal and cannot conquer that tragic hazard, mortality', that 'even the totality of human genius is no less mortal than the individuals who provide it.' The search for beauty, hope in the value of the poet's creative act, are counter-balanced by deep metaphysical doubt, and one may wonder whether he ever finally escaped from the dichotomy of 'le Néant' and 'le Beau' which he expressed in 1866:

Oui, *je le sais*, nous ne sommes que de vaines formes de la matière, mais bien sublimes pour avoir inventé Dieu et notre âme. Si sublimes, mon ami! que je veux me donner ce spectacle de la matière, ayant conscience d'être et, cependant, s'élançant forcenément dans le Rêve qu'elle sait n'être pas.

Much the same was true of other Symbolists—of Jules Laforgue, poet of despair and ironic mockery, yearning for the Ideal but ending (as above all *Les Moralités légendaires* (posth. 1887) suggest) in nihilism; of Maeterlinck, whose retreat from idealism is especially clear; less pessimistically, of Paul Valéry, whose thought resembles logical positivism in its dismissal of metaphysical questions. Even in aesthetic theory the Symbolists do not wholly—or even largely—escape from the positivist outlook.[1] One finds in several of them (though not in a Verlaine or a Claudel, both of them largely non-rational in their original acceptance of Catholicism) a contrast between the anti-positivism of their aspirations and the apparent positivism of their actual views on religious and metaphysical matters. Most of them are perhaps in reality idealists only in one sense of the term. We may distinguish two 'idealisms': the first, taken from 'ideal', supposes belief in a transcendent reality or an objective moral order; the second, taken from 'idea' (i.e. 'subjective idealism'), is the view that we can know only our own mental states, that (in the words of Schopenhauer) 'the world is my representation'.[2] To make a no doubt too sweeping generalization, many of the Symbolists aspired to idealism in the first sense, but often ended in idealism in the second sense. 'Moi n'étant pas, rien ne serait', Mallarmé declared, a view explicitly shared by Laforgue. Rimbaud, too, concluded that his 'visions' were not of a world outside but 'hallucinations' within his own mind alone. And it is important to note that this subjective idealism does not challenge any part of the positivist system except Comte's own epistemological contention—not essential to strict positivism—that the world is in reality as we perceive it to be. Even Naturalists like Zola and Maupassant can accept something of the subjectivist view—as when they define a work of art as 'un coin de la création vu à travers un tempérament'.

If, then, the nineteenth-century positivists were in some ways divided minds, as we saw, the same was true of many of those who reacted against their ideas, their aspirations being undermined by a persisting positivism of outlook. The 'idealist reaction' was as intellectually ambiguous as the positivists' movement to scientism: the positivist spirit was present in both, albeit in very different ways

[1] A. G. Lehmann concludes that Symbolism is in an intermediate position between 'two contrasting moments of aesthetic history, the contemporary and the positivist' (*The Symbolist Aesthetic in France*, 2nd ed., 1968).

[2] For a contemporary statement of this distinction, linking subjective idealism with materialism, cf. Remy de Gourmont, 'Les Racines de l'idéalisme', *Promenades philosophiques*, 3 vols., 1905-9.

and moods, and so was its antithesis. Conflict and tension were as clear within the minds of individuals, however varying their primary commitments, as in the intellectual life of the age as a whole, and to assign its separate writers over-simply to one philosophical group or another is to overlook much that is central, moving, and fascinating in their work.

NOTE

AUGUSTE COMTE, 1798–1857, was educated at the École polytechnique and became both disciple and secretary of Saint-Simon, from whom he derived some of the basic concepts of his philosophy. After quarrelling with Saint-Simon in 1824, he lived by part-time teaching and examining and with the help of admirers who attended his private lectures later published the *Cours de philosophie positive* (1830–42), his most important work. In later life he developed a religion of Humanity whose tenets are summarized in his *Catéchisme positiviste* (1852) and also stated in *Système de politique positive* (1851–4).

ERNEST RENAN, 1823–92, was educated for the priesthood but broke with the Church in 1845. Thereafter he became a notable scholar of Hebrew religion, his major work being the *Histoire des origines du christianisme* (1863–83), of which the first volume was his controversial *Vie de Jésus*. But he was even more influential as a speculative thinker, with works like *L'Avenir de la science* (1890, written about 1848) and *Dialogues et fragments philosophiques* (1876), and numerous articles, including an 'Examen de conscience philosophique' (*Revue des Deux Mondes*, 1889).

HIPPOLYTE TAINE, 1828–93, achieved fame over a wide range: in literary history with books on La Fontaine (1853), Livy (1856), and his *Histoire de la littérature anglaise* (1863–4); in philosophical polemics with *Les Philosophes français du dix-neuvième siècle* (1857), an attack on eclecticism in particular; in art history (he was a professor at the École des Beaux-Arts from 1864); in psychology with *De l'intelligence* (1870); and in history with his vast work on *Les Origines de la France contemporaine* (1875–93). Underlying all these works there was a unity of method and aim, a basic philosophy, which made him a dominant intellectual influence and a highly controversial representative of scientific determinism.

Criticism. General surveys of nineteenth-century French thought include A. Cresson, *Les Courants de la pensée philosophique française*, vol. ii (1931), J. A. Gunn, *Modern French Philosophy (1851–1921)* (1922), D. G. Charlton, *Secular Religions in France, 1815–1870* (1963), and I. Benrubi, *Les Sources et les courants de la philosophie contemporaine en France*, 2 vols. (1933). Studies of the French positivists include D. G. Charlton, *Positivist Thought in France during the Second*

Empire, 1852–1870 (1959) and, on Comte, L. Lévy-Bruhl, *La Philosophie d'A. Comte* (1900), G. Cantecor, *Comte* (n.d.), J. Delvolvé, *Réflexions sur la pensée comtienne* (1932), and H. Gouhier, *La Jeunesse d'A. Comte et la formation du positivisme*, vol. iii (1941). Two very perceptive nineteenth-century studies are J. S. Mill, *A. Comte and Positivism* (1865) and É. Littré, *A. Comte et la philosophie positive* (1863). General studies of Taine include V. Giraud, *Essai sur Taine* (n.d.), M. Leroy, *Taine* (1933), and—more difficult but rewarding—G. Barzellotti, *La Philosophie de Taine* (1900), and A. Chevrillon, *Taine: Formation de sa pensée* (1932). His approach to literary study is examined in S. J. Kahn, *Science and Aesthetic Judgement: A Study of Taine's Critical Method* (1953). Renan is best treated in P. Lasserre, *La Jeunesse de Renan* (1928), J. Pommier, *Renan* (1923) and *La Pensée religieuse de Renan* (1925), Ph. Van Tieghem, *Renan* (1948), and M. Weiler, *La Pensée de Renan* (1945). The impact of science and positivism on nineteenth-century literature is examined by R. Fath, *L'Influence de la science sur la littérature française dans la seconde moitié du 19ᵉ siècle* (1901), and C. A. Fusil, *La Poésie scientifique de 1750 à nos jours* (1918). For the idealist reaction against positivism see A. Aliotta, *The Idealistic Reaction against Science* (1914), D. Parodi, *Du positivisme à l'idéalisme*, 2 vols. (1930), and A. Fouillée, *Le Mouvement idéaliste et la réaction contre la science positive* (1896). On the literary expressions of this reaction one may consult G. Fonsegrive, *L'Évolution des idées dans la France contemporaine* (1920), D. M. Knowles, *La Réaction idéaliste au théâtre depuis 1890* (1934), and, on the Catholic revival, J. Calvet, *Le Renouveau catholique dans la littérature contemporaine* (1931), R. Griffiths, *The Reactionary Revolution* (1966), and H. Guillemin, *Histoire des catholiques français au dix-neuvième siècle* (1947).

2. Poetry and Pure Art: Gautier, Leconte de Lisle, and Heredia

IF the French Romantics are at present out of favour, it is probably true to say that in this country the Parnassians have never been in. Art for Art's sake has no parallel in English literature, whose practitioners, even when in opposition, have usually retained strong and detailed ethical concerns. In France a wholesale rejection of all that is suggested by bourgeois life and values was almost a premiss of nineteenth-century literature. Whatever their interest in the surface activity of the bourgeois world, writers as different as Stendhal and Flaubert worked from a much more detached vantage point than a Dickens or a George Eliot. Satire is the normal mode, art the natural standard of comparison. If this seemed a legitimate approach for the novelist, how much more was the ivory tower the natural home of the poet. But the English tradition contains no Flaubert or Leconte de Lisle, no representative of the lofty, stoical pursuit of formal perfection. Art may be justified with the moral–mystical fulminations of a Ruskin, but otherwise its spokesmen have tended to be the exquisites, easy prey to the robust ridicule of a W. S. Gilbert. And if the aims of Art for Art's sake are uncongenial, there is also perhaps a more technical impediment to the English reader's admiration. However well he understands French versification, it is unlikely that he will be sensitive enough to the difficulties of its composition to bestow praise for, say, the conquering of the special problems of the alexandrine. Even the tepid French critic will spare a word of congratulation for the *facture des vers* of the Parnassians—and may well go as far as seeing this in itself as earning them a place in literary history. The English reader is unlikely to be able to make such appraisals. Yet even here the problem is only partly technical. Ultimately it may be that we do not willingly see qualities like solidity of structure and richness of rhyme as having very much to do with genuine poetic achievement.

In other words, the rejection of 'l'art pour l'art', though often formulated in rather a philistine way, may well contain a sound intuition. For, in the event, Art for Art's sake proved not so much undesirable as impossible. Such a statement could be contested on the ground that none of the writers rigorously defined the *beauté* which was their object, that we have no right to infer a precise definition from scattered expressions of their ideals and exclusions. Nevertheless, the lack of a definition of such a constantly recurrent word is itself significant. If, as a start, the three chief Parnassian poets aimed at the approximation of poetry to the pictorial and the statuesque, the elimination of subjectivity and moral judgement, then—in varying degrees—they singularly failed in their attempt. But their failure may well coincide with our idea of success. And we should certainly not dismiss these poets in advance simply because we hold that the ideals implicit in titles like Gautier's *Émaux et camées* and Heredia's *Les Trophées* are not worth pursuing or incapable of being achieved. Whatever else they are these poems are not merely essays in the pictorial, the hard delineation of outline, the evocation of colour and posture, which the aesthetic of Gautier's poem 'L'Art' might suggest. Nothing seems to characterize the *Émaux et camées* less adequately than the notion of the artist chiselling away laboriously at ungrateful materials to produce a monument that will outlive the ravages of time. On the other hand, the aesthetic is not irrelevant to the discussion of these poets. It can provide a framework in which to appreciate their successes, and an awareness of it often helps us to define their failures in terms of the conflict between the objective aspirations and the necessarily subjective nature of the writing of poetry.

Gautier's literary career is essentially that of a Romantic who lowers his sights. He started as a militant supporter of Hugo, and though, from the first, he dissociated himself from the political and social sides of the movement, it was only gradually that he became the exclusive spokesman of Art in the narrower sense. Many of his early poems are on the stock 'big' Romantic themes of love, death, and transitoriness, and they have the merit at least of having contributed to the fund of image material which Baudelaire transformed and made his own in *Les Fleurs du mal*. Thus in 'L'Horloge' (in the collection *España*) local colour gives way to a fairly familiar sort of moral reflection, with a range of tones reminiscent of Hugo—world-weary and heroic, colloquial and expansive ('Oui, c'est bien vrai, la vie est un combat sans trêve / Un combat inégal contre un lutteur caché. . . . Naître, c'est seulement commencer à mourir', etc.), together with a somewhat more resonant note, almost a Baudelairean foretaste ('Et dans nos cœurs criblés, comme dans une cible / Tremblent les traits lancés par l'archer invisible'). But Gautier was manifestly not a Baudelaire; and perhaps it was also a sure sense of literary expediency, of the exhaustion of the Hugo style, rather than a wholly positive ideal, which made him move towards the more restrained style of the *Émaux et camées* (1852, enlarged 1872). At any rate there is no total and abrupt move from the sentimental to the pictorial; the evolution can rather be described as a narrowing of scope, an extreme caution both over subject-matter and form, a determination not to make a romantic fool of himself. The pre-Baudelairean 'L'Horloge' gives way to the authentically Gautieresque 'La Montre'. But though the watch exercises the descriptive powers of the miniaturist, the main theme is the forgetfulness of the poet, whose self-absorption makes him omit to put 'au trou de rubis la clef d'or'; followed by a rather routine and inconclusive contrast with God, who never fails to rewind the human heart. This is a surprisingly common pattern for the Gautier poem; it is rather as though the poet had not suffi-cient confidence in his ability to put his aesthetic into practice—description has to be supplemented by morality. So, in 'La Rose-thé', the celebration of the stylish weakens into the traditional precious praise of the natural ('La peau vaut mieux que le pétale', etc.); while the famous 'Symphonie en blanc majeur', which Gautier, by a title unusually pretentious for him, offered as cross-ing new frontiers in art, in fact repeatedly falls into the purest clichés of seventeenth-century gallantry:

> Dans ces grandes batailles blanches,
> Satins et fleurs ont le dessous,
> Et, sans demander leurs revanches,
> Jaunissent comme des jaloux.

Gautier has in fact returned to an old tradition of French poetry, in which pictorial description is combined with whimsical reflection and moralizing, which aims to be apposite and ingenious rather than personal and complex. The comparison with the seventeenth century is not an arbitrary one, since Gautier much admired the poets of the early part of that century and wrote an attractive collection of essays (*Les Grotesques*) about them. The closer one looks at the poetic technique of the *Émaux et camées*, the more it seems to resemble—and perhaps to be indebted to—these predecessors. Description as such is less prominent than the stock devices of the seventeenth-century observer. With the latter, metaphor and simile are not detached and definitive but rather part of a procedure of endless apposition, periphrasis, and re-definition. Gautier, who can call a watch-spring a 'papillon d'acier' and who describes the snow-capped mountains as an assembly of magistrates in ermine whose 'blanc tribunal examine / Un cas d'hiver se prolongeant' would have been at home and honoured in the Hôtel de Rambouillet. Gautier's proclaimed intention of the *transposition d'art* is often taken to characterize the nature of his actual achievement. In fact the simulation of painterly techniques is much less common than the appeal to the reader's own power of analogy ('On dirait une femme nue'—the 'on dirait' form is recurrent) or to shared cultural associations:

> Comme, au clair-obscur de Corrège,
> Le corps d'Antiope dormant . . .
>
> Reflet de la beauté première,
> Sœur de 'l'éternel féminin'.

Such a characterization need not mean that we are condemning Gautier; but our judgement will depend in part on our ability to savour a certain sort of preciosity; it will not be so much the absence of sentiment as its very particular sort of presence that provokes our admiration or irritation. For Gautier, again as for many of the early-seventeenth-century poets, the poem is a caprice, part description, part whimsical response and speculation; and the responses most relished, the subjects most cultivated, are those where the poet can indulge the pleasure of a mixed reaction, where the material is a starting-point for paradoxical or bizarre reflection. Life is a carnival, a masquerade which the poet watches, not dispassionately, but still with little deep emotional engagement. It is always the marginal and the miniature, the mixed and the ambivalent which are called on to supply the starting-point—the contralto voice, 'bizarre mélange', Carmen with her 'laideur piquante', the dead child's toys, 'ce mélange / Puérilement douloureux'. Such a response may of course be completely authentic and acceptable. But the acceptability of Gautier's poetry depends in part on the tact with which he chooses the material on which his limited responses are to operate. In 'Les Vieux de la vieille', where he is dealing with human beings, we may feel that the response is maudlin and trivial. The spectacle of the old soldier is a familiar one in Romanticism from Rousseau onwards. Gautier both looks back to the sentimental imperialism of the young Hugo and forward to Baudelaire's sense of the poetry of the urban scene. But the scene is turned very promptly into pure spectacle and matter for precious reflection; he relishes, without the Baudelairean element of horror, the mixed sensations of this 'ridicule héroïque', and the contrast between the bodies and the uniforms generates yet another series of paradoxical juxtapositions:

> Nobles lambeaux, défroque épique,
> Saints haillons, qu'étoile une croix . . .

When, as in 'Variations sur le carnaval de Venise', the subject is a masquerade proper, we are much more willing to share the observer's reactions. His reactions are still of a precious, paradoxical order ('plaisir mortel', 'jovial et mélancolique'), but the ingenious, analogical mind here establishes a real and convincing series of moods and sensations. Here the term of comparison would be Verlaine rather than the Parnassian ideal, it is 'de la musique' rather than 'de l'art', there are distant premonitions of symbolism:

> A l'air qui jase d'un ton bouffe
> Et secoue au vent ses grelots,
> Un regret, ramier qu'on étouffe,
> Par instants mêle ses sanglots.

Gautier in fact excels at suggesting movement, mystery, imprecision, as with the ghostly figure of 'Inès de las Sierras':

> Peigne au chignon, basquine aux hanches,
> Une femme accourt en dansant,
> Dans les bandes noires et blanches,
> Apparaissant, disparaissant,
>
> Avec une volupté morte,
> Cambrant les reins, penchant le cou . . .

Here the urgent, suggestive rhythms cut across the restraints of the octosyllable and admirably convey Gautier's vision of 'l'Espagne du temps passé'. Indeed it is noticeable that, perhaps precisely because of his analogical obsessions, he tends to reduce the living to a series of postures ('L'Aveugle', 'Le Château du souvenir'), but to give convincing life to the inanimate or the imagined. This much is true of the common view of Gautier, that he is best inspired by works of art—not, however, so much to pure pictorial transcription as to reflection and analysis. But here again, the *Émaux et camées* show a narrowing of scope; the very impressive interpretation in 'A Zurbaran' gives way to the more whimsical though still delightful 'Les Néréides'.

In general, one feels that Gautier is a poet who does not quite bring to expression his potential range of feeling, that caution as well as artistic restraint dictates his mature style. The praise given him in his lifetime, notably by Baudelaire, now seems excessive. One wonders—and the final remarks of Baudelaire's essay give some support to the speculation—whether the praise is not in part due to admiration for the rare man of letters who is 'successful' in a way that a Baudelaire can admit to be valuable; who manages to lead a humane, ordered, and unembittered life without in the least selling out to the enemies of art. But the same good nature means that 'le bon Théo' achieves a rather facile domination of his world; and inevitably, in the huge shadow of Baudelaire, such intimations as he has of 'l'héroïsme de la vie moderne' seem superficial, perhaps deliberately kept superficial. 'Une mansarde est toujours triste; / Le grenier n'est beau qu'en chanson', he remarks in a good-humoured poem on the artist's life. It is the nearest we get to the 'horreur de mon taudis' which returns after Baudelaire's escape into his *rêve parisien*. And though Gautier exclaims in 'Les Vieux de la vieille' at seeing 'des spectres en plein jour', this is not the world where 'le spectre en plein jour raccroche le passant' and imperiously invades his consciousness; where 'tout devient allégorie' in a way less comfortable than the conscious seeker after analogy, even with his 'curiosité dépravée', would wish to experience. Not that there is anything necessarily more 'profound' in the working out of the more metaphysically pretentious theories of correspondence; the limitations of a poem like 'Affinités secrètes' could of course, if one wished, be defined in terms of failure to lay bare a higher reality. I should prefer to say that, even taken on its own terms as one man's *madrigal panthéiste*, it remains, in spite of some delicate images, a somewhat schematic and precious compilation.

All this is not to say that Gautier is not a sensitive and in many ways congenial writer. But the nature of his achievement is often misrepresented—either because the programme is taken for the practice, or because the cultured and fastidious reader tends to give extremely generous collaboration to this sort of poet. In Wilde's *Dorian Gray* the hero turns the pages of the *Émaux et camées* ('Charpentier's Japanese paper edition, with the Jacquemart etching') until he comes to the stanzas on Venice: 'How exquisite they were! . . . Leaning back with half-closed eyes he kept saying over and over to himself:

> Devant une façade rose,
> Sur le marbre d'un escalier.

The whole of Venice was in those two lines.' Exquisite these and the preceding lines certainly are, with their delicate and ingenious personification of 'La Vénus de l'Adriatique', its domes like 'des gorges rondes / Que soulève un soupir d'amour'. But one would have to know one's Venice to attribute to them any very particularized pictorial power. And the writer who can be praised for the picturesque quality of lines like

> Aux blanches terrasses de Malte,
> Entre l'eau bleue et le ciel bleu

TRINITY COLLEGE
LIBRARY

is certainly reaping to the full the dividends of a shared cultural tradition.

There is nothing lightweight or trivial about the figure who most fully represents the ideals of the loosely constituted Parnassian school. Far from lowering the sights of poetry, as Gautier does, from the philosophical to the delectable, Leconte de Lisle appears from the first as the saviour of art from the various forms of degeneracy and misuse into which he claims it has fallen. From the preface to the *Poèmes antiques* (1852) onwards he castigates in turn the personal effusions of the Romantics (which, even when sincere, he considers to be an unworthy offering to 'la plèbe carnassière'); the harnessing of poetry to political and social ends, 'je ne sais quelle monstrueuse alliance de la poésie et de l'industrie'; and the dangers of 'le didactisme rimé, cette négation de toute poésie'. Even the poets who have looked to the past rather than to themselves for inspiration have gone about it the wrong way. Hugo, in *La Légende des siècles*, for all his grandiose achievements, forces history to subserve his own highly subjective creed of evolutionary progress; and Vigny, though 'un très noble esprit, un profond penseur' and (significant indication of Leconte de Lisle's view of nineteenth-century literary history) 'un précurseur de notre renaissance littéraire', is criticized for using the story of Moses as a vehicle for his own feelings and misrepresenting 'le vrai personnage légendaire qui nous apparaît aujourd'hui, le chef théocratique de six cent mille nomades idolâtres et féroces, errant affamés dans le désert'. The wider context for these rejections is an idealized vision of the Greek world and its art which (among other things) the coming of Christianity destroyed. In so far as he sees any future for degenerate and divided modern man, it must be through a revisiting of the antique sources rather than through still further introspective and prophetic activity. Poets must join with the new generation of scientific archaeologists, anthropologists, and philologists to fulfil the most hopeful task of the century, which is to 'réunir les titres de famille de l'intelligence humaine'. Though the poet may one day recover his Greek status of popular singer and prophet, the most urgent need for writers, and perhaps for their readers too, is what Leconte de Lisle rather dauntingly calls a period of 'épreuves expiatoires'.

What he himself will offer—and the formula does not change essentially after the *Poèmes antiques*—is a poetry which shall be 'archaïque et savante', attempting to recreate pictorially and atmospherically the history and legends of the past.

Such a sketch is inadequate to deal even with the terminological problems raised by Leconte de Lisle's views and aspirations. It does, however, introduce us to what looks like a fundamental contradiction in them. On the one hand we have a man of rather acidulous and doctrinaire temperament with highly subjective—and extremely pessimistic—views of life: history for him is at worst—in Vigny's phrase which he quotes approvingly—'un accident sombre entre deux sommeils infinis'; at best, a story of continuous decline from Greek harmony to medieval and modern barbarity, momentarily redeemed only by a few acts of courage, virility, and defiance. On the other we have the artist who preaches 'soumission à l'objet', the patient study of the past as a *source* of objective truth and intrinsic beauty.

Given these divergent tendencies, it seems impossible that Leconte de Lisle should not, in the selection and treatment of his material, be guilty of the very fault—if fault it be—that he attributes to Vigny. And this is in fact what happens. Sometimes, if the 'meaning' of the story does not emerge clearly, he allows himself an explicit gloss—as in 'Nurmahal', where a complex and circumstantial oriental narrative ends with the stanza:

> Gloire à qui, comme toi, plus forte que l'épreuve,
> Et jusqu'au bout fidèle à son époux vivant,
> Par un coup de poignard à la fois reine et veuve,
> Dédaigne de trahir et tue auparavant!

Or else, as in 'Qaïn', the main character is a transparent spokesman for the poet's own hatred of the God who invented and conferred upon man the power to sin.

That Leconte de Lisle should break his own implied rules is of course not important in itself; only in so far as it impairs the artistic force or unity of what he writes. Qaïn's speeches may be eloquent protest in the Romantic-Promethean tradition; but at the same time the initial 'Q' is there making its claim for the objective and

B

erudite nature of the poem, and introduction of the Cain story through the bizarre vision of Thogorma seems to be an attempt (like Flaubert's stained-glass window in *La Légende de Saint Julien l'Hospitalier*) to disclaim responsibility for the philosophical implications of the subject-matter. So that when we come to the patently subjective point, the elaborate lead-up seems, in retrospect, a rather pretentious piece of mystification. The more circumstantial the legend the odder the juxtaposition appears to be. In another ambitious poem, 'La Légende des Nornes', it is something of a relief, among the obscure details of Yggdrasill, 'le frêne aux trois racines', to come upon more lyrical and seemingly personal passages reflecting on the transience of human achievement and evoking a spectacle of the eventual destruction of the world. But this very lyricism—it is comparable to that of the short, overtly personal poem 'L'Illusion suprême'—makes us the more suspicious of the value and relevance of the archaic framework. If this is essentially what the poet has to say, why doesn't he say it straight out?

As we read Leconte de Lisle's poetry, then, a certain *air de famille* begins to emerge under the diversity of names and settings. Cain's evocation of his happiness in the morning of the world strangely resembles that of characters as ostensibly individualized as Khiron in the *Poèmes antiques* or the old chieftain in 'Le dernier des Maourys'. A common line of development in the poems is the opening introduction to a brooding, emotionally or metaphysically discontented character; then the building up of an atmosphere of foreboding, followed by a single violent action; and a final statuesque tableau with elegiac or fatalistic implications. For all their orthographic authenticity and individuality, we sense—and eventually begin to anticipate—the homogeneity of these characters' dramas:

> Vingt Cipayes, la main sur leurs pommeaux fourbis
> Et le crâne rasé ceint du paliacate,
> Gardent le vieux Nabab et la Begum d'Arkate,
> Autour danse un essaim léger de Lall-Bibis.
>
> Le Mongol, roide et grave en ses riches habits . . .

The unintelligible opening gives way to the all too familiar fifth line, the Mongol joins the series of grave hieratical figures—Angantyr, 'pâle et grave'; Akhab, 'l'œil sombre et dur'; Djihan-Guir, 'rêveur et les yeux graves'—who people the 'sombre accident' that is mortal life.

Yet the tenacity with which Leconte de Lisle pursued the preparatory studies for his work is surpassed only by Flaubert's, and goes far beyond what a purely artistic ideal of internal consistency and coherence could demand. There is something strange and tragic about a writer who in 'La Maya' proclaims the illusoriness of all appearance, yet attaches such fanatical importance to its details. One feels that in a sense the 'épreuves expiatoires' of a Leconte de Lisle or a Flaubert are penance not only for the sins of past writers but also for their own nihilism; having condemned the world as meaningless and banished most forms of art as ignoble, they seem to feel that if, in the last remaining area of activity, they keep their tempers and concentrate hard on the object, the products of their virtue will receive the magic touch of poetry. But the last area itself remains available only through a philosophical inconsistency: the exact reconstruction of the past finds its only true apologists in the optimistic, positivistic spirits of the time, like the young Renan; dogmatic belief in the *Maya* makes mockery of history and legend as anything but escapist entertainment.

And even assuming the aim of escape into pure art, into the rich and strange for its own sake, legend will prove an unsatisfactory medium. For legend lives on in large part through its allegorical qualities, it cries out for interpretation, its selection by a modern writer seems to promise such interpretation. It is difficult for the reader to adopt a mental posture in which he will not see the descriptive as mystification (if sustained) or delay (if eventually superseded). For there is a vast difference between the random accretion of detail in the original variants of a legend, and their considered reproduction in a modern work of art. The concept of authenticity has little validity in relation to legend; the whole notion of the authentic transcription of what is already fictional is a dubious one. In any case, many of Leconte de Lisle's 'sources' have since proved to be spurious—and some he knew to be already.

Again there is nothing intrinsically wrong with his having exploited them; one merely feels that a less pretentious aesthetic, a less ponderous stance in the presentation of material, would have been appropriate to the man who drew the opening vision in 'Qaïn' from an obscure prose epic-writer named Cailleux, who in his turn had made sorties into a rocky area near Marseille in order to 'document' the landscape of the antediluvian world.

The ballad form and style is in fact the best way in which legend can flourish in modern poetry: the brief setting, the rapid narrative line, the subject-matter which deals with such simple and universally appealing emotions that the question of the personal presence or absence of the teller hardly arises in a significant critical way: all these are the surest preventives of the sort of failure to which Leconte de Lisle is subject. This of course is a way of rejecting much of his content as well as his form, since not every story can be adapted to ballad treatment. When he does choose material suitable to such a form he produces some of his most complete successes—and we are struck by the way the ballad suits his heroic–fatalistic temperament—expresses in fact what he essentially has to say. 'Ekhidna', under its Greek trappings, is at once (we suspect) his view of the eternal feminine and his version of the 'Lorelei' motif: a little heavy-handed perhaps, but notably less so once the opening classical genealogy has been got out of the way. 'Le Cœur de Hialmar' is even more uncluttered. And the elegiac and heroic are simply conveyed in the confidential fellowship with the crow ('Viens par ici . . . mon brave mangeur d'hommes'), the evocation of past fraternity ('Dans Upsal, où les Jarls boivent la bonne bière / Et chantent, en heurtant les cruches d'or, en chœur'), the radiant certainty of immortality ('Jeune, brave, riant, libre et sans flétrissures, / Je vais m'asseoir parmi les Dieux, dans le soleil!').

Many of Leconte de Lisle's best anthologized poems follow this pattern of desolate scene and striking single figure or group of figures. The overtly personal poems tend to run to the merely abusive ('Aux Modernes' or 'L'Anathème') or the rhetorically apocalyptic ('Solvet saeclum'); though beside this latter class, in 'La Fin de l'homme' ('Qaïn' without the trappings, and the better for its undisguised subjectivity), we have a splendidly sonorous

lament for the world as it was before God wilfully corrupted his own
creation. Brief poems like 'Les Éléphants', 'Les Hurleurs', 'Le
Sommeil du condor' do create suggestive landscapes and suggestive symbols, half-understood figures suffering, ruminating, or
disdainful, in a hostile or neutral world 'marqué du signe de colère'.
The landscape is less localized than in the more ambitious poems,
but at the same time there is perhaps a more truly 'scientific' spirit
at work, the vision of the endless, ageless universe and the bizarre
predicament of its inhabitants perhaps translates in part the spirit
of the historical, geological, and evolutionary speculation of the
time. 'Sacra fames' is a poem actually *about* the survival of the
fittest, while 'Midi' offers the view of nature of one who has gone
beyond the Romantic responses, both pantheistic and protesting.
But the mood is not sustained and, to a greater extent than he would
wish, Leconte de Lisle remains an eloquent late Romantic, re-
clothing Vigny in multi-racial splendour, his thesis as unhistorical,
and as obtrusive—though less unabashedly so—as that of an Hugo.

  With José-Maria de Heredia we meet a much more congenial
figure, whose work belies the portents of its title and layout. *Les
Trophées* (1893) suggests an essay in the purely pictorial or sculptural, while the division of the collection by historical periods seems
to threaten us with another tendentious legend of the centuries. In
fact, Heredia is a much more attractive, unpretentious, and eclectic
poet than his literary exterior and his almost idolatrous discipleship
of Leconte de Lisle would suggest. Their poetic worlds are basically
similar: there is the same lament for an idealized Greek world, the
same disillusion and feeling of the emptiness of the universe (once
well peopled with the comforting familiars of polytheism), the same
slightly inconclusive admiration for the grand gesture which gives
temporary meaningfulness, the same overriding sense that nullity
and oblivion are the only reality. But this vision is played on by
a temper less systematic, more truly artistic than Leconte de
Lisle's. Heredia's pessimism lacks the fierce doctrinaire quality
which, whether suppressed or given rein, is such a decisive factor
in his master's poetic undertaking. The cult of impersonality is
followed in so far as there is no effusive display of the 'moi'; but,
in general, Heredia's admirations, regrets, and reveries are more

straightforward, less inhibited by the aspiration to do in poetry
what had never been done before.

One of Heredia's *partis pris*, deriving from his pride in his own
Spanish ancestry, is his admiration for the *conquistadores*, whose
feats exercised such a fascination on him that he spent a substantial period of his life translating one of their earliest chroniclers.
It is this world that he evokes in the group of sonnets, *Les Con-
quérants*, of which the first is the finest:

> Comme un vol de gerfauts hors du charnier natal,
> Fatigués de porter leurs misères hautaines,
> De Palos de Moguer, routiers et capitaines
> Partaient, ivres d'un rêve héroïque et brutal.
>
> Ils allaient conquérir le fabuleux métal
> Que Cipango mûrit dans ses mines lointaines,
> Et les vents alizés inclinaient leurs antennes
> Au bords mystérieux du monde Occidental.
>
> Chaque soir, espérant des lendemains épiques,
> L'azur phosphorescent de la mer des Tropiques
> Enchantait leur sommeil d'un mirage doré;
>
> Ou penchés à l'avant des blanches caravelles,
> Ils regardaient monter en un ciel ignoré
> Du fond de l'Océan des étoiles nouvelles.

Here we have poetic diction which rises above any suspicion of the
laboured erudite exercise. The opening simile is discreetly archaiz-
ing but forceful and appropriate; and the form of the rest of the
quatrain completes what the image has suggested, the potential
vigour, the dammed-up instincts of the bird of prey finding release
in the delayed and emphatic 'partaient' of the fourth line. The
second quatrain, with its sonorous adjectives, widens the horizon,
fills out the grandiose nature of the *rêve*, conveys, by the wonderful
trouvaille of the 'vents alizés' (our prosaic trade-winds, but benefit-
ing from the association with *ailés*), the excitement of their swift
progress into the unknown. The tone now subsides, and the poem
seems inconclusive beside the fully developed moralities of Baude-

laire's 'Le Voyage' or Dante's magnificent account of Ulysses' last journey; to the latter of which, at least, Heredia seems to owe something. But it is the inconclusiveness of Heredia's personal philosophy, in which the desire to find human aspirations valid is inhibited by a more sombre realism. The character of the sailors remains unresolved, it is both 'héroïque' and 'brutal'; their hopes may be fulfilled, but probably the mirage is a mirage only, they await epic tomorrows, but their only actual discovery is the new constellations, tokens of their progress but at the same time reminders of the frightening infinity of the universe and the littleness of man. The poet, in addition to expressing his admiration, has also made the conquerors partly in the image of himself; the eagle eye of stout Cortez is clouded over with Heredia's own brand of heroic melancholy.

But Heredia also has means for dominating this melancholy. Indeed his enthusiasm for the Brittany coast tricks him into language which, though energetic, is oddly like that of an over-literary travel-poster:

> Pour que le sang joyeux dompte l'esprit morose
> Il faut, tout parfumé du sel des goëmons,
> Que le souffle atlantique emplisse tes poumons;
> Arvor t'offre ses caps que la mer blanche arrose.

More authentically, he sees the landscape as partaking of some of the significance of the god-forsaken scenarios of Leconte de Lisle's poems; yet as giving access to artistic and imaginative consolations:

> L'Hiver a défleuri la lande et le courtil,
> Tout est mort. Sur la roche uniformément grise
> Où la lame sans fin de l'Atlantique brise,
> Le pétale fané pend au dernier pistil.
>
> Et pourtant je ne sais quel arome subtil
> Exhalé de la mer jusqu'à moi par la brise,
> D'un effluve si tiède remplit mon cœur qu'il grise;
> Ce souffle étrangement parfumé, d'où vient-il?

It is a striking and personal variation of the Parnassian landscape with its metaphysical desolation and its redeeming phenomena;

and one cannot help feeling, though this is perhaps to make a point about personalities rather than poetry, that Heredia faces the situation more resourcefully than Leconte de Lisle, and that the *aubaine* that the winds bring him is a more accessible and rewarding one than the 'sombre volupté' offered to the select few at the end of 'Midi'.

The difference of temperament is further brought out in the way in which the two poets put forward their contrast between the classical and the present age. While Leconte de Lisle vituperates against *les modernes*, Heredia is more like the archaeologist who reluctantly admits that everybody cannot share his tastes, but wishes that at least they would be a bit more careful where they tread. 'L'homme indifférent au rêve des aïeux' is treated very much more in sorrow than in anger, and in the very last poem, 'Sur un marbre brisé', Heredia actually offers the reader a poetic initiation into the technique of his archaeological and aesthetic pleasures. And these are not in fact simply points about personality; this moderation and sense of proportion are connected with the qualities that allow him to adopt so easily and authentically the unemphatic epigraphic style he learnt from the Greek Anthology, to run the whole range of elegiac emotion from the wry laments of 'Hortorum Deus' to the tolerant melancholy of 'La Source'. Heredia successfully runs the risk of the miniature and the precious, and we feel a great deal more comfortable with his eloquent centaur ('Les monts Thessaliens étaient mon vague empire / Et leurs torrents glacés lavaient mon poil vermeil') than with Gautier's talking obelisks.

To prefer these poems is to go against the usual judgement of Heredia, which praises him for his ability to render colourful action, the geographical dimension and the historical turning-point within the narrow compass of the sonnet; poems like 'Antoine et Cléo-pâtre' are indeed impressive, but the tendency to rely on the 'big' sculptural final line becomes rather routine and has something of the bogus air of the fade-out of a bad film, claiming significance without having really earned it. The sonnet form at least ensures that the dangers of the painterly cannot get out of hand; even so, Heredia's most successful poetic dealing with it is in a poem which is not directly pictorial, but which evokes the activity of the pictorial artist. 'Rêves d'émail' gives a wonderful impression of the artist's self-sufficiency, confidence, and absorption:

> Et sous mes pinceaux vit, naît, court et prend l'essor
> Le peuple monstrueux de la mythologie,
> Les Centaures, Pan, Sphinx, la Chimère, l'Orgie
> Et, du sang de Gorgo, Pégase et Chrysaor.

Perhaps it is the fact that he has no space in which to proceed to the actual *peinture* that leaves our admiration completely intact.

Heredia is not a major figure in the development of literary history. Though much of it was written in the high Parnassian period, his work was not finally published till 1893. Perhaps in spite of his continued allegiance to Leconte de Lisle he also learnt something from the successive poetic movements which passed by in his lifetime, learnt to see that, like the transient civilizations they 'studied', the Parnassians' aesthetic too was a temporary phenomenon, that the true sources of poetry were as ever personal, unpredictable, and unrelated to public announcements of impending artistic renaissance. At least he had a sound intuition that, in returning to one of the most traditional forms of French poetry, he was avoiding a multitude of poetic sins.

NOTE

THÉOPHILE GAUTIER, 1811–72, was an ardent supporter of the Romanticism of 1830 and his first poems are in the Romantic manner. However, he soon moved to a narrower, dominantly pictorial conception of poetry and became the chief spokesman of the doctrine of 'Art for Art's sake', which he aimed to exemplify in his most famous work, *Émaux et camées* (1852, enlarged 1872). His vast literary output was mostly journalistic; but 'le bon Théo', as he was called, held a position of unique respect among his literary superiors.

CHARLES MARIE RENÉ LECONTE DE LISLE, 1818–94, was born in the island of Réunion, which perhaps stimulated his taste for the colourful and exotic. After being active in the 1848 revolution he moved, like Gautier, towards a more aristocratic conception of the poet as creator of timeless beauty. He was the chief figure in the mid-century Parnassian group of poets (so called because of their occasional anthology *Le Parnasse contemporain*), who rejected the sentimental and political concerns of the Romantics in favour of the pursuit of formal perfection.

JOSÉ-MARIA DE HEREDIA, 1842–1905, Leconte de Lisle's most fervent disciple, came also from an exotic background. Born in Cuba of a French mother, he was directly descended through his father from the Spanish *conquistadores*. Though his poems were well known in Parnassian circles they were only finally collected in *Les Trophées* (1893).

Editions. The Garnier edition of Gautier's *Émaux et camées* (ed. A. Boschot, 1954) contains a biographical sketch and a selection from Gautier's other poetry. The standard editions of Leconte de Lisle's four collections (*Poèmes antiques*, 1852, *Poèmes barbares*, 1862, *Poèmes tragiques*, 1884, and *Derniers poèmes*, 1895) and of Heredia's *Les Trophées* are those of Lemerre, and have been reprinted. There is a useful selection of Leconte de Lisle, *Choix de poèmes* (ed. E. Eggli, 1943) and an edition of *Les Trophées* by F. W. Stokoe (1942).

Criticism. A. Cassagne, *La Théorie de l'art pour l'art en France* (1906), is an excellent introduction to the period. Gautier has attracted little literary critical attention, but J. Richardson, *Théophile de Gautier, his Life and Times* (1958), is a reliable account of his literary career. On Leconte de Lisle, A. Fairlie, *Leconte de Lisle's Poems on the Barbarian Races* (1947), is scholarly and specialized, but the concluding chapter has interesting general remarks. See also I. Putter, *The Pessimism of Leconte de Lisle* (2 vols., 1954, 1961), and I. Brown, *Leconte de Lisle* (1966). The only detailed study of Heredia is M. Ibrovac, *J. M. de Heredia : sa vie, son œuvre* (1923), and *J. M. de Heredia : les sources des 'Trophées'* (1923).

3. Realism and Reality in the Novel

HOW 'real' is realism? Suppose that I wished to incorporate into a novel the reality of the room in which I am now writing. I should doubtless have to indicate, say, that there is a long bookcase facing me with a white radiator to the left of it, but would my 'realistic' description require me to list the titles of the hundreds of books in the bookcase, or give the cubic capacity (which I happen not to know) of the white radiator? And suppose that in the name of a dedicated realism I contrived to do this, at what point—before I get involved in expounding the principles of gas-fired central heating or copying out faithfully the hundreds of thousands of pages contained in the bookcase—might I reasonably allow myself to draw the line?

One has only to compare 'realistic' conversation in a novel with the straggling nature of actual conversation as tape-recorded, to consider the concentration of time involved in treating a human life in two hundred pages, or to remember the necessary limitations of experience and perception of any single novelist to confirm that reality, in any literal or complete sense, cannot possibly be rendered in the novel. The novel is a game—of make-believe, in the first instance—and like all games it depends upon rules or assumptions. Realism—like classicism, symbolism, or any other 'ism'—is one form of presentation, means of persuasion, or literary convention. It offers not so much reality as the *illusion* of the real—and, of course, a fragile illusion at that.

For the illusion, obviously, is itself a convention—the reader will abandon it soon enough for a more real reality if a helicopter lands in his garden or flames start licking up his drawing-room door. Again, if only because he is aware that the illusion has been contrived by a single individual, he knows that the writer is necessarily selecting and re-ordering, that even within the illusion the realism is essentially a matter of emphasis, that he is not so much being offered reality as *sign*—the writer says that the hero got off the train in an agitated state at Victoria Station and the willing reader, in order to keep the game going and, indeed, whether he has ever been there or not, can in practice be relied upon to *assume* the complex reality of central London. Why then does the reader 'believe' in this very conventional 'illusion' of reality? He does so to the extent that he accepts it as a necessary field of suggestion or demonstration: as the indication of an implicit *frame of reference*. And since we are not as yet concerned with the philosophy associated with the nineteenth-century phenomenon of Realism with a capital 'R', but rather with the assumption implicit in the provision of the illusion itself, this frame of reference may be said broadly to be governed by a simple underlying *idea*: that human life cannot be represented in a fully meaningful or truthful manner without taking account of the pressures brought to bear upon the individual by his milieu, by the particularity of social situation and historical circumstance.

Realism, then, is a matter of literary pitch, a stylization which carries the implication of a certain necessary relationship between man and his natural or social environment. In so far as it remains a literary convention, however, it is not of itself more real or more true than other conventions—'truth' and 'reality' are functions of the compulsion of a particular work and of its relationship with a particular readership. Again, in so far as a particular convention may dominate a form at any one time in such a way as almost to define it, the realistic mode may be adopted by writers who might be expected to be unsympathetic to the philosophical implications inherent in or associated with the style itself—very many Christian novelists, for example, have written in a realistic idiom. In practice, it may be said very broadly that the use of the style is governed— and whether this be accepted positively or antithetically—by the *relevance* of the idea implicit in it to the culture at large at any one time.

There was always an element of realism associated with comedy, of course, since this genre tends naturally to see man in a social context, and the technique of illusion is to be found at certain moments in older art—in Hellenistic art, for instance, or the medieval *fabliaux*, or Dutch painting. But in literature proper, for obvious reasons, the great move towards realism coincides broadly with the fundamental general shift from the old God-centred view of the world towards our own distinctively man-centred culture, and from an absolutist view of an immutable 'human nature' towards a relativist view of the conditioned individual and the 'human situation'. The neo-classical stylization of the theatre of Racine, for example— even if Molière's comedy coexisted alongside it and, indeed, if the rigorously conventional Unities were defended on realistic grounds—depends, even in its innocent assumption of a central cultural continuity extending from Ancient Greece to seventeenth-century France, upon the background Christian belief in a God-given human nature which is determinant independently of environment or cultural conditioning. This idea of a fixed human nature, briefly, passes through certain intermediates—such as a still essentialist view of 'character', for example—until with Zola, say, two hundred years later, it has been transformed into the idea of man as the product of hereditary and environmental factors.

At one level, of course, it may seem that there is a curiously similar pessimism about the view of the individual as the victim of original sin on the one hand, and of impersonal social and biological forces (or our more recent Freudian fatalities) on the other, but the difference remains fundamental in that any remedy to the human predicament is now seen as lying not with God but with man him-self—in the *understanding* of these forces of necessity, in social and political action, and so on. And what has intervened in these two hundred years between Racine and Zola, it need hardly be said, is the collapse of the feudal order, the collapse of Christianity as a dimension of government and as a universally held belief, the industrial revolution, the development of scientific and sociological thinking, the theory of evolution—in fact all that has gone towards the making of our own relativistic agnostic culture. The development of the novel form itself is coextensive with the history of modern realism as it reflects this radical transformation of the culture; and realism has not only been the distinctive mode of the form but remains the dominant stylization of the novel, taken over all, up to the present day.

The whole subject of realism remains a complex and paradoxical one, however, and two major difficulties may be stated at once. The first of these concerns the use of the term itself. Quite apart from the consideration that all art must obviously see itself as being concerned with reality in some form, there is the fact that 'realism'—perfidiously elastic as such literary terms frequently are—has tended to escape its narrow identification with nineteenth-century social or biological determinism to accommodate subsequent developments in the culture, as the novel form itself has developed in sophistication to incorporate them. The descriptive techniques of an anti-novelist such as Alain Robbe-Grillet, for example, may not unreasonably be seen in terms of 'neo-realism', while innovations ranging from the 'stream of consciousness' to the *tropismes* of Nathalie Sarraute are often classed as 'psychological realism'. 'Realism', in fact, has tended inevitably enough to follow a changing sense of reality and, being thus extensible as a term, cannot in practice be considered bound to the particular assumptions underlying self-conscious Realism or Naturalism of the nineteenth century.

The second major difficulty is implicit in the simple impossibility of fully rendering reality and in the merely conventional nature of the 'illusion of reality', already indicated. Reality, or its illusion, implies objectivity—the world itself rather than the author's view of it. Yet it is entirely clear that the novelist—like the illusionist on a stage—is tied to the game of telling a convincing lie, that he must select and re-order and interpret, that he is limited to his own perception of things: that the novel, in a word, can only be the expression in projection of an individual subjectivity. If criticism has not satisfactorily resolved this apparently contradictory relationship between objectivity and subjectivity—the central problem of literary realism—it is not entirely surprising. While it is in France that the central engagement in the battle over realism—perhaps the most spectacular in the history of literature—was fought, Flaubert, Zola, and the other great writers involved were never able, at the theoretical level, to solve this basic problem themselves.

To some extent, of course, this was due to the cultural agitation of the time in which these writers lived. If the broader movement towards realism came relatively late to France—largely because neo-classicism had been artificially maintained by the nature of the régime, and because the reaction to it had initially taken the form of a Romantic subjectivism—it partly overlapped the Romantic period itself and came with considerable force into a richly explosive social, political, and cultural situation. Indeed, the new trend in the novel developed over the sixty years between 1830 and 1890 amid a confused kind of permanent revolution of which the political events themselves—the revolutions of 1830 and 1848, the *coup d'état* of Napoleon III, the Franco-Prussian War, the Commune— merely constituted the surface. With the growth of the industrial revolution, the rise of a new financial bourgeoisie, the phenomenon of proletarization, the development and the hardening of the class conflict, the society in which these novelists were writing was changing in depth. And the intellectual and moral climate was being transformed by accompanying changes in the culture: the spread of Positivist ideas, the development of scientific methodology, the growth of an evolutionary, environmental view of man and of optimistic, progressive social philosophies—in fact the whole new and often naïve enthusiasm for the scientific and sociological rationalism conveniently rendered by the word 'scientism'.

The 'triumph' of Realism may well be situated in the mid-1850s, with the exhibition of Courbet's paintings, the scandal surrounding Flaubert's *Madame Bovary*, Duranty's review *Le Réalisme*, and Champfleury's influential collection of essays of the same name. As for the more applied and overtly determinist Naturalism—the name combined the modern association with zoology and botany with an older usage of the word in the sense of materialism—it may be said to emerge with the 'clinical' *Germinie Lacerteux* (1864) of the Goncourt brothers and with Zola's study of remorse as an 'organic disorder' in *Thérèse Raquin* (1867). It assumed physical form in a group of writers surrounding Zola and continued on its highly controversial course well into the 1880s. Given the confusion of the period—the terms 'Realist' and 'Naturalist' were differently and often interchangeably employed— it is retroactively that modern literary history has imposed this broad pattern of Realism, Naturalism, and Reaction, and no such pattern was very clear to the major novelists themselves. They were writing essentially out of the usual combination of talent and a certain imperialism of the imagination itself frequently related to a particular condition of the personality—the arrested emotional development of Flaubert, of Balzac, or even of Stendhal, for example—and driven to impose their own vision upon the world. They possessed no more than the layman's knowledge of science itself, and their aesthetic views were often propounded only under the pressure of controversies with moral and political overtones; but in an age when even such writers as Flaubert and Baudelaire could feel that art must become increasingly 'scientific' they tended naturally to justify their activity, not only to the public but to themselves, in the intellectual terms dominating their cultural situation.

While there was broad agreement about the more obvious features of realism—the inclusion of the whole range of society and of experience, the emphasis on the representativeness of fictional characters, the reliance on observation and on documentation—a significant dialectic of division and confusion emerges over the half-century in question in relation to this central problem of reconciling the apparent contradiction between subjectivity and an increasingly 'scientific' objectivity.

What each writer had to do, in effect, was to provide some sort of theoretical basis for objectivity from within the terms available to him at his own particular stage of the culture, while yet taking account of his own existence as a man with his own individuality and world-view. For Balzac, in a sense, there was as yet no problem. He provides his theoretical basis by adapting Saint-Hilaire's theory of milieu differentiation into a kind of poetic zoology within which he studies the various 'social species', but since he saw himself happily as a novelist-historian-scholar-philosopher (though he was in fact a richly confused visionary Romantic fascinated by the real, and a compulsive story-teller if ever one existed), he felt no need whatever for the writer to conceal his own moral, political, or social convictions. It will fall to his admirer Champfleury to react against him in this connection and to argue that the novelist must turn himself into a clear unclouded lens, able in an impersonal *style transparent* to render man in his everyday ordinariness with a kind of ideal photographic exactness.

With the Goncourts and with Flaubert, the pendulum swings back towards the *style artiste*, but only thereby to pose the problem more dauntingly than before. Flaubert himself, although he brought about the decisive shift towards the complete 'illusion of reality'— towards the work of art as object or world-in-itself rather than the mere illustration of a world-view—could not solve it at the theoretical level. Harshly contemptuous of the idea that art should serve any explicit moral, social, or utilitarian purpose whatsoever, he was nevertheless fiercely anti-subjectivist in his opposition to any expression of private emotion in the novel. It is only at a level of symbolical abstraction—where the imposing semi-platonic entities which he called *le Vrai*, *le Beau*, and *la Justice* can quite simply be equated—that Flaubert can stabilize the contradiction. And he tends somewhat innocently to justify a Parnassian or 'art for art's sake' type of impersonality and objectivity in terms of a very idealist view of the 'precision of science'.

His successor Zola was perhaps more aware of the contradiction, even if he was no more successful at resolving it. While, armed with Claude Bernard's experimental physiology and with Lucas's treatise on heredity, he proceeded to set up his Rougon-Macquart series of novels as a vast, controlled, 'scientific' experiment plotting the combined effect of heredity and environment, he nevertheless knew that the writer's 'temperament' was decisive, and even argued, as against Flaubert, that the writer must express his own individuality. If Zola later grew out of his 'scientism', it was left to Maupassant—the only major writer of the period who appears to have understood the profound change which the novel form was undergoing—to point out that each writer has his own sense of reality, that the great writer is one who convincingly imposes his own reality upon the world, and that the Realists were really 'Illusionists' bringing about through the *technique* of the *appearance* of reality a decisive sophistication of the expressive possibilities of the form.

What is one to say today about this failure of the major realists in the novel from Balzac to Zola—and they were after all intelligent, highly gifted and dedicated men—to resolve intellectually the apparent contradiction between objectivity and subjectivity?

One very common approach is to say in effect that the contradiction cannot be resolved, that Realism with a capital 'R' is an absurdity, and that these were considerable novelists *despite* the fact that they were Realists or to the extent that they did not implement their own aesthetic. Some critics—remembering, perhaps, that in France itself the Naturalist movement was followed immediately by what was in part a spiritualist reaction—tend further to see in the confusion of the Realists the bankruptcy of the scientific humanism of the nineteenth century and to assume tacitly that the growing subjectivism of Western art thereafter is the function of a new, if inchoate, philosophical idealism. This approach, however, is hardly a convincing one. In the first place, while it may be granted that at the philosophical level the objectivist pretensions of Realism are indeed something of an absurdity, it is entirely clear that the artistic achievement of Flaubert or Zola, say, would have been inconceivable if their romantic temperaments had not been disciplined by the realist aesthetic. In the second place, if it is true that the mechanistic determinism of nineteenth-century 'scientism' has been superseded, it is rather obvious that—as indeed the extension of the term 'realism', already noted, itself suggests—it has in fact been superseded by a more open and sophisticated form of the same world-view, and that the growing subjectivism in art is the function of an individualism sanctioned by an increasingly agnostic and relativistic culture. The problem is not to be solved quite so easily.

Nor is it to be solved by identifying, as does Erich Heller, *two* realisms in modern literature—a realism, relating to external reality, of the great nineteenth-century novel, and one, relating to human inwardness as the only reality, of a line of poets ranging from Baudelaire to Rilke. For this is to force the language unduly, to turn a matter of emphasis—itself to some extent explicable in terms of generic differences of pitch—into a false dichotomy and thereby, in effect, to simplify our whole culture. All art, obviously, is the function of a tension between an inner sense of reality and the totality of the real, between a subjectivity and the world. Zola, for example, is as much a *poète de la vie moderne* as is Baudelaire, and the 'world' of his writing is in the end as intimately personal. A more fruitful approach, perhaps, is to follow the good sense of Maupassant and consider this central paradox underlying literary realism in terms of the development of the novel form itself.

It is obvious, of course, that a literary form cannot have an independent history, but its inner development tends to be a surer guide than the opportunist rationalizations, movements, manifestos, swings and counterswings which agitate the surface of literary history. To approach the matter in this fashion is perhaps to see how Flaubert, in the midst of the dilemma which enabled him to say at once, and in fact quite rightly, 'Madame Bovary n'a rien de moi' and 'Madame Bovary c'est moi', not only established the realist novel but also, in some sense, the modern novel itself; to see why the anti-Realist Proust should have expressed his debt to him, and why even the 'anti-novelist' Robbe-Grillet should look back to him as the fountainhead. It is also perhaps to see, beneath the dialectical 'party warfare' of Romanticism, Realism, Reaction, and so on, the essential continuity underlying our complex culture.

To understand the mutation in the novel brought about by the Realists—or Illusionists, as Maupassant preferred to call them— one may think for a moment, since he has already been mentioned, of the high stylization of the theatre of Racine. The writer's sensibility may be expressed in every line and he may even be dramatizing his own conflicts on the stage, but he *is* dramatizing them: the projection is complete. The play has as it were its own separate reality, and there can be no question of Racine walking up and down his own stage telling us what he thinks of Britannicus, say, or distancing himself prudently from certain views expressed by Phèdre. Yet this, in effect, is very much what the novelist before Flaubert had tended to do, and it was the absence of this interpretative comment on the part of the author rather than the very routine theme of adultery—the apparent coldness of the 'impersonality' engendered by Flaubert's attempt to achieve total projection, or the complete 'illusion of reality'—which disconcerted many of the original readers of *Madame Bovary*. Flaubert was not respecting the rules of the game.

But then, at a time when the novel was taking over from the theatre as the representative literary genre of the culture, the existing rules were already out of date. The novel, in fact, had until then been something of a bastard form—a kind of illustrated treatise, in the main, in which the writer tended to act as chorus to his own action, mediating the whole through his own explicit world-view and, indeed, larding his 'imitation of life' with ingratiatingly 'noble' prefaces, philosophical interludes, moral aphorisms, and so on. However, with the increasing sophistication of the reader, the break-up of the old cultural unity, and the hardening of the division of opinion within society, the novelist who showed his hand too clearly was becoming increasingly vulnerable. The reader could all too easily reduce the total impact of the work to argumentative terms, identify the world-view, and reject it. By moving towards a complete illusion of reality, on the other hand, the novelist could disarm the reader and, indeed, come close to brain-washing him by appearing to offer not just the illustration of a world-view or even an *interpretation* of the world, but the world itself: *la force des choses*. If this shift towards objectivity came under the pressure of a new social reality and the sense of its conditioning impact, it in any event represented a necessary improvement in technique if the novel—in view of its new importance within the culture—was to become a high art form.

Given this new sophistication, of course, the game becomes a much more demanding one for the novelist to play. Since he cannot render the world itself, creating a complete illusion of reality is in effect creating a world *plausible* enough to take over in the reader's mind from the world itself. He soon discovers that the realism of detailed notation—the time of arrival or the agitated gestures of our hero at Victoria Station, if you like—is only the surface of his task; that what he really has to do is to create a fictional world which suggests the depth and the consistency which the reader postulates for the world itself. It is for this reason that the emphasis shifts insensibly from the surface of the work to the structure of the work, from direct correlation with external reality to the internal coherence, the separate total relativity of the created world. By a series of succulent ironies, therefore, Realism leads

towards the technique of illusion, and the technical exigencies of
the illusion lead towards the idea of the separate reality of the
illusion—until we have Flaubert himself dreaming of writing a
novel which could stand up by the perfection of its structure and
style alone without having to depend upon correlation with anything external to it: the 'father of realism' dreaming of the 'novel
about Nothing'!

All that has taken place, of course—as Racine could doubtless
have pointed out—is that through all the confusion of a changing
cultural situation the novel has in some sense blundered towards
the apparent autonomy, the completeness of stylization which
characterizes high art. For any real autonomy—the impossible
dream of Flaubert as of Robbe-Grillet—is obviously out of the
question. The novel manifestly has to be about *something* and, in
practice, about human beings, if only by implication and because
there really is not, to date, very much else that it could readily be
about. It is also clear that the so-called autonomy can only be the
form achieved in projection by a human awareness. What has really
happened—and the contradiction is only apparent—is that the
realist novelist, through this new discipline of objective rendering,
has found the means of expressing more fully his own subjectivity.
Like the debate about whether the characters are more or less
important than form or structure in the novel—if the characters
are unconvincing the form cannot impose itself; if the form is
unsatisfactory the characters lose their force of conviction—the
apparent contradiction between objectivity and subjectivity turns
out, in practice, to be a false problem.

From Stendhal, who saw the novel as a 'mirror of life', to Proust,
who saw that genius lay rather in the quality of the mirror than in
the quality of the life reflected, the progression over this whole
period is clear. But if Stendhal was somewhat innocent about the
clarity of his mirror, the subtlety of Proust's reflective and refrac-
tive capacity cannot exist without something to reflect; from subjectivity at one end of the process and the world at the other there
can be no escape. And the point about realism is that it deepened
that relationship between them which the novel, simply, is all about.
Driven by a set of social and cultural pressures towards an objective

rendering of the world, the nineteenth-century novelist, as we have seen, is led towards complete projection, the 'illusion of reality'. He indeed provides a more complete and objective picture of the world than before, but the technical demands of the illusion require him in effect to set up an alternative or 'autonomous' world; and this totality, in turn, challenges his subjectivity more profoundly and confronts him more completely with himself.

For now that the will to objectivity or 'impersonality' has in practice eliminated from the work the explicit world-view which had previously mediated not only between himself and the reader but between himself and his own fiction, it is in depth that he is confronting himself. Projecting himself beyond the immediate 'defence mechanisms of the ego', to adopt psycho-analytical parlance, it is *organically* that he is giving shape and coherence to his 'autonomous' world—so much so indeed that he may find himself establishing his vision of things even at the cost of the break-up of his explicit world-view. For the 'autonomous' world, even if it looks like the world itself, is in practice *his* world—to the very extent that he realizes it in terms of the world he is structuring and achieving his own subjective awareness. So that whether we talk about the realization of a subjectivity in terms of the objective world, or about the rendering of the objective world under the profound control of a subjectivity—whether we call realism a rectification of reality in the service of a private vision or the concretizing of a private vision in terms of the real—the objectivity and the subjectivity go hand in hand, are necessarily interfused. It is because the self cannot be eliminated but only transmuted, because it is most profoundly expressed in total projection that, though for Flaubert 'Madame Bovary n'a rien de moi', nevertheless 'Madame Bovary c'est moi'. Indeed, he might almost, and more profoundly, have said it of the whole work: '*Madame Bovary* c'est moi.' It is for this reason too that Champfleury—whatever his arguments, and all differences of individual talent, of course, set aside—was entirely right to place the *roman réaliste* above the introspective novel or *roman personnel*. And whether or not the intellectual terms in which they conceived of their activity were inadequate, it is not despite the fact that they were realists, but *because* they were realists that the great writers associated with this international trend in the novel achieved what is at once, probably, the fullest picture of the modern world and one of the highest expressions of Western subjectivity in modern literature.

Implicitly, of course, the paradox underlying realism is recognized today even in our critical clichés—as when, however real our interest in the historical setting itself, we talk about 'the world of Zola', for example. And since in the one work, *Madame Bovary*, as will be indicated in the next chapter, Flaubert pioneered the basic techniques of the high art form to be exploited so successfully by such writers as Proust, Joyce, and Thomas Mann, the line of development of the novel from the realists onwards is a fairly straight one. Whether we think of the continuing central stream of realism in the novel or of the 'autonomous' world of certain antinovelists, the essential continuity of the form seems clear. And there remains perhaps to say something, however briefly, about the problem of experimentation in the present-day novel.

Far from being dead, as some critics appear to imply, the broad and simple assumptions indicated at the outset as being implicit in the realistic stylization itself would seem more and more to be those upon which our civilization depends. It would be hazardous indeed, in practice, to maintain that realism was disappearing from a culture compounded of colour reportage, technological advance, the popularization of the social sciences, 'science fiction', 'godless theology', and virtually round-the-clock multi-channel TV, straight and semi-documentary! The 'dilemma' of the novel is paradoxically a function rather of this very fact, of what one is tempted to call the *over-relevance* of the broad idea implicit in realism to the culture at large. And any deviation from formal realism in recent fiction has to be viewed in the light of the fact that the novel, in a culture increasingly dominated by the 'realism' of the powerful mass-media developed over the past hundred years, is obliged to adapt itself to changing—and in many ways reduced—circumstances.

Not only has the depiction of social reality in the novel lost its shock value, but it may well, given the development of the

TRINITY COLLEGE LIBRARY

audio-visual media, have lost its *raison d'être*. If in 1885 the appropriate form for Zola's treatment of a mining community in *Germinal* was obviously the novel, the situation is rather different today. It is true, of course, that there is still a surprising amount of reportage in the novel, to say nothing of the new kind of enhanced documentary which has recently emerged with Truman Capote's *In Cold Blood* and John Berger's *A Fortunate Man*. Nevertheless it might seem that, except under the pressure of urgent social and political issues as in the 1930s and 1940s, the novel has been supplanted in its traditional domain. More than that, there are ex-novelists such as Sartre who maintain that psychological exploration in the novel has been largely superseded by the science of psychology itself. And even if we were to say that the novel can still convey the 'existential feel' of living in the world, some would argue that the cinema is at once more richly equipped for this purpose and more universal in its application. In this somewhat daunting situation, the signs are that, just as the high theatre, helped, of course, by a sense of destiny deriving from a dramatic world situation, has tended to survive competition from the cinema over the past thirty years or so by becoming more of a metaphysical 'theatre of language', the novel is now aspiring to become in some sense the new poetry of our culture.

If this is the case, one is tempted to think that it will not be easy. Even the 'autonomous' novel cannot easily aspire to the freedom of poetry or of the plastic arts, in that it is tied by its very physical presentation to a sense of sequence. By simply stating two different happenings, the writer implies a sense of time and the sense of a behavioural pattern; and the sense of behaviour in time by implication lets in the historico-social and the moral, whether the writer likes it or not. That realism, which is in some sense the *meaning* of the novel form, is not easily superseded, and the new novel itself—as the term 'anti-novel' eloquently suggests—is still dependent upon it antithetically. Nor is it easy for the novel to escape the intellectual pressures of the culture at large. Whether we think of Flaubert or Proust or Virginia Woolf, experimentation in the novel has in practice correlated fairly directly with precise intellectual developments in the culture at large and, in the case of the new novel itself, the emphasis on the separate totality or on the 'autonomy' of language would seem to correspond readily enough to a proliferation of gestalt psychologies and to the growing importance in so many fields of the rapidly multiplying sciences of linguistics. And there is one final point to be made.

Whereas the anti-novel is dependent antithetically not only upon the traditional form but upon the sense of reality which the reader derives from the many other media now acting upon him, a great realist novel such as *War and Peace* combined a profound realization of a subjectivity with an inclusive and direct rendering of the world and of the historical and social fatalities bearing upon the situation of the reader. Part of its authority, indeed, came from the fact that it was often, if in its own way, imparting simple information about the world. The historic achievement of the great realist novel was a function of its central and privileged position within the culture: it *at once* stated and re-ordered the world. And even if the novel did contrive to 'save itself' by transforming itself in effect into a different genre, it is difficult to see how it could ever again occupy the central position in the culture which it enjoyed in the heyday of Balzac and Flaubert and Zola.

That the novel, born of a realism itself born of the decisive change in human culture, should in the medium term be in danger of dying, as it were, of excess of realism in our civilization is obviously a sad and ironical thought. However, this would simply mean that it had in effect been replaced by other modes of artistic expression, and certainly—to say the very least—this final irony would be a fitting climax to the paradoxical history of the form.

NOTE

Biographical and bibliographical details for Balzac, Flaubert, and Zola follow the appropriate chapters in the present volume and in vol. 4.

CHAMPFLEURY (pseudonym of Jules François Félix Husson), 1821-89, was influential through his collection of essays *Le Réalisme* (1857) and through his many other publications. His more successful novels include *Les Bourgeois de Molinchart* (1855) and *Monsieur de Boisdhyver* (1856). Also interested in art, he was appointed curator of the Sèvres museum in 1872.

Criticism. Since the critical writing in this field is very extensive, the best initial approach is probably through works which combine documentary material with a critical presentation, such as G. J. Becker (ed.), *Documents of Modern Literary Realism* (1963), which includes Proust on realism and Erich Heller on 'The Realistic Fallacy'; H. S. Gershman and K. B. Whitworth, *Anthologie des préfaces de romans français du XIXᵉ siècle* (1965); J.-H. Bornecque and P. Cogny, *Réalisme et naturalisme* (1958).

Useful short treatments are to be found in the relevant chapters of P. Van Tieghem, *Les grandes doctrines littéraires en France* (1946), and R. Wellek, *Concepts of Criticism* (1963), while there is a good article by A. J. Salvan, 'L'Essence du réalisme français', in a symposium on realism in *Comparative Literature*, vol. iii, no. 3, Summer 1951.

Standard literary histories include R. Dumesnil, *Le Réalisme et le naturalisme* (1955), C. Beuchat, *Histoire du naturalisme français*, 2 vols. (1949), and P. Martino, *Le Naturalisme français* (1923). B. Weinberg's well-documented survey, *French Realism: The Critical Reaction, 1830–1870* (1937), has since been supplemented by M. Iknayan's *The Idea of the Novel in France: The Critical Reaction, 1815–1848* (1961), while M. Raimond's *La Crise du roman: du lendemain du naturalisme aux années vingt* (1966) provides an excellent pendant to G. Reynier's *Les Origines du roman réaliste* (1912). Among other works of interest are E. Auerbach, *Mimesis* (1953); J. Chiari, *Realism and Imagination* (1960); H. Levin, *The Gates of Horn* (1963); G. Lukács, *Studies in European Realism* (1964); and F. W. J. Hemmings (ed.), *The Age of Realism* (1974).

4. Flaubert

IT is enough to glance again at the Imperial Advocate's speech for the prosecution at the ludicrous trial of Flaubert in 1857 for *offenses à la morale publique et à la religion*—or for that matter at Maître Sénard's speech for the defence—to be reminded, not only of the moral necessity of a dash of realism in a hypocritical society, but of the simple newness of what Flaubert had achieved in *Madame Bovary*. The reminder is a salutary one for several reasons.

In the first place, if he still tends to be classed among the world's 'great novelists', Flaubert is hardly the one most likely to appeal to an audience accustomed to the rather self-conscious literature of the 'human situation' of our own time. For one thing, the famous 'agonies of style' may seem a trifle quaint. For another, Flaubert's scepticism may appear to be so all-embracing as to be self-defeating. His thunderous denunciation of his time may be thought to be not so much constructive as the expression of a convenient, even complacent, 'catastrophism' on the part of a comfortably secluded and very bourgeois anti-bourgeois. To a century which has had to try to come to terms with real catastrophe there may in fact appear to be a certain innocence about Flaubert—and not only about a semi-Platonic pursuit of the Beautiful in a form tied to the depiction of human behaviour. There is surely also something a little innocent about thunderings against a nineteenth-century bourgeois order which by their very intensity tend implicitly to lend to that order a kind of eternal stability—as about a bitter emphasis on human stupidity which tends to preclude any real sense of human evil and, thereby, any very real possibility of good. The present-day reader may find this particular old master more ornate than profound. Indeed, he may even feel that the fine feathers of Style are the consecration, rather than the redemption, of a nineteenth-century world-view which is essentially negative, self-protective, and confused.

Nor is that all. For if Flaubert's role in the development of the novel—already indicated in the previous chapter—cannot seriously be called in question, this in itself may tend paradoxically to operate against him. By one of the many ironies surrounding this 'novelist's novelist'—as Henry James called him—the reader approaching *Madame Bovary* for the first time may be so conditioned to a fictional method deriving largely from Flaubert himself as to be a little bemused by talk of its originality. In fact, at a time when the novelist André Malraux speaks of Flaubert's 'beaux romans paralysés' and the critic Martin Turnell describes him as 'a great literary engineer rather than a great novelist'—and when Jean-Paul Sartre and others have been taking a cool look at the old sentimental picture of the 'hermit of Croisset' as the sanctified incarnation of the lonely integrity of the Artist in a philistine society—it is doubtless all too easy to be unfair to this 'martyr' of the modern novel.

For after all, however great the division of critical opinion regarding them may now have become, at least three of Flaubert's works—*Madame Bovary*, *L'Éducation sentimentale*, and *Bouvard et Pécuchet*—remain major landmarks in the history of the novel. And the more we are surrounded by anti-novels, the clearer does it become that Flaubert's contribution to the development of the fictional form was a fundamental one. It is not too much to say that he brought about a kind of mutation in the novel. As has been suggested at some length in the preceding chapter, it seems clear that he did this not simply by treating 'realistic' subjects, or by bringing to the whole task of writing a dedication which has become legendary, or even by submitting the writing of prose to the disciplines of poetry. Essentially, he did it by creating an apparently impersonal art whereby his 'perpetual absence', as Taine put it, might become 'all-powerful'. In the one novel, *Madame Bovary*, he effected the decisive shift towards the artistic 'autonomy' of the work, the complete projection of the action into the 'illusion of reality'—the necessary shift from the old bastard form of the novel as the illustration of an explicit world-view to the novel as 'object', or world eloquent of itself.

It is possible to take a short passage almost at random from
Madame Bovary—as I have seen a French professor of literature do
with great verbal skill, a wealth of background knowledge, and
superb, if discreet, mimicry for an hour and a half—and demonstrate, for example, how a particular kind of carriage, the clothes
of the people inside it, the ruts on the roadway, the height of the
hedges, the gauche gesture of the girl of fifteen, or the shaving-scar
on the face of the man who has had to prepare hastily for the journey
in the morning twilight, all correspond to a precise historical and
human reality. This, of course, is a perfectly natural tribute to
Flaubert's skill as a writer, but it is not perhaps the shortest way to
an understanding of this realist for whom reality was only a 'spring-
board'. Flaubert's art does not depend upon the accumulation of
detail, but upon the idea of the interdependence of every element
in the construction: upon what he called the 'harmony of the
whole'. The detail on the surface may well correspond to observable
reality—and of course needs to, if the *illusion* is to convince—but it
is in theory subservient rather to the complex concealed architecture, or symphonic orchestration of the totality of the work itself.
Flaubert's art is not an imitation of the world, but a subordination
of the world—disguised by the apparent accuracy of the illusion of
reality and the *apparent* lack of comment—to a controlling 'conception', or idea. And the idea or theme underlying this particular
story—of the degradation and final self-destruction of a woman
whose vague Romantic aspirations are betrayed by her own
limitations and by those of the provincial world in which she lives—
is simply the theme underlying Flaubert's own experience of life.

His first task is to set up a kind of alternative world in answer to
his idea. Historically, the two broad philosophical possibilities of
his own world, as of that of Emma Bovary, were the somewhat
diminished Church on the one hand and the new anti-clerical progressive 'positivism' on the other. Accordingly, this opposition
provides the clumsy, imperceptive priest Bournisien on the one
side, and the unforgettably comic Homais, an apothecary who is a
kind of provincial monster of the new 'scientism', on the other. By
using them as terms of reference, by balancing the opposition between their different forms of futility—they end up by having a

grotesquely pedantic argument at Emma's deathbed before nodding off to sleep in a sort of pathetic fellowship—Flaubert already goes far towards creating the world demanded by his idea. He now has to find a way of giving general validity to his provincial situation and does this by making the story move smoothly outwards from Tostes through Yonville to Rouen, with its suggestion of Paris beyond, in such a manner as to make this situation suggest the macrocosm of the whole society. There remains to build into the work a sense of the biological, social, and psychological variety of life itself. This he achieves in a way which calls for special comment.

He sets up an immensely elaborate network of controlled opposi-tions and parallels among the characters, ranging from that be-tween Emma and her honest plodding husband Charles, or that between the two lovers Léon and Rodolphe, to that between the predatory old notary Guillaumin and the infatuated young Justin. Yet here again he is not simply setting up a one-to-one corre-spondence with life itself: far from it. It is rather that the *principle* underlying this complex geometry of contrast and parallel suggests the depth and the consistency which the reader *postulates* for the world itself. The world of experience is a confused and shifting place, where action operates in fits and starts. The 'autonomous' world which Flaubert derives by extrapolation from his controlling idea has something of the precision of the well-made watch, and action within it flows with smooth necessity. This almost mathe-matically ordered world is potentially *more* compelling than the world itself.

However, it still has to be made 'lifelike'. The first and relatively easy task—though it obviously involves lengthy observation and documentation—is to provide enough accurate detail to make it lifelike on the surface. The second and much harder task—and it is this which brings us to the real originality of *Madame Bovary*—is to make it lifelike in depth. In fact, of course, Flaubert has already gone a long way towards this by making his world more structured than life itself. It is, paradoxically, in one sense *more* lifelike in that it corresponds to our *idea* of the world, if not to our actual experience of it; but he has also decided that it cannot be lifelike so long as it impinges as something which is being *told*. He must therefore make

this alternative world eloquent of itself, give to the illusion of
reality the force of persuasion of the world itself. He must, if you
like, make the work say what he wants it to say without having to
step in and say it—or at least without allowing the reader to catch
him saying it. And this 'impersonality' called for a new set of techniques. It is fair to say at once that as yet Flaubert's practice is not
perfect—he does intervene to some extent and some of his ironical
effects are by present-day standards a trifle heavy—but this may
largely be explained by his knowledge that the public would have
difficulty in reading the new conventions. The skill with which he
manipulates them remains formidable.

   In describing this new method, one is led inevitably into analogies
with music and painting. Just as the old 'hierarchy of subjects' was
collapsing in painting, here too the subject—and nothing could be
more routine than this story of adultery—gives way to *treatment*.
If it is still true that 'the novel tells a story', it is now less told
through narrative than it *emerges* from an elaborate web of suggestion—the symphonic organization of themes, the controlled
opposition and parallelism of characters and events, the delicately
reverberant counterpoint of symbols and images. The sense that
the world of the novel, however rigorously ordered it may actually
be, possesses the *relativity* of the world itself is provided in a
variety of ways: by a clever modulation of point of view superseding
the 'flat-on' approach of the older 'omniscient' novelist, by building
up a character progressively rather than by the once-and-for-all
monolithic presentation of a writer such as Balzac, by giving each
character his own distinct style of speech, and so on. Flaubert contrives to a large extent to 'make the author disappear' by a subtle
use of the imperfect tense which enables him to slide in and out of a
character's consciousness without showing his hand too clearly.
But he also contrives to avoid direct comment through a most complex use of irony—the ironical juxtaposition of events, of ideas
expressed in conversation, or of images thronging in people's
heads; ironical comparisons of all kinds; and a certain ironical over-
precision which he uses tellingly for comic effect. It is by such means
as these, all answering to the same principle, that Flaubert—before
finally sealing off his world within a rhythmic perfection of language

which has little to do with the speech of the real world—gives coherent life to the 'alternative world' of an illusion of reality set up essentially in order to impose upon the reader an *idea*. Postulate some kind of ordered meaning for the world, believe in the reality of the gauche gesture of the girl of fifteen or the shaving-scar of the man who had to get up early in the morning . . . and you are on the way to believing that there is no room for individuality or the aspiration towards beauty in nineteenth-century bourgeois society. That is the mode of persuasion of Flaubert's 'realism', and the ultimate tribute to his skill is paid by the French professor who so eloquently demonstrates the reality of the illusion. *Madame Bovary* is not simply a historic construction: it is an intricate, sumptuous, and compelling one.

What, then, of the 'beaux romans paralysés'? If I feel that Malraux's term is indeed applicable to Flaubert's other major novels, I do not see it as applying to *Madame Bovary*. The criticisms that the work is too destructive and that the heroine does not have sufficient stature to involve the reader fully in her situation tend perhaps to leave out of account a certain fruitful ambiguity in this novel. It is true that Flaubert destroys Emma very systematically, but then, since he also lays waste the world about her in the process, the memory of her longings seems to linger over the ruins as being at least symbolical of a valid human aspiration, which might have found fulfilment in a woman of finer nature and in a different society. Emma, in fact, wins by default. And this, of course, is only the negative aspect of the real ambiguity pervading the work—the tension, amounting almost to a love–hate relationship, between Flaubert and his own heroine. For in *Madame Bovary* the frustrated Romantic was writing about himself; hunting down, as it were, an intimately familiar butterfly. One feels the *unity* of the cruel perception and the secret complicity of the hunter—and the butterfly remains profoundly, at moments miraculously, alive. The cold disciplines of 'impersonality' were won at a price. As Jean Prévost put it, 'une source pleure sous ce marbre'.

It is with the next two novels—*Salammbô* (1862) and *L'Éducation sentimentale* (1869)—that the 'problem' of Flaubert really presents itself. It need hardly be said that he can only be judged by the very highest standards—his own, in fact—but he himself had doubts about the conception of each of these works, and fundamental criticisms of them in retrospect. And I feel that he was right.

At the time of the composition of *Salammbô* he saw himself as writing 'in order not to live'. And the logic of his disgust leads him not only to reconstitute 'a cleaner *milieu* than the modern world'—an uncomplicated world of primitive savagery in which he himself, one cannot help thinking, would hardly have felt very much at home—but to attempt the artistically impossible. In an art-form which, being tied to the behavioural, cannot escape emotional and moral meaning, he is attempting a 'pure art' which will 'prove nothing' and even 'say nothing', a kind of non-meaningful monumentality. He does indeed achieve a Parnassian type of monumentality in this long account of the struggle between Carthage and the rebel Mercenaries in the third century B.C. The language is often magnificently handled, there are superb descriptions, and some of the episodes are excellently achieved. The monumentality, however, is a hollow one, in that it is soon felt to have been attained at the expense of both collective and individual truth. Deceptively, the opening of the novel suggests an exciting new departure—as though we were reading a sort of nineteenth-century anti-novel—in that the remorselessly flat treatment implies the hard, slow truth of historical time as opposed to standard fictional 'duration'. But it soon emerges that this is not time as the characters themselves live it, any more than this Parnassian Carthage is Carthage as they themselves experience it. In fact it soon appears that the historical situation has been flattened into an exotic backcloth—coloured up with every conceivable kind of eruditely documented and fastidiously rendered brutality—for the essentially sub-romantic love-story of the rebel leader Mathô and the princess Salammbô. Neither the individual nor the collective aspect of the work is satisfactory, nor do the two sides seem to cohere. *Salammbô*, one feels, is a somewhat gory Turkish Delight dreamed up by a man seeking to escape the burden of individuality of the modern world. It could perhaps all too readily be translated on to the screen, with a 'star cast', as a glossy great 'Vistavision Spectacular'.

C

Is this due to the fact that Flaubert was taking a holiday from the 'grisaille bourgeoise'? Will he be back to normal and on 'home ground' in *L'Éducation sentimentale*, his ambitious attempt to fuse the study of a particular failure in human relationships with what he sees as the sad history of a whole period: 'l'histoire morale des hommes de ma génération'? Strangely enough, and the more significantly this time, the same hybrid quality, a similar kind of flatness and structural incoherence, still seem to be present, even though this is an infinitely more attractive novel. Once again, of course, we have some very fine moments and a number of superb 'impressionist' descriptions and other painterly effects in the writing—reaching even greater heights on occasion, perhaps, than *Madame Bovary*. Once again, however, the interaction between the individual situation and the background is fundamentally unsatisfactory, and it was this which led Henry James to feel that the novel was a dead one in comparison with *Madame Bovary*.

If we take *L'Éducation sentimentale* as a 'straight novel', it is clear that it is profoundly lacking in tension. Flaubert is obviously treating a part of his own life and his own impossible love for Madame Schlésinger—he wrote to Schlésinger himself at one point on a matter of detail—but he remains too close to his material. He does not so much transpose and project in depth as simply disguise. Not only does he tend to use Frédéric as a mere peg, but he is personally so close to him as to appear in certain scenes almost to forget his existence within the relativity of the situation. By his own aesthetic, he starts very correctly by setting up two contrasting characters—Frédéric and Deslauriers—as twin pillars to support his ambitious edifice. With unconscious self-indulgence, however, he tends to throw the whole weight on to Frédéric, and thereby sacrifices his novel. If he wishes to suggest to us that time wears people down and makes a mockery of the aspirations of a generation, we might be entirely disposed to believe him, so long as the failure impinges as a *real* one. But Frédéric himself, upon whom the novel so heavily depends, is too exceptionally passive and feminine to stand convincingly for the aspirations or endeavours of a generation—even without the self-consciousness which leads Flaubert, self-laceratingly but in the end self-protectively, to undermine his position as a central character with a constant and often savage surface irony. The results of this basic lack of conflict are that there can be no development and no 'education', and that the book has gone flat well before the events of 1848.

Here again, as with *Salammbô*, there is initially the exciting suggestion—in the superb summary dismissal of Frédéric's first, empty year in Paris—that Flaubert is attempting in an anti-fictive manner to tell the undramatic truth about the average life; to give us a nineteenth-century anti-novel of failure. Even if one reads the novel in this way, however, and disregards the still considerable problem of how Frédéric relates to the very ambitious framework, it hardly seems any more coherent. For the treatment of time in the short chapter mentioned virtually makes nonsense of the laboured treatment which ensues, while the very 'period' Great Irony of Fate which prevents the lovers from coming together at long last at the end of Part Two would in this perspective smack of artistic vulgarity. *L'Éducation sentimentale* will certainly continue to engage the interest of critics and of historians of ideas, but it is difficult to see it as an artistic success. Nor is the loss, once again, of the 'harmonie de l'ensemble' the effect of a simple confusion of stylizations—novel, anti-novel, disguised autobiography, and even sheer history. The 'anti-novel' aspect of the work is essentially the negative by-product of Flaubert's inhibitions in approaching his subject. He himself, of course, came to see that he had failed to project his material—that the book was 'too true' and lacking in what he excellently called 'la fausseté de la perspective'.

Yet this can only add to the mystery of what has happened. For the basically similar kind of structural failure and overall incoherence to be found in these two very different novels is quite manifestly a function of the fact that Flaubert did not implement his own aesthetic; but why not, since he had *invented* it? Why this slackening of tension? Why has the documentation *underlying Madame Bovary* begun to drift to the surface in flat stretches of mere historical erudition? Why did it take him ten years after publication to see what was wrong with *L'Éducation sentimentale*? Why did he only see it, as though it were a revelation, when someone pointed it out to him? At the circumstantial level, these

questions take us back to the intellectual confusion surrounding the
emergence of Realism as discussed in the previous chapter. It
would seem that Flaubert got his neo-platonism so mixed up with
the new 'scientism' as to believe, for example, that he could achieve
an almost scientifically objective view of a situation by wading
through a mass of often very secondary documents, or that in some
kind of final or philosophical sense there really was a *mot juste*.
However, since he did in fact implement his aesthetic in *Madame
Bovary*, whether he urderstood it fully in intellectual terms or not,
the 'mystery' leads us back inescapably to the very life-style of this
writer who for so long symbolized the correct attitude of the Artist
in the modern world. And the interest is more than biographical.
For nobody could exemplify more poignantly than Gustave
Flaubert himself the monumental paradox of literary realism.

'J'ai été lâche dans ma jeunesse,' he told George Sand in a letter
in 1874, 'j'ai eu peur de la vie.' And indeed, whether we follow the
standard approach to Flaubert's life in terms of his purely private
situation—his hermit-like existence following upon his illness, his
close relationship with his mother, his bisexuality—or whether, like
Sartre, we approach it through concrete social analysis, we seem to
divine some kind of inner defeat, or refusal. Two years after this
handsome young 'Apollo' was struck down at the age of twenty-two
by a hysterical convulsion and forced to give up Paris for the silence
of Croisset—two years of real uncertainty about his mental as well
as his physical health—he told a friend that they had been the best
years of his life. It is as though the lightning attack on the road
between Trouville and Rouen had come as the confirmation of a
pre-existing secret choice. Already in adolescence, the Romantic
passion for the much older and married Elisa Schlésinger—an ideal
unconsummated love which had the effect of depriving him totally
of sexual awareness for three years—had led him to wall off 'Love',
and perhaps 'Life', within an inviolable 'royal chamber'. Yet even
in the seclusion of Croisset it was against life (with a small *l*) that
he had to defend himself. And even without his own sad testimony
of later years there is much to indicate that he defended himself only
too well. For about Flaubert at every level—his surface personality,
his world-view, even his insistence on 'impersonality'—there is a

strong suggestion of disguise and self-protection; and more than a hint, since he describes himself at one point as a *saltimbanque*, or showman, that at bottom he was aware of this.

Certainly, the rich contradictions of this Romantic who forced himself to be a Realist, of this sentimentalist who tended to shy away from true feeling and its responsibilities, are obvious enough. The nervously sensitive man variously described as a 'hysterical big girl' and a 'hysterical old woman' is so often transmuted into a hearty, blustering, almost Rabelaisian father-figure in the *Correspondance*. At heart a mystic, as he says, he 'believes in nothing'; himself a self-conscious bourgeois, as the Princesse Mathilde easily discerned, he detests the 'Bourgeois'; sentimentally fond of individuals, he sneers at 'Humanity'. He decrees that the society around him is irretrievably vulgar and mediocre, that Humanity is universally stupid, that life is 'une chose tellement hideuse que le seul moyen de la supporter c'est de l'éviter'—or to treat it as being merely the raw material of Art. Sadly, his own inability to live and his own pride, as it might seem, leave him little option but to decree that living is beneath him. He knows at bottom that he is posturing, cheating himself. He even sees the grim irony that all the 'agonies of style' are in the service of—not to say the privileged cultural expression of—the 'ignoble Bourgeois'. But he clings desperately to this refusal of life until he becomes a kind of perverse upside-down-Bourgeois, a prudent, emotionally tight, self-protectively resourceful Cassandra of a Bourgeois. Life itself battered him, of course, particularly in his last years, but it never quite broke down his defences. He seems, in a sense, to have paralysed himself.

Now one might well say with Flaubert himself, however romantically, that this rejection of life was the condition of attaining to the transcendence of Art; and it is obviously true that, had his whole situation been a different one, there might have been no writing in the first place. Yet the ironies surrounding Flaubert's realism are more complex and more painful. Even granting the probable relationship between his general situation and the fact of his writing, it still has to be said that it is to the extent that he paralysed himself that he, in the main, paralysed his art. The realist novel, in so far as it presents human behaviour in the 'real' world, depends in its very composition upon tension and conflict, whereas the principle underlying Flaubert's life-style and nihilist world-view is the avoidance of conflict with the real world. This means that, however great his gifts as a stylist, he will only write great novels—indeed, only implement his own aesthetic—when he can break the paralysis and get beyond the carefully engineered untruth of the self-protectively negative world-view. But how can a man who opts for a non-life so resolutely armoured by pride, seclusion, and the vicious logic of frustration itself ever be brought to do this? Between them, life itself and the ironical logic of this 'impersonal' form which he invented have an answer, and a brutal one.

Flaubert, in practice, implements his own aesthetic, achieves a coherent relationship between his central character and the world, attains the necessary structural harmony—and even, by a most significant irony, the necessary *impersonality*—only when the pressure of life upon him is such as to smash the protective shell and force him to write about himself. He does not then write about himself shallowly, in thinly veiled transposition as in *L'Éducation sentimentale*, where the very knowledge that he is writing about himself inhibits his structural sense and leads him to intervene with constant self-irony; rather, he writes about himself in depth, in total projection as the aesthetic demands, *pursuing the artistic autonomy of his creation until he is led beyond the self-protective world-view*. It is in this sense that he could truly say 'Madame Bovary, c'est moi', whereas *L'Éducation sentimentale*, by being in the narrow sense 'trop vrai', lacked that 'fausseté de la perspective' which might have enabled it to attain artistic coherence—and truth.

Given Flaubert's carefully contrived situation, of course, those moments of pressure when he was driven to challenge the whole world in relation to the self could only be rare. However, the period of the writing of *Madame Bovary* was such a moment. He had been deeply humiliated, for he had written a book which he had seen as the triumphant vindication of his stand against the world until two trusted friends, with all the authority of friendship, had told him to put it in the fire where it belonged. This was the second chance. He was writing to salvage his pride as an artist, to save his dignity as a man, and perhaps even to save his mind, since it is largely through the writing of this novel that he seems to have conquered his hallucinations. He could hardly have avoided writing profoundly about himself in *Madame Bovary*, where he alienates himself and—as the subtle Baudelaire could be trusted to divine at once—in some sense *realizes* himself as a Romantic woman defeated by her own sensibility and by the reality of the world. It is surely this which infuses organic life into his novel, until a world of symbolical oppositions deriving from the heroine's—and Flaubert's—dilemma comes to have the force and cohesion of the world itself. But the very writing of *Madame Bovary* relaxed the pressure and restored the pride. And thereafter we have the drift towards structural weakness, confusion with regard to point of view, the loss of impersonality, and the general blockage of the artist's vision by the self-protective world-view. By the time we come to the final version of *La Tentation de Saint Antoine* of 1874—a dramatic or, rather, undramatic survey of the inadequacy of the metaphysical hopes of all mankind —Flaubert has arrived at a point of virtual dissociation. The lack of human tension is now such that there is no real temptation, and practically no Saint Anthony. For all its visionary appearance, this work is *nothing but* the expression of his own world-view. As always with the later Flaubert, it has some beautiful moments, but as a totality it is dead.

The irony of all this is brought out with particular poignancy by the work of Flaubert's last years. The world hit him very hard in the mid-1870s with a whole series of disasters: the double humiliation of offering and then failing with a play in Paris; the death of a number of old friends; the near-ruin of this landed proprietor through a family involvement in industry, which brought him to the unbelievable pass of thinking that he might have to write for money. He was in despair, in doubt about the rightness of his whole solitary existence, thinking that he should perhaps have married, had children, been like everybody else—and this very real despair perforce involves him in living again. However, by a further irony, the erosion of his nihilism comes too late to save the astonishingly ambitious *Bouvard et Pécuchet*. It merely completes its artistic destruction.

As so often with this writer, *Bouvard et Pécuchet* starts more than promisingly. The almost insolently stylized beginning, and the hint that these two retired clerks will innocently but rigorously undertake nothing less than the debunking of human culture, suggest excitingly that, not content with attempting a nineteenth-century anti-novel, Flaubert has set his sights on a great and revolutionary work of literature of a kind undreamt of by his contemporaries. But as so often, again, he blurs the writing with insignificant detail, he frequently descends to a facile 'take-off' of scientific theories long since superseded, and, by introducing actual historical events, he throws away the whole stylization. But then the real trouble with this work is that there are no less than three incompatible forms fighting and destroying one another within it. There is, basically, an intellectually conceived attempt at a total *non-novel*—designed to extend the nihilist demonstration of *La Tentation de Saint Antoine* to cover the whole field of human knowledge and activity. There are occasional suggestions—as in the highly stylized beginning—of the extremely sophisticated *anti-novel* which is the only medium through which he could artistically have realized his ambition. Finally, there are the lineaments of the traditional *novel* into which he started turning the work halfway through, when the softening of his world-view under the pressures of the mid-1870s led him to begin to take some human interest in his own characters. *Bouvard et Pécuchet* is a disaster, even if that very fact has much to do with its perennial fascination. It is perhaps the most grandiose wreck in modern literature.

However, there is a swan song, and of a different order. In the darkest days of this testing period Flaubert started writing some stories, just to keep himself going. And even though he gains in any case from the shorter form in these *Trois Contes*, one of them—in which almost everything has been found to relate back to his own life and in which, probably unconsciously but significantly, he transposes his first attack of hysteria—comes close to perfection. It is the story of the hard life of a servant-woman who, at the end, becomes so attached to a stuffed parrot that she dies identifying it triumphantly with the Holy Ghost. Flaubert makes no concessions to sentiment: he calls his poor old servant Félicité. But in the ending of *Un Cœur simple* no irony is intended. For Flaubert has perhaps made the essential discovery: that it may not too much matter

whether the aspiration is answered by a stuffed parrot or by the
Holy Ghost; that the aspiration may be valid in itself; that people
may have dignity simply because they endure, because they exist.
Yet it is only as artist that this simple heart led by pride to become
the suffering old servant of letters can accept the discovery—and he
will die defiant.

A writer who writes best when he is at his most impersonal, who
is at his most impersonal when he is writing in deep projection
about himself, who writes in depth about himself when he is writing
about a woman . . . —and these are only the first ironies of the hall of
mirrors of this 'illusion of reality', this 'autonomous' realist novel
which sets out to achieve truth through the medium of the totally
convincing lie.

What matters about an author of Flaubert's importance—since
at this level we are in the end more interested in the writer and his
total achievement than in individual books—is not that a particular
novel should be great and others unsatisfying, but rather the scale
and significance of the whole enterprise. By this criterion Flaubert
is a very big writer indeed—and the greatness and the weakness are
part of the same study. He in effect invented this new novel of a
century ago, he established it at the highest level of practice, and,
inevitably perhaps, he was himself its first battleground. The
'lesson' of Flaubert, both positively and negatively, remains a
fundamental one. And a moving one.

NOTE

GUSTAVE FLAUBERT, 1821–80, was a surgeon's son. He found no vocation in
law studies and, after the first attack of a nervous illness in 1844, devoted himself
solely to literature. After his father's death in 1846 he lived a secluded life with
his mother at Croisset, near Rouen. He rarely left this retreat, though he did
travel abroad to North Africa and the Near East.

Works. Flaubert's first published and best-known novel, *Madame Bovary*,
appeared in 1857 (he and the editor of the periodical in which it first appeared
were tried for offences against public morals, but acquitted). Then followed
Salammbô (1862), with its Carthaginian setting, and *L'Éducation sentimentale*
(1869), a partly autobiographical novel about his own time. The final version of

La Tentation de Saint Antoine was published in 1874. (It was the condemnation of a first version of this by his friends Louis Bouilhet and Maxime Du Camp, in 1849, which had led him towards realistic writing.) His other fiction consists of the *Trois Contes* (1877) and the unfinished and posthumously published *Bouvard et Pécuchet* (1881). The collection of trite sayings which he assembled during his life, *Dictionnaire des idées reçues*, was to have formed part of *Bouvard et Pécuchet*.

Editions. The definitive *Œuvres complètes*, published by Conard from 1910 onwards, comprise ten volumes plus thirteen volumes of correspondence. The novels and short stories occupy two Pléiade volumes edited by A. Thibaudet and R. Dumesnil (1936) and six separate 'Classiques Garnier' volumes, all edited by E. Maynial. A selection from the voluminous correspondence, highlighting Flaubert's views on writing, is edited by G. Bollème, *Gustave Flaubert: Extraits de la correspondance, ou préface à la vie d'écrivain* (1963).

Criticism. Since the number of studies of Flaubert is legion, the reader may conveniently turn in the first place to such collections as the 'Twentieth Century Views' *Flaubert* (1964), edited by R. Giraud, which contains helpful essays by E. Auerbach, G. Lukács, Baudelaire, and J.-P. Richard in particular, and *Madame Bovary and the Critics* (1966), a collection of essays edited by B. F. Bart. Among the more recent studies in English may be mentioned V. Brombert, *The Novels of Flaubert: a Study of Themes and Techniques* (1966), E. Starkie, *Flaubert: The Making of the Master* (1967), and *The Master* (1971), the relevant section in M. Turnell, *The Novel in France* (1950), and A. Fairlie's helpful short study, *Madame Bovary* (1962). Standard studies in French include A. Thibaudet's still suggestive *Gustave Flaubert* (1922), R. Dumesnil, *Gustave Flaubert, l'homme et l'œuvre* (1932), E. Maynial, *Gustave Flaubert* (1943), C. Digeon, *Flaubert* (1970), V. Brombert, *Flaubert par lui-même* (1971), and D. L. Demorest's very systematic *L'Expression figurée et symbolique dans l'œuvre de Gustave Flaubert* (1931). Henry James's views may be found in *French Poets and Novelists* (1878), while Jean-Paul Sartre has published a massive study of Flaubert, *L'Idiot de la famille* (1971-3), in three volumes.

5. The Drama of Money and Class

FRENCH drama of the nineteenth century oscillates between two major conventions. The first might be styled as idealistic, transcendental, hospitable to heroic aspiration. It is present in the melodrama's naïve image of the struggle between good and evil; in the grandiose strivings of Hugo's mysterious and doomed heroes; in the vague spiritualism of Maeterlinck's legendary figures; in Claudel's theatrical enactment of Christian myth. With the exception of melodrama, none of these forms attains the dominance over the larger theatre-going public which is achieved by the second convention: the play about social life. It is this kind of play that reflects the prosaic concerns of the age which is ushered in by the French industrial revolution.

Within this second mode, the emphasis may fall either on the surfaces of social life or on the tensions and conflicts of value which arise from shifts and changes in the position of the classes. Louis-Benoît Picard, Eugène Scribe, and Théodore Barrière are all, in their different ways, adept at conveying the surfaces of social life and all, with varying degrees of stylization, concentrate on social mannerisms and stereotypes and on the transient fashions of the day. Farce-writers of the second half of the century, like Eugène Labiche and Georges Feydeau, are equally adroit at rendering the surfaces of society, but they intensify the mechanical aspects of social behaviour in a spirit of extravagant, and sometimes explosive, fancy. The alternative emphasis within this convention falls on the serious, and often didactic, analysis of social and moral attitudes. Such an emphasis, which is more concerned to understand the nature of the forces at work in society, finds expression in Alexandre Dumas *fils*'s problem-plays; in Émile Augier's social comedies; and, though with much less artifice and sentimentality, in the flat austerity of Henri Becque's realistic studies of manners, notably

Les Corbeaux (1882). The tradition continues in the harsh satire of business life represented by Octave Mirbeau's *Les Affaires sont les affaires* (1903); in Eugène Brieux's sensational treatment of syphilis, legal corruption, gambling, and other social ills; and in the rather bloodless theatre of ideas produced by François de Curel. Whatever its aesthetic limitations, the distinctive achievement of this serious social drama can only be gauged by contrasting it with the superficiality of the popular theatre which preceded it, a theatre of which Scribe must be accounted the prime architect.

With Eugène Scribe (1791–1861) drama displays the apotheosis of plot. Plot functions like a self-regulating mechanism, alone creating the illusion of life on the stage while soliciting our admiration at every point for the ingenuity of the playwright who stands outside his artefact. This goes much further than Romantic drama, which always, no matter how confusedly, implies larger moral concerns and a strong sense of human bafflement and pain. The almost automatic reconciliation of conflicts which we encounter in Scribe's plays (when such conflicts are not actually short-circuited by artificial devices) has no counterpart in the—slightly ridiculous—blood and anguish of the Romantic theatre.

Scribe, one might say, is all craft and no vision while a Romantic dramatist like Hugo has more vision than craft. Scribe is a superb entertainer and though his plots are ingeniously complicated and ramifying rather than neat and elegant, he still strikes one, by comparison with Hugo and the elder Dumas, as a maker of intricate toys. What Scribe lacks is that passion to understand human experience which alone can raise drama beyond the level of mere spectacle and contrivance. What he conspicuously possesses is an acute sense of the immediacy of theatrical effects. He can judge precisely what impact a particular bit of stage 'business' will produce and the way in which the audience can be maintained in a constant state of expectancy through a succession of clever theatrical strokes. His skill is in the making of ingenious connections and in manipulating striking local effects rather than in creating a unified dramatic structure, an over-all 'shape' that is aesthetically satisfying and psychologically coherent. He manages very successfully to excite us about trivia: who, for example, will be waiting in the conservatory or what the discovered letter will reveal. Trivia, that is, by any reckoning of significant human experience, but not in terms of the theatrical 'game' which he has set up and which is articulated about the interplay of just such trivia. The contrivances of plot create problems that the ingenuity of the playwright has to resolve. If each contrived problem is given a plausible solution by the dramatist, few of his audience are churlish enough to complain that the elaborately constructed puzzles do not really add up to a meaningful statement about human life. The spectators become the willing accomplices of the playwright and, in Scribe's plays, the recurring motifs of chess and playing-cards tend to emphasize the game-like character of the whole enterprise.

The structure of the plot in *Adrienne Lecouvreur* (1849) will serve admirably to illustrate Scribe's manner. The play, which is set in Paris, involves Adrienne, a promising young actress at the Comédie-Française, the dashing military commander Maurice of Saxony, son of the King of Poland, and the Princesse de Bouillon, Maurice's former mistress. In the opening scenes of Act I between the Princess and a worldly and scandal-mongering priest, and subsequently between Maurice and the Princess, we learn that her husband the Prince, who is an amateur scientist and has participated in the discovery of a lethally poisonous powder at the Académie des Sciences, is having an affair with the actress Duclos, Adrienne's rival on the stage, whom he has set up in a house at Grange-Batelière. The Princess herself is revealed to be still in love with Maurice. She suspects that the posy worn by Maurice when he joins her is the gift of a new mistress and she employs the Abbé to discover the latter's identity. In Act II love ripens between Adrienne and Maurice, whose true identity is not at this point known to her. The process is aided at the artists' foyer of the Comédie-Française, by a coquettish scene in which Adrienne seeks to improve Maurice's French by reciting La Fontaine's 'Les deux pigeons'. The Prince, who has also arrived at the theatre, intercepts a note from his mistress Duclos inviting Maurice to her house. Not knowing that the note has been written at the Princess's request, the Prince concludes that Duclos is unfaithful to him and invites all the actors back to Grange-Batelière in the hope of surprising

Duclos and Maurice together. In Duclos's house, at the opening of Act III, the meeting between Maurice and the Princess, who has come to warn him of debts which may ruin his political ambitions, is interrupted by the arrival of the Prince, the Abbé, and the actors, including Adrienne. Adrienne learns for the first time of Maurice's true identity and agrees to help him by giving his lady visitor, whose identity is unknown to Adrienne and who has been obliged to hide in an adjoining bedroom, a key which will give her access to the garden while the other guests are at supper. Because of the dark, the two women fail to recognize each other but they exchange words and the Princess accidentally drops a bracelet while leaving. The bracelet comes into Adrienne's hands and, hearing that Maurice has apparently followed his mysterious guest, she faints as the curtain falls.

In Act IV Maurice, who has been imprisoned for debt through the machinations of the jealous Princess, is released through the intervention of Adrienne who pawns her jewels to purge the debt (an effect likely to produce a thrill of sympathy in an investing public). He supposes that his anonymous benefactor was the Princess and goes to her house to thank her. A reception is being held at which Adrienne has been invited to recite. Bracelet and voice enable the women to identify each other as the person present at the fateful meeting in the darkened room. They engage in a bitter exchange of words in which Adrienne's histrionic talent gives her a temporary advantage as she declaims appropriately contemptuous lines from Racine's *Phèdre*. Finally, in Act V, the jealous Princess, who has acquired the offending posy, sends it back to Adrienne, liberally dusted with the Prince's poisonous powder. Adrienne, interpreting the return of the posy as proof of Maurice's rejection of her, kisses the flowers with lingering regret and survives just long enough to die in the arms of Maurice himself who has now discovered from Adrienne's loyal friend, Michonnet, the truth about his release from prison.

It is clear from this summary of the plot that Scribe has placed formidable obstacles in the way of our granting him a 'willing suspension of disbelief'. Why, for example, should the identity of so dazzling a public figure as Maurice remain unknown to Adrienne until the moment he reveals it to her? And is there not something a little preposterous about a Prince who just happens to be an amateur scientist specializing in lethal powders? This ineffable concoction of coincidence, misunderstanding, and carefully 'planted' props is, perhaps, no sillier than Hugo's *Le Roi s'amuse*, from the point of view of plot, but it was seen by contemporary audiences as a great deal more plausible, in spite of a *grand guignol* ending which rivals Hugo himself. What impressed the public was a technique in which every scene was functional, in the sense that it foreshadowed and prepared for another. Nothing depends on memorable language, power of characterization, moral insight, intellectual or emotional coherence, or even verisimilitude. Everything rests on a lethal powder, a carefully preserved posy of flowers, the accident of a darkened room, and a dropped bracelet. It is not too much to say that the poison, the posy, and the bracelet overshadow in importance the hollow characters. The skill and timing with which these objects are introduced, withheld, and finally produced again is what really connects the acts and gives the play the highly artificial continuity it possesses. Physical events crowd in on one another; shock follows on shock in a carefully controlled tempo, and the curiosity of the audience as to how the complications are to be unravelled is kept unflaggingly alive.

There is no 'life' here apart from the life of the theatre, but pace, inventiveness, a firm grasp of the mechanics of entry and exit, and an exact sense of how long revelations can be deferred before the audience becomes bored or baffled, confer on this stage movement a temporary credibility. The same is true of another of Scribe's most popular historical plays, *Le Verre d'eau* (1840), in which, as its sub-title 'Les effets et les causes' suggests, the game is to show how great events spring from trivial causes. The disgracing of the Duchess of Marlborough, the collapse of the Whig party, the rise of Bolingbroke, and radical changes in British foreign policy, are all shown to stem from complicated and trivial personal intrigues, symbolized by the 'glass of water' which Queen Anne asks of her young admirer Masham and which spills over the Queen's dress as the jealous Duchess grabs it. In this play, as in a number of others, the action is dominated by two brilliant conspirators (the Duchess of Marlborough and Bolingbroke), who create a web of deceit and misunderstanding by means of secret assignations, rumours, eavesdropping, so as to use the unsophisticated and unsuspecting young lovers, Masham and Abigail Churchill, as pawns in furthering their own ends.

The general character and technique of these two plays suggest well enough Scribe's contribution to nineteenth-century French and, indeed, European drama. In spite of the degree to which they finally transcend him, both Ibsen and Bernard Shaw learned much that was valuable from the plot-making of this virtuoso who was to provide the modern commercial theatre with its standard recipes. This remains true even though Shaw savages Scribe's natural heir, Victorien Sardou (1831–1908), who tightens up and tidies up Scribe's technique so as to produce plays of undeniable craftsmanship in which elaborately complicated plots and striking theatrical effects mask a total absence of true feeling, insight, or distinction of mind. Their tinsel and cardboard quality was exactly what Shaw epitomized in his derisive label 'Sardoodledom' and is what one encounters in Sardou's comedies of manners, like *Les Pattes de mouche* (1860); his melodramas, like *Tosca* (1887), already so close to the operatic convention that Puccini found no difficulty in adapting it; and his immensely popular historical plays, like *Madame Sans-Gêne* (1893), in which a laundress who has married one of Napoleon's marshals demonstrates, with a carefully contrived raciness of idiom, the vigour and good sense of the common people.

In so far as Scribe himself can be said to have a moral view, it may be located in a settled habit of mind which saw human nature in a consistently trivial and mediocre light, and was suspicious of any large idealism. It was a kind of grocer's-eye-view of the world which commended itself to his middle-class audience as the acme of shrewd and worldly judgement. It is the view that informs a play like *Bernard et Raton* (1833) in which political principle and revolutionary idealism are ruthlessly debunked. Elsewhere it expresses itself in a bluff common sense which is hostile to all flights of fancy and exposes the claims of passion as aberrations potentially disastrous to property and family life. Such is the case with *Le*

Mariage de raison (1826), where a prudent union between a lady's maid and an old soldier with a wooden leg is preferred to a heady misalliance between her and an aristocrat. This is not to say that Scribe's theatre is the stern voice of morality, as Dumas *fils*'s was to be. On the contrary, the formidable skill he displays in managing the contrivances of plot empties the drama of everything except its mechanics and a general blandness and insipidity. So in *Une Chaîne* (1841), which deals with a man trying to discard his mistress in favour of a fresh and innocent young girl, the mechanisms of evasion and deceit (intercepted letters, secret meetings, mischances) effectively displace any sense of the complexity of the moral life or the life of feeling.

Scribe could judge to a nicety, because he shared them, the ethical and aesthetic limitations of the conventional middle-class public he had made his own. He never questioned property or matrimony, but was able, on occasion, to permit himself a little naughtiness at the expense of the Church since that too was a consecrated middle-class sport in France. He lacked both insight and the curiosity to understand human beings, but he possessed a sharp eye for the surfaces of social life and the minutiae of social transactions, and he conveyed these through stereotypes who are quite wittily sketched: stockbrokers, retired generals, lawyers, dashing young officers who have shed the coarseness of the mess, and spoilt daughters of rich and besotted fathers. Scribe captures these much in the spirit of Gavarni's early sketches of Parisian life. His comedies of manners are full of leases, deeds, marriage contracts, investments, and dividends. Money is the theme that galvanizes them and, as much in what they omit as in what they choose to include, his plays mirror the rising middle classes of the Restoration and the July Monarchy, though with much indulgent fun so long as he is dealing with men of the golden mean, solid citizens in trade, manufacturing, or the professions, and not long-haired aesthetes (like the Romantics) or doctrinaire politicians. Everything is prettified. There is no vein of genuine feeling, but frequent judicious doses of sentimentality and carefully prepared injections of chauvinism, as the old soldiers wax lyrical about the Imperial past. Above all, the dominant classes are reconciled in alliances which bring breeding to the Stock

Exchange and badly needed funds to families of good birth. As the critic Jules Janin wrote at the time: 'la noblesse et la finance ont été les héroïnes de ses pièces.' This makes it all the more piquant that, with the growth of literacy and comparative prosperity among the Parisian artisans of the Second Empire, these figured increasingly among Scribe's admirers in the galleries of the Vaudeville and Gymnase theatres.

The reduction of the play to an ingeniously complicated mechanism of plot effectively anaesthetizes it as an instrument for exploring and interrogating significant human experience. In this sense, Scribe's plays minister to the complacency of his middle-class public and confirm it in its moral and intellectual inertia. Paradoxically, French farce, which pushes this conception of plot to its mechanical limit, can often function in such a way as to undermine temporarily the settled conventions of society. For example, in the hands of Eugène Labiche (1815–88) and Georges Feydeau (1862–1921) farce is catastrophe diverted. It embodies the spirit of carnival, a permitted flouting of the rules of respectable society. Farce grants a temporary licence to aggression and destructiveness; it outrages both family piety and public propriety and though, in its resolution of the plot, it leaves the hallowed institutions of society standing, they are not unscathed. In Feydeau's *L'Hôtel du libre échange* (1894) it seems entirely appropriate that the title should ambiguously refer to an economic principle of the period and to the character of its marital infidelities; both involve transactions for gain. In his *Feu la mère de Madame* (1908), normally repressed desires (the wife's sexual exhibitionism, the husband's unfeigned acceptance of his mother-in-law's 'death' as a stroke of luck) find an outlet before the world of normality and conventional codes is restored. In a similar way, Fadinard's frantic search for the married lady's compromising straw hat in Labiche's *Un Chapeau de paille d'Italie* (1851) effectively demonstrates the hollowness of social respectability. Both writers concentrate on man as a social animal and derive their comic energy from the tensions that are produced when the structure and values of established society are challenged by exhilarating and irreverent games which hover on the brink of outrage.

No doubt the 'outrage' performed by farce depends for its effec-
tiveness on the vitality of the values and institutions (especially
marriage) which are assaulted but, and here it differs from traditional comedy, farce does not imply a stable norm but the more
disturbing idea that such norms as exist may be precarious and
threatened with anarchy. Bourgeois marriage, in particular, with
its dowry system and its tendency to become an instrument for
transmitting property, is perpetually threatened by the fantasies
released by French farce in the second half of the nineteenth century.
However, though the giddy entertainments of Labiche and Feydeau
may lay a few depth-charges under respectable French society,
their view of it is too heavily stylized, their tempo too breathtaking
for us to see them as other than playfully subversive images of
kinds of moral and social strain that are spelt out for us, in more
prosaic form, elsewhere in the French theatre of the nineteenth
century. Two figures dominate all others: Alexandre Dumas *fils*
(1824-95) and Émile Augier (1820-89). Both playwrights need
initially to be set within the framework of the economic and social
life of the Second Empire. They have to be related to a rapidly
growing investing public; to the mania for speculation on the
Stock Exchange, and to the development of Paris as a cosmopolitan
centre of pleasure which results from the striking expansion of the
French railway system during this period. The plays of Dumas *fils*
and Augier reflect the intense bourgeois interest in the workings of
high finance and in the morality of money-making. As a conse-
quence of the expansion of the railways, the normal, middle-class,
theatre-going public of Paris was swollen by appreciable numbers
of foreign tourists and holidaying provincials, avid for spice and
excitement. It is likely that these helped to give the period audiences
of the boulevard theatres something of that febrile and sensation-
hungry character which some contemporary observers testify to
and which Dumas *fils*, in particular, responded to in his theatrical
manner and choice of theme.

The circumstances of Dumas *fils*'s illegitimate birth and his life
in the raffish and disordered household of his natural father, Dumas
the Elder, make him an impassioned moralizer, obsessed with the
problems of illegitimacy, adultery, and prostitution. His temper is

fiercely didactic in every play except his first, *La Dame aux camélias*
(1852), which is saved from abstraction by the youth, spontaneity,
and sheer incandescent feeling of the lovers, Marguerite and
Armand: 'it is all champagne and tears', in Henry James's phrase.
Elsewhere, his theatre sets out to demonstrate the subversive and
dangerous effects of illicit love and to show that no excuse can be
made for it. The one element that humanizes these rigorous
sermons is his moving and indignant pity for the wronged and
exploited woman who suffers from the 'double standard' which
society casually applies to the sexual misdemeanours of the male.

So intensely partial a view of human life necessarily limits the
range and interest of Dumas *fils*'s plays. These are deliberately
designed to have a utilitarian purpose; to effect a practical change
in society, whether in its divorce laws or in its treatment of illegitimacy. His plays embody the answers to moral dilemmas defined
with clarity and assurance. A respectable family should refuse to
share in the dubious profits of a speculator who has deceived them
into joining dishonest schemes (*La Question d'argent*, 1857);
society should rehabilitate a repentant 'fallen woman' and approve
of her marriage to a man of impeccable character (*Les Idées de
Madame Aubray*, 1867); a worthy illegitimate son should be placed
on the same footing as his legitimate brother (*Le Fils naturel*, 1858).
The 'lesson' is not incidental but central to all of these plays. The
action and the characters simply serve as illustrations of ideas and
have no life outside the ideas they embody. In Sarcey's neat formulation, they are 'théorèmes vivants et passionnés'.

At one level, then, Dumas *fils* is a 'realist', preoccupied with
depicting contemporary types and conditions in the observable life
of society around him. This kind of realism is echoed in his stage
sets, usually conventional middle-class drawing-rooms with large
double doors at the back. Such sets and social problems contrast
strongly with the Romantic theatre or with Scribe's historical
dramas, both of which create the illusion of reality through an
elaborate display of 'local colour', an accumulation of picturesque
detail in costume, setting, and language. Yet, on inspection, Dumas
fils's 'realism' emerges as strikingly artificial. A clue to the nature of
this convention, as he handles it, is contained in his preface to *Un*

Père prodigue (1859): 'Le réel dans le fond, le possible dans le fait, l'ingénieux dans le moyen, voilà ce qu'on peut exiger de nous.' This reference to the element of 'ingenuity' points to Dumas *fils*'s pre-occupation with technique, with the artifices of plotting learned from Scribe. In fact the plays of Dumas *fils* are shaped not by the logic of feeling nor by a coherent imaginative vision of the world, but by a kind of externalized or theatrical logic. To put it in other terms, the denouement of each play represents both a resolution of the complexities of the plot and a ready-made solution to the animated problem which is embodied in the play. The playwright begins with his solution and works backward from it. The end is known in advance and determines the entire structure of the action. In this sense, Dumas *fils*'s plays offer an essentially rhetorical structure, an appropriate form for affirming deeply felt insights or prejudices rather than for exploring experience. For example, the proposition that has to be demonstrated in *Diane de Lys* (1853) is that nothing can justify adultery: neither the system of arranged marriages, nor a cold, unsympathetic, and legalistic husband, nor the absence of divorce. It therefore follows that the impulsive young artist, Paul, will be shot for his adultery with Diane by her injured husband, the Count, no matter how this violates our humane instincts or runs counter to the sympathies excited in us by the characters themselves. In much the same way, the demands of a kind of debating-society logic make it inevitable that the charity of the exemplary Madame Aubray, in *Les Idées de Madame Aubray*, will be tested in the most graphic fashion when her own son asks to marry the 'fallen woman' of the play. Here the concrete rendering of life is wholly subordinated to a formal and mechanical working out of moral premisses to their logical conclusion.

This sense of contrivance is intensified for us by a style that is almost relentlessly 'brilliant', which is to say, witty, aphoristic, and charged with glittering paradox. There is little attempt, except in *La Dame aux camélias*, to catch the inflections of natural speech or to individuate characters by an appropriate idiom. The voice of the author unifies these plays stylistically, lends them their distinctive force and concentration, and produces what Henry James describes as 'the curious dryness, the obtrusive economy of his drama—the hammered sharpness of every outline, the metallic ring of every sound...' This hardness of tone tends to mask the equivocal aspects of Dumas *fils*'s theatre. The ambivalent, and insufferably superior, de Ryons of *L'Ami des femmes* (1864), who acts as director of conscience to the erring Jane de Simerose and reconciles her with her neglectful husband, is a kind of moral *voyeur* whose task it is to protect women from their own weakness and to defend the institution of marriage, though he himself is a bachelor man-about-town. Similarly, the breeding and integrity of Olivier de Jalin, Dumas *fils*'s preferred 'raisonneur' in *Le Demi-Monde* (1855), are never called into question though he seems to spend most of his time in a clandestine gambling-saloon run by a discredited lady of the aristocracy. Dumas *fils*'s manner of combining the exemplary punishment of social and moral transgressors (adulterous wives, shady financiers, society whores) with an avid interest in their vices recalls rather too forcibly the homilies contained in those 'shocking revelations' lasciviously purveyed by the Sunday Press of France and England. Even if one excepts the hysterical, and almost apocalyptic, vision of *La Femme de Claude* (1873) in which Claude, representing morality and conscience, kills his wife Césarine, the Beast who symbolizes the adulteress undermining French society, one is forced to recognize that Dumas *fils*'s art is stultified by the narrowness of his personal obsessions. He falls victim to the rhetorical machine he himself created to expose the 'horrors' of sexual promiscuity.

'O père de famille, O poète! je t'aime.' The celebrated line from Émile Augier's early verse-play, *Gabrielle* (1849), suggests the fulsome praise of conjugal bliss which represents one aspect of his theatre. We are a long way from the appalling stage families of Cocteau or Anouilh and, though these too represent a convention, it is a convention that seems less fatuous to a modern sensibility than Augier's. Yet it would be unfair to judge all Augier's drama by this expression of sentimentality. He can be a serious and adroit defender of the best in the middle-class way of life, though often sharply critical of its complacency, philistinism, and corrupt politics. He is a writer of true comedy in the sense that he sets the failings and vices of his middle-class characters against a code of decency which he believes expresses the 'true' bourgeois spirit, a spirit which reverences hard work, thrift, and personal integrity, and abhors easy money, vulgar display, and social pretensions. No doubt this spirit idealizes the ethics of the class to which Augier belonged, but he strikes one as an honest man whose plays reflect the craving for an acceptable moral order consistent with the nature of French capitalism under the Second Empire. Contrary to Augier's intentions, the modern reader of his plays may well be driven to conclude that his examples of moral dilemma simply emphasize that a satisfactory personal morality and the economic and social order of Augier's day can be reconciled only with difficulty.

Something of Augier's moral confusion and uncertainty can be gauged from one of his most important comedies, *Le Gendre de M. Poirier* (1854), in which he collaborated with Jules Sandeau. The play clearly sets out to be a satire on the conflict between the hereditary aristocracy and the rising new-rich, but the attack on Gaston de Presles, who symbolizes an idle, frivolous, and arrogant nobility obsessed with its own genealogy, is neutralized by Augier's harsh portrait of the upstart draper Poirier as an oafish social climber, odious in the power of his wealth. Indeed, Gaston's positive qualities (grace, wit, cultivation) contrast strongly with Poirier's grossness and philistinism, and help, purely at the level of feeling, to reconcile us to the young nobleman. We are further alienated from Poirier by his tendency to manipulate his spirited and un-affected daughter, Antoinette, without any proper regard for her personal inclinations. In this respect, the structure of human feel-ing in the play tends to work against its declared bourgeois standards of morality. The other, more sympathetic, examples of bourgeois and aristocratic life (Verdelet and the duc de Montmeyran) effec-tively cancel each other out and so do not radically alter the symbolic significance of the conflict between Gaston and Poirier. The result is that Poirier, who is honest, hardworking, and thrifty, forfeits our sympathy because he lacks delicacy, restraint, and imagination while Gaston de Presles, who is a waster and the prisoner of a spurious and trivial conception of honour, contrives to touch our sympathy by what is, after all, simply an elegant and heedless style of life.

In all this interplay of feeling, Antoinette stands out as a key figure. By a singular paradox, her final magnanimity toward the erring Gaston, who has treated her shabbily while living off her father, can be read, not so much as typifying bourgeois moral sensibility, as transcending it. In eventually permitting Gaston to fight his duel, she might even be said to reveal the degree to which she has accepted the empty conventions of her husband's class as valid moral ideals. In this sense, *Le Gendre de M. Poirier* is profoundly conservative in content, and its vision of a purse-proud and laborious bourgeoisie perpetually subservient to a stylish nobility given over to conspicuous consumption is clinched for us in the sentimental twist of the plot by which Verdelet buys Antoinette the Presles' ancestral home as a wedding present.

The adequacy of the aristocratic ethos as a rule of life, which is patently left unexamined in *Le Gendre de M. Poirier*, is no more fully or persuasively scrutinized in *Le Mariage d'Olympe* (1855) where our sympathy is solicited for the old marquis de Puygiron when he shoots dead a society whore, Olympe Taverny, who has passed herself off as a respectable farmer's daughter and made a clandestine marriage with his nephew, Henri. The trouble is that the marquess and his lady are simply conventional stereotypes of domestic virtue, dispensing a rather patronizing old-world charm. They do not offer the play a convincing moral centre, any more than Henri himself, who is a priggish booby. Olympe is admittedly a slut and a blackmailer, but her nerve and appetite for life do, at least, suggest an energy and vitality that are singularly absent from the static and moribund world of the Puygirons. In failing to persuade us that idolatry of family constitutes a vital moral tradition, the play inevitably fails to compel the sympathy of the modern reader for the summary execution of an offending outsider. Cold-blooded murder is not really effaced by the spectacle of honour vindicated, especially when the content of honour is so vague and uncertain. The savagery of the denouement is more plausibly explicable as a symbolic punishment meted out by the possessing classes to those who seek to deprive them of their status and gains rather than as an expression of aristocratic pride.

It is also true, of course, that Olympe symbolizes the acquisitive appetite, the lust for easy money. It is this human failing which Augier excoriates most. He attacks it in Roussel, the millionaire who has made a fortune by playing the market (*Ceinture dorée*, 1855) and who finds that the only disinterested suitor for his daughter's hand is the well-born de Trélan whose father has been ruined by one of Roussel's financial schemes. Here again, the pursuit of money is set against a traditional order of morality embodied in a young noble-man whose delicate moral scruples will not allow him to marry Caliste Roussel until her father has lost all his ill-gotten wealth. To what degree de Trélan's rectitude is coloured by the impulse to revenge his father is nowhere explored by Augier.

In Augier's plays, the speculator emerges as the great bogy-man of Second Empire society. Vernouillet of *Les Effrontés* (1861) not only manipulates the market but also controls the press from the proceeds of his financial operations. It is true that he is finally thwarted in his hopes of a brilliant marriage but, as Augier shows with satirical verve, this in no way inhibits him or prevents him from extending his newspaper empire. As Augier presents them, Roussel and Vernouillet are almost mythical embodiments of the period mania for speculation, but they are not offered as means of totally discrediting capitalist society. On the contrary, their greed and folly are seen as essentially eccentric departures from the solid and worthy norm of the bourgeoisie and not as inherent in its fierce acquisitive individualism. This central flaw in Augier's picture of society is what prevents him from achieving the status of an impressive moralist in the theatre. He is too much the prisoner of the values of the investing class to which he belongs to see the malaise of his society clear and whole. He fails to recognize that thrift, family solidarity, and commercial probity, though useful social virtues, are not large enough values to live by. He is too imperfectly aware that social and moral orthodoxy might need to be tested against a higher moral law or that the idealistic spirit can be outraged by the meanness and materialism of this society, even when its affairs are conducted according to the rules.

Consequently, his work lacks both intensity and poetry, though it conveys a fuller sense of life than that of Dumas *fils* because it is much freer of rigged demonstration, crude didacticism, and rhetorical strain. At the same time, Augier never quite rids himself of Scribe's sentimentality, facile patriotism, and love of happy endings. *Le Gendre de M. Poirier* neatly illustrates all three, with the duc de Montmeyran expressing the mystique of the flag: 'Le premier coup de canon défonce les blagues, et le drapeau n'est plus un chiffon au bout d'une perche, c'est la robe même de la patrie.' Augier, then, is formally uninventive and persists in using, even in plays with serious pretensions, some of Scribe's more contrived tricks of plotting, though he is without Scribe's (or Sardou's) meretriciousness. In *La Contagion* (1866), for example, everything turns on a letter which is twice lost, hidden for several weeks, and produced, with great sleight of hand, in order to set off a scandal and a spectacular conversion. As against these weaknesses, Augier's strength lies in a genuine fund of comic observation, in the impressive range of memorable characters he creates, and in his acute feeling for the changing life of his society. He puts on the stage not only the familiar period themes of adultery (*Les Lionnes pauvres*, 1858), prostitution (*La Contagion*), and divorce (*Madame Caverlet*, 1876), but also the larger social questions of the irresponsibility of the press (*Les Effrontés*), the conflict of social classes, and the dangers of clerical obscurantism (*Le Fils de Giboyer*, 1862). In his hands, the drama of money and class really comes into its own and emerges as the theatrical form most perfectly attuned to the solid bourgeois public of the day.

Sentimentality and moral improvement characterize much of the theatre of Dumas *fils* and Augier. So does moral debate or the tendency to locate moral principles in individual characters so as to allow of their dialectical play. Yet it is by no means certain that Dumas *fils*'s problem-plays or Augier's social comedies are really to be accounted a drama of ideas, in the fullest sense. After all, a true drama of ideas (Shaw's or Ibsen's, for instance) implies the radical questioning of received values and ideas in a spirit of critical doubt. For all the scandalous nature of certain episodes and situations which shocked contemporary audiences, the theatre of Dumas *fils* and Augier remains a theatre of orthodoxy. In the end, the principal social and moral assumptions of the dominant middle classes are vindicated and proffered as eternal verities.

NOTE

Editions. For Scribe, the standard edition of the plays is *Œuvres complètes* (76 vols., 1874-85). A convenient edition of the plays of Dumas *fils* is *Théâtre complet* (10 vols., 1868-92), while Augier's social comedy may be read in *Théâtre complet* (7 vols., 1890). The standard collection of Sardou's plays is *Théâtre complet* (15 vols., 1934-61). A useful anthology is J. L. Borgerhoff (ed.), *Nineteenth Century French Plays* (1931, reprint 1959).

Criticism. Important modern studies include M. Descotes, *Le Public de théâtre et son histoire* (1964), chaps. 9-10; M. Lamm, *Modern Drama* (1952); J. R. Taylor, *The Rise and Fall of the Well-made Play* (1967); and P. Voltz, *La Comédie* (1964). Older, but still valuable, general studies include R. Doumic, *De Scribe à Ibsen* (1893); E. Faguet, *Propos de théâtre*, 4ᵉ série (1906); A. Filon, *De Dumas à Rostand* (1898); L. Lacour, *Trois théâtres: E. Augier, A. Dumas fils, V. Sardou* (1880); J. Lemaître, *Impressions de théâtre* (10 vols., 1888-98); B. Matthews, *French Dramatists of the Nineteenth Century*, 5th ed. (1914); H. Parigot, *Le Théâtre d'hier* (1893); F. Sarcey, *Quarante ans de théâtre* (8 vols., 1900-2); J.-J. Weiss, *Le Théâtre et les mœurs* (1889); and É. Zola, *Nos auteurs dramatiques* (1881). Ernest Legouré, *Soixante ans de souvenirs* (2 vols., 1886-7), is informative.

On Scribe the most useful critical studies are N. C. Arvin, *Eugène Scribe and the French Theatre 1815-1860* (1924, reprint 1967), and C. Duckworth, 'Comment Scribe composait *Le Verre d'eau*', *Revue de la société d'histoire du théâtre*, iv (1959), pp. 315-26.

On Dumas *fils*, useful studies include N. C. Arvin, *Alexandre Dumas fils* (1939); Henry James, 'Dumas the Younger', in *The Scenic Art*, ed. A. Wade (1957); P. Lamy, *Le Théâtre d'Alexandre Dumas fils* (1928); and F. A. Taylor, *The Theatre of Alexandre Dumas fils* (1937).

For Augier two studies are especially valuable: H. Gaillard, *Émile Augier et la comédie sociale* (1910), and P. Morillot, *Émile Augier* (1901).

6. Verlaine

VERLAINE'S originality as a poet reaches its finest development in his fourth collection, *Romances sans paroles*, published when he was thirty. I want to trace three stages in the growth of this originality, illustrating each stage by a particular poem, or poems. Since artistic development is not as tidy as our schematic reconstruction of it, the poems are not always quoted in chronological order, but they all belong to the first four collections.

The first stage is represented by a sonnet from *Poèmes saturniens* in which Verlaine uses a clearly defined description to convey a mood which is essentially indefinable:

Après trois ans

Ayant poussé la porte étroite qui chancelle,
Je me suis promené dans le petit jardin
Qu'éclairait doucement le soleil du matin,
Pailletant chaque fleur d'une humide étincelle.

Rien n'a changé. J'ai tout revu : l'humble tonnelle
De vigne folle avec les chaises de rotin . . .
Le jet d'eau fait toujours son murmure argentin
Et le vieux tremble sa plainte sempiternelle.

Les roses comme avant palpitent, comme avant
Les grands lis orgueilleux se balancent au vent.
Chaque alouette qui va et vient m'est connue.

Même j'ai retrouvé debout la Velléda
Dont le plâtre s'écaille au bout de l'avenue,
—Grêle, parmi l'odeur fade du réséda.

After an absence of three years the poet enters a garden which he once knew well, and finds that everything is as he remembers it.

The attention is caught by sharply focused detail: the narrow door is shaky on its hinges, there is a wet point of light on each individual flower, the plaster is peeling from the frail statue. Yet the very intensity of focus gives the objects an aura of unstated significance. Verlaine's exploration is unconsciously purposeful, following the perspective of the garden through to the statue at the end of the avenue. Before he reaches it, only his eyes and ears have been attentive, but in the last line a third sense is suddenly engaged by the scent of the reseda, at once heavy and penetrating. The archaic use of the preposition 'parmi' with a singular noun (a characteristic device) produces a close yet at the same time indefinite spatial relationship between the material and the immaterial, between the visually precise impression of the statue's frail limbs and the diffuse ubiquity of the perfume. Verlaine has achieved the aim described in his 'Art poétique', published sixteen years later, of situating his effect at the point where 'l'Indécis au Précis se joint'. It is as though a subliminal awareness of the perfume is suddenly made conscious, so that it expands instantaneously to fill the garden, enveloping all the separately named objects in a single atmosphere and so forming an almost tangible element in which the poet's mood exists.

This mood is never explained to us. We do not even know whether the poet is glad or sorry to be back. We retain only a half-formed impression built up out of a number of hints afforded by the nature of the objects themselves. First, there is the gentleness of the sunlight, which has a peaceful effect. Next, there is a reassuring familiarity, suggested by 'l'humble tonnelle' and concentrated in the to-and-fro movements conveyed through the rhythms of the first tercet. Finally, the whole is coloured by a faint melancholy, since the garden is clearly neglected and succumbing to the slow attrition of time. 'Même' in line twelve indicates not only the statue's focal importance, but also the poet's surprise that it hasn't tumbled down. The mood is as frail and precarious as the statue itself. And we suddenly become aware that what has been pressing uneasily for our attention as we read the poem is a series of unasked and unanswered questions about the people who sat in the chairs or walked along the avenue. Who and where are they? We see that it is their absence which gives the poem its elusive poignancy. The aura surrounding the things in the garden was caused by their human associations. Despite the clear outline exposition of the poet's situation and the sharpness of the observation, we are left wondering about the circumstantial causes of the mood whose quality has been so vividly suggested to us by that of the objects associated with it. The poem is about an experience deeply felt but only dimly understood.

Nevertheless the clarity and perspective, limited though they are, represent a link with conventionally descriptive verse. A second stage in Verlaine's development is marked by a series of poems in which the technique of identifying objects with the mood they evoke is taken considerably further (though the technical advance does not necessarily mean an aesthetic improvement on the beautiful 'Après trois ans'). In these poems the outside world is internalized, or conversely, objects are invested with the quality of the consciousness which perceives them. This technique, which is an aspect of symbolism—indeed, some would say the essence of symbolism (cf. Chapter 9)—derives from Baudelaire, and the title of 'Crépuscule du soir mystique' pays frank homage to Baudelaire's 'Crépuscule du soir':

Crépuscule du soir mystique

Le Souvenir avec le Crépuscule
Rougeoie et tremble à l'ardent horizon
De l'Espérance en flamme qui recule
Et s'agrandit ainsi qu'une cloison
Mystérieuse où mainte floraison
— Dahlia, lys, tulipe et renoncule —
S'élance autour d'un trellis, et circule
Parmi la maladive exhalaison
De parfums lourds et chauds, dont le poison
— Dahlia, lys, tulipe et renoncule —
Noyant mes sens, mon âme et ma raison,
Mêle dans une immense pâmoison
Le Souvenir avec le Crépuscule.

(From *Paysages tristes*, in *Poèmes saturniens*)

The device of the recurring line or lines which impose a visible

unity on the stanza or, as here, on the whole poem is frequent
in Baudelaire. But Verlaine is being more Baudelairean than
Baudelaire (even in a poem like 'Harmonie du soir'), systematically
working the elements of his poem into a complicated, dynamic
pattern.

The poem conveys a struggle in the mind between Memory and
Hope, the first associated with, and therefore loosely symbolized
by, the dusk, the second by the lurid colours of the sunset. Memory
and darkness triumph. Yet there is no narrative progression, but
rather a gradual intensifying of the same mood, the same moment.
The verbs keep the poem's single sentence steadily moving through
a series of new impulses, so that it is never arrested into a definitive
profile, but flashes its interconnected facets towards us one after
the other. The verbs either suggest a process of dynamic change
('recule', 's'agrandit', 's'élance') and thus press on towards the
climax, or denote intermittent but continuous movement
('rougeoie', 'tremble'), or, finally, move progressively into the
idea of fusion ('noyant', 'mêle'). The poem's forward movement,
therefore, does not preclude an impression of simultaneity. Memory
takes on the colours of Hope, and shares the latter's trembling,
precarious existence as a flame. The flame is ambiguous, both
receding and growing. The images grow together out of loose
associations: the wall, originally connected with the idea of Hope,
suggests a trellis with climbing flowers, which in their turn are
associated with Memory. The symbolic equation breaks up and
the poisonous scent, combining delight and disgust, sweeps
him away—mind, soul, and body—into a swoon in which
Memory and dusk, mind and world, have become indistinguishable. For, whereas in the first line the relation between the two
was only suggested by 'avec' used in a loosely conjunctive role,
in the last, 'avec' is a preposition governed by the verb 'mêle'.
Thus the final line, as in 'Après trois ans', concentrates all
the states invoked through the poem into a single moment of
time.

Nevertheless, the consciousness here is divided into components
(Memory, Hope) which are no less abstract than those used in the
rationalist tradition of psychological analysis: 'L'esprit est toujours

la dupe du cœur' (La Rochefoucauld). Memory and Hope are concepts which, although used as units in a dynamic pattern, are in themselves static and opaque. Similarly in 'Le Rossignol' (also from *Paysages tristes*), we have a complex image of a mental experience: the poet's memories are birds settling in the tree of his mind, his regrets are figured by the dull sheet of water in which the whole is reflected, the nightingale's voice is the memory of his first love, whose languid purity emerges from the clamour of the other memories. The use of the multiple image reminds us of a highly cerebral sixteenth-century sonnet like Du Bellay's 'Je suis semblable au marinier timide' (*L'Olive*), in which the poet is a sailor, his thoughts are the sea, the sighs and tears of unrequited love are the wind and the rain, while his lady is the star which will guide him out of the storm.

The basic technique of these two poems, written at an interval of more than three hundred years, is exactly the same. Both poets use the multiple image to show the interrelation of the different components of their experience. But whereas Du Bellay's poem gives us a diagram of his relationship, an external analysis which tells us nothing of his feelings at any given moment, Verlaine's takes us inside a changing consciousness, showing how the breeze rising from the waters of regret progressively stifles the shrillness of the flock of memories:

> et puis la rumeur mauvaise
> Qu'une brise moite en montant apaise,
> S'éteint par degrés dans l'arbre.

By his brilliantly elliptical fusion of concrete and abstract, Verlaine makes us feel how one element of mental experience acts upon another. (The process is shown consecutively in 'Le Rossignol', simultaneously in 'Crépuscule du soir mystique'.)

Nevertheless, in these poems regret, memory, and hope are still rationally apprehended as named concepts. Before Verlaine could achieve the total illumination of the interior of consciousness, these hard abstract lumps had to be refined away. When this happens, especially in *Romances sans paroles*, the third stage of the development of Verlaine's originality is reached. The result is poetry which,

even more than Lamartine's, seems purged of external substance
and rational structure:

> Je devine, à travers un murmure,
> Le contour subtil des voix anciennes
> Et dans les lueurs musiciennes,
> Amour pâle, une aurore future!

> Et mon âme et mon cœur en délires
> Ne sont plus qu'une espèce d'œil double
> Où tremblote, à travers un jour trouble,
> L'ariette, hélas! de toutes lyres!

> O mourir de cette mort seulette
> Que s'en vont, cher amour qui t'épeures,
> Balançant jeunes et vieilles heures!
> O mourir de cette escarpolette!

Here there is no longer an explained situation, as there was
partly in 'Après trois ans', nor a logical ordering of the complex image as in 'Le Rossignol', nor yet a dynamic manipulation
of psychological abstractions as in 'Crépuscule du soir mystique'.
Memory and hope are no longer conventional counters. They
have their own internal dimensions. External rational perspective has been almost abandoned, and the artistic organization is
much less apparent. Indeed, the expression is elliptical to the
point of obscurity. It is clear from the last line (and this is sup-
ported by the original title of the poem, 'Escarpolette') that the
poet is on a swing. This provides a basic image of *balancement*,
and the poem uses both connotation of the word: indecision
and oscillation, thus extending an image already consecrated in
the language.

The poet swings between the past and the future, between,
so we gather from the word 'amour' in the fourth line, an old
love and a new one. Both come to his consciousness through
a sort of haze. The old love appears as familiar *voices* whose
delicate *outline* is guessed at through the general murmur of
other memories. The intermingling of the different senses accom-
panies the intermingling of concrete and abstract to produce an

D

TRINITY COLLEGE
LIBRARY

impression of the undifferentiated content of the consciousness. The device brilliantly conveys the workings of memory, at once vivid and impossible to focus. So, too, the new love is the pale promise of a new dawn, immensely distant and unattainable —merely the *musical* promise of furtive gleams of *light*. The statement compresses a complex and confused experience into a single image.

The second stanza gives the characteristic effect of a deliberately blurred vision. The poet's whole interior being becomes a sort of agonized squint taking in the superimposed images of past and future. The blur of sight shades off into the vagueness of a future expressed as an infinite series of haunting tunes. The specific alternatives are absorbed in a musical shimmer of hope, and the movement from the visual to the auditory perfectly expresses the loss of definition. The form of the *ariette* (a tune from a light opera) has the undidactic, tenuous quality which the *Romances sans paroles* consciously attempt to reproduce.

In the third stanza the sensation of swinging induces a return to a deliciously irresponsible infantile state, an extension of the to-and-fro movements of 'Après trois ans'. The impression is reinforced by words like 'tremblote' and 'seulette', diminutives which suggest the cosy reassurance of baby-talk. The deliberately strained syntax ('mort' is the object of 's'en vont balançant') makes the death-wish itself partake of the oscillation which precludes any terminating resolution. The movement of the swing is an image for the evasion of adult responsibility, the refusal to halt at either of the two poles of choice, the refusal to focus either alternative into the exact image of what it has to offer so that the process of rational calculation on which choice could be based would become possible. This is a withdrawal from life, the desire to fade dreamily into oblivion, soothed by the rhythmic alternation between the alluring images of past and future. But in terms of adult experience the desire for infantile oblivion leaves the poet solitary, self-enfolded, shy of the living tensions of human contact. The theme of *Fêtes galantes*—and perhaps also of *La Bonne Chanson*—is that love is a dreamy game, a masquerade whose mournful gaiety is a cloak for solitude.

In *Romances sans paroles* Verlaine is the poet of uncertainty:

> Dans l'interminable
> Ennui de la plaine,
> La neige incertaine
> Luit comme du sable.
>
> Le ciel est de cuivre
> Sans lueur aucune,
> On croirait voir vivre
> Et mourir la lune.
>
> Comme des nuées
> Flottent gris les chênes
> Des forêts prochaines
> Parmi les buées.
>
> Le ciel est de cuivre
> Sans lueur aucune,
> On croirait voir vivre
> Et mourir la lune.
>
> Corneille poussive
> Et vous, les loups maigres,
> Par ces bises aigres
> Quoi donc vous arrive?
>
> Dans l'interminable
> Ennui de la plaine,
> La neige incertaine
> Luit comme du sable.

The first stanza could be rewritten as follows:

> Dans l'interminable ennui
> De la plaine
> La neige incertaine luit
> Comme du sable,

which gives a secondary form hidden in the ostensible form. The verb 'luit' takes on intense stress both from being a *rejet* from the previous line and because of its internal rhyme with 'ennui'. It appears at once as the culmination of a sense-unit in the secondary form, and as the opening word of the line in the primary form. Thus there is a concealed latent rhythm cutting across the external rhythmic pattern, which contributes to the impression of uneasy half-focus given in the meaning of the words. The very word which is stressed by the secondary rhythm, 'luit', connotes a general, diffuse impression, and indeed this is one of Verlaine's favourite words.

The whole statement of the opening stanza creates a doubt about the actual texture of snow, and in stanza two there is a similar uncertainty about the dull copper sheen of the sky. It is not even clear whether the moon is shining or not; the impression of fitful flickering is conveyed in a deliberately disconcerting image whose harsh sounds do not come comfortably to the tongue: 'on croirait voir vivre . . .' The colour of the trees is a typically indeterminate grey; they mingle with the mist, detached from substance and precise location.

In the process of losing their independence of contour and texture they become dream-like, no longer placed in the orderly scheme of a world rationally accounted for—and therefore relegated to the habitual inattention of our daily response—but uneasily immaterialized. Compare:

> L'ombre des arbres dans la rivière embrumée
> Meurt comme de la fumée
> (from *Romances sans paroles*)

in which we can trace this dissolution of matter. The trees here are only shadows of themselves, the shadows are reflected in the water, the reflections are almost absorbed in the mists on the water's surface. Furthermore the tree itself is an image, a reflection, of the poet's mind. This is the spectralization of reality in the endless recessiveness of misty reflections, the process by which matter becomes mind, by which the world comes to symbolize a mental state. It is Verlaine's achievement to have made this process so familiar to us that in a poem like 'Dans l'interminable ennui de la plaine' it functions without any of the detailed machinery of allegory we saw in 'Crépuscule du soir mystique'. The whole landscape represents aspects of the single mental state of *ennui*. Thus, by a striking compression of his method which is habitual to Verlaine, the abstract noun is given a concrete adjective—or at any rate, here, one which has concrete as well as abstract application: 'interminable ennui'. The *ennui* is at once never-ending—for so boredom affects us—and spatially limitless, a dreary interior extent. Thus, anything that is said about the landscape adds to our picture of the state of boredom. Typically, the origin of the boredom is not described. There is only the anxiety of the question which does not expect an answer: 'Quoi donc vous arrive?' addressed to the skinny wolves and hoarse raven who figure the gloomy premonitions of a mind which is so immersed in its mood that it cannot find its causes.

Unanswered questions are also a feature of one of Verlaine's most perfect and poignant poems, again from *Romances sans paroles*:

> Le piano que baise une main frêle
> Luit dans le soir rose et gris vaguement,
> Tandis qu'avec un très léger bruit d'aile
> Un air bien vieux, bien faible et bien charmant
> Rôde discret, épeuré quasiment,
> Par le boudoir longtemps parfumé d'Elle.
>
> Qu'est-ce que c'est que ce berceau soudain
> Qui lentement dorlote mon pauvre être?
> Que voudrais-tu de moi, doux chant badin?
> Qu'as-tu voulu, fin refrain incertain
> Qui vas tantôt mourir vers la fenêtre
> Ouverte un peu sur le petit jardin?

Again the questions ask: 'what is happening to me?'—the semi-anxious response to powerful memories stirred in him by the woman's singing, but never reaching the pitch of urgency which would demand the awakening of the rational part of his mind to throw off the spell and find an answer. Here the technique of precise imprecision is totally successful. This time there is a circumstantial frame, but it is reduced to a disembodied minimum: the caressing touch of a delicate hand, the gleam of the piano keys in the muted light of evening, the sound of the tune and the perfume of the boudoir, all blending into a single, psychologically continuous experience. The typically loose preposition 'par' suggests the usual directionless ubiquity, and the sound, like the scent in 'Après trois ans', becomes almost tangible in its lingering persistence. Yet we never lose our acute awareness that it is soft and elusive to the point of being imperceptible. It cannot be grasped. When, where does it end? The soft colours suffer a further loss of clarity because they are not even applied to specific objects, but to the evening in general, so that we get the impression of a diffused glow.

The adverb 'vaguement' further attenuates what is already tenuous, whilst its position at the end of the line also has the effect of prolonging the diffusion of the colour in time and space, contributing to the carefully established weightlessness of the whole. Conversely, the emphatic adverbs 'très' and 'bien' are used to intensify what is indeterminate. In any case the grammatical function of 'vaguement' is not clear-cut, since it could qualify the verb 'luit' or the adjectives 'rose et gris'. The latter reading would be odd, but it is suggested by the omission of the comma after 'gris'. It is as if Verlaine were deliberately holding back from any definitive formulation of his subject, allowing a relaxed freedom of response. Grammatical ambiguity is the linguistic equivalent of Verlaine's artistic enterprise, which is to capture the elusive and evanescent quality of experience rather than to record the neat patterns into which it is organized by the process of conceptualization.

Some readers will object, with Julien Benda, that such attempts to portray the sophisticated extremes of modern sensibility revert to a kind of primitivism or infantilism which is the opposite of sophisticated. Thus, writers like Verlaine can be seen as betraying the precious heritage of human evolution. What is the value of a poem which seeks to reconstitute the pre-rational consciousness of a baby? We are, after all, not babies. The experience of a civilized adult is recuperable from the blur of sensory response precisely because he has learned to stand outside the shadowy turmoil of primitive consciousness in order to judge and analyse.

In one way this type of criticism is justified. The extraordinary success of poems like 'Le piano que baise une main frêle' is dependent precisely on the absence of the critical perspective of which vestiges remained in 'Après trois ans'. The limits of Verlaine's powers can be marked by comparing 'Le piano que baise une main frêle' with a poem by D. H. Lawrence on a similar theme, 'Piano' (*Selected Poems*, Penguin, 1950, p. 30). Lawrence places a similarly intense experience of involuntary memory in a conceptual context and a mature moral perspective, and although we can lose ourselves in Verlaine's poem as we cannot in Lawrence's, some people will prefer the more grown-up approach. Yet it is Verlaine's very limitations as a moral being which release his power as a poet.

This is not to say that he is a 'natural' poet, an instinctive purveyor of mindless jingles. It should be apparent from the recurrence of certain techniques in the poems I have quoted that Verlaine's tenuous, impressionistic effects are obtained by the intelligent exploitation of his own stock of poetic devices. In the opening stanza of 'Chanson d'automne', for example, he organizes half a dozen vowel sounds (é, õ, ã, eu, open and closed o) into a controlled pattern of verbal harmonics:

> Les sanglots longs
> Des violons
> De l'automne
> Blessent mon cœur
> D'une langueur
> Monotone.

One notices especially the way in which the muffled nasal rhyme of the first two lines is transposed into a clearer register by its ringing feminine equivalent in the third and sixth.

The Benda point of view, if we are to apply it to Verlaine, will need serious modification. A poem like 'Crépuscule du soir mystique' traces the drowning of reason in the swirl of consciousness and sensation, but it does not give us the verbal equivalent of subliminal existence. Verlaine is not mesmerizing himself with words. There may be no logical organization of the experience, but there is a rigorous artistic organization of the poem. The elusive rhythms of 'Escarpolette' subtly avoid the temptation of transposing the image of *balancement* into an over-obvious metrical regularity. This is to say that the lack of moral perspective is balanced by a high degree of artistic responsibility. The Verlaine of the first four or five collections is a master of his means.

It is striking that this mastery was achieved precisely in *Romances sans paroles*, written when Verlaine was living and working with Rimbaud. Rimbaud, with the splendid arrogance of adolescence, found that all previous attempts by French writers to give literary expression to the inexhaustible richness of imaginative experience had been hopelessly feeble. He therefore sought with a kind of frenzy for new forms and a new language to express the wealth within. This meant that he was never satisfied with what he had done, or indeed with what he was doing, so that he passes with disconcerting rapidity from one experiment to another. It is likely that it was his example and encouragement which led Verlaine, who, although he was Rimbaud's elder by ten years, appears to have played the submissive, feminine part in their relationship, to explore his own art to its limits in *Romances sans paroles*.

But he conspicuously lacked Rimbaud's fierce integrity, and when, after they had parted, he was left on his own, it is as though his artistic and moral growth had been virtually arrested. After *Sagesse*, he alternates between two conflicting attitudes which, though opposites, are both curiously conventional. On the one hand, Verlaine the saint, the simple-mindedly pious Catholic; on the other, Verlaine the satyr, the impenitent drinker and eroticist. This is a continuation, on a wider scale, of the *balancement* which I analysed in 'Escarpolette'. Verlaine, as the title of his eighth collection, *Parallèlement*, indicates, cultivates the two halves of his personality as two separate and autonomous departments, reflected in two parallel streams of inspiration which rarely meet. Both manners strike us as superficial and, since they persist right through the remainder of his voluminous output of poetry, depressingly monotonous. Neither reflects his inner experience as honestly and deeply as the poems of *Romances sans paroles*.

Even those, however, were inspired by the example of the iconoclastic energy of Rimbaud and, although the younger man's influence worked in the same direction as Verlaine's natural talent, impelling him towards self-discovery as a poet, it is clear from Verlaine's failure to develop further after the break that he was dependent on the sanction of an external authority. Before Rimbaud, he had hoped to find in marriage a framework for living which would

somehow transform him into a model husband content with a
tranquil bourgeois existence (*La Bonne Chanson*). The contrast between this and Rimbaud's ideal of self-fulfilment through the
deliberate conspuing of conventional values, is a measure of
Verlaine's pathetic instability and lack of self-knowledge. After
Rimbaud he looks to the authority of the Church on the one hand,
and on the other to the sanction of a certain potentially tedious
tradition of bohemian eroticism. Neither corresponds to any
mature attempt to define himself and his own morality, though
some critics claim that after the dreamy self-abandonment of
Poèmes saturniens, *Fêtes galantes*, and *Romances sans paroles*,
Sagesse marks the beginning of a conscious attempt to lay hold on
things as they are.

In one or two poems of *Sagesse* he comes close to achieving a
truer kind of poetry which would reflect his conflicting impulses
together, not as beatifically separate but as an agonized interior
struggle; for some, this, rather than the earlier work, is the apogee
of Verlaine's achievement:

> Les faux beaux jours ont lui tout le jour, ma pauvre âme,
> Et les voici vibrer aux cuivres du couchant.
> Ferme les yeux, pauvre âme, et rentre sur-le-champ :
> Une tentation des pires. Fuis l'infâme.
>
> Ils ont lui tout le jour en longs grêlons de flamme,
> Battant toute vendange aux collines, couchant
> Toute moisson de la vallée, et ravageant
> Le ciel tout bleu, le ciel chanteur qui te réclame.
>
> O pâlis, et va-t'en, lente et joignant les mains.
> Si ces hiers allaient manger nos beaux demains ?
> Si la vieille folie était encore en route ?
>
> Ces souvenirs, va-t-il falloir les retuer ?
> Un assaut furieux, le suprême, sans doute !
> O va prier contre l'orage, va prier.

The temptation to return to the wild adventures of the past has
shimmered like a mirage, flashed like lightning in the clear sky of

the convert's new-found serenity, beating down like hailstones of fire on the carefully nurtured growths of his new life. These are the 'lueurs musiciennes' of 'Escarpolette' transformed into a destructive and menacing force, and the quatrains make use of the technique, perfected in the poetry written before conversion, of using external phenomena to symbolize mental experience. It is noticeable that the tercets, on the other hand, give a more prosaic statement of the predicament, so that the conflict between past adventure and present order is reflected in the form of the sonnet. We may well feel that in the more deliberate language of the tercets something of Verlaine's poetic power is being lost, but the poem is satisfying precisely because it embodies the difficulty, for a man of violent feeling like Verlaine, of living a spiritually ordered life.

By contrast the poems which reflect only one side of the two parallel inspirations of the later collections are increasingly perfunctory. It is true that he goes on producing the occasional fine poem, and the professional dexterity with which he handles a great variety of verse forms is impressive and often entertaining. He also experiments a little with *argot* or phonetic spelling, lines with eleven, thirteen, fourteen, and once even seventeen syllables, mixed rhythms, inverted sonnets, poems with a subtle blend of rhyme, half-rhyme and assonance, and occasionally no rhymes at all. But Verlaine's inventiveness is playful, and stops a long way short of radical innovation. He is a master of the *vers libéré*, which extends the prosodic freedom developed by Hugo from the example of Chénier, but his experiments are no more than variations of the traditional metrical models, and Verlaine was convinced that rhyme and metre were an indispensable ingredient of French poetry.

His experiments in any case are far outweighed by a kind of artistic inertia whose typical expression is self-parody, sometimes taking the form of the palinode (the poem which repudiates past attitudes). But, as with Musset, deliberately ironical self-parody is not easy to distinguish from unwitting self-parody, and a great deal of the later work comes under this dreary heading. The devices which made up the originality of the earlier poems are pitilessly overworked. Deliberate simplicity of utterance degenerates into

insipidity, while the automatic use of the final adverb can give a
lamentably lame effect:

> La cathédrale est grise admirablement,
> Tandis que le jour luit adorablement
> Et que les arbres sont verts tout doucement.

Similarly, the subtle verbal harmonies of the earlier collections fall
only too readily into a sort of flat jingling:

> Sur la plume et le bitume
> Paris bruit et jouit.

The yearning for a return to childhood irresponsibility declines
into a longing for babyhood—or perhaps we might coin the word
bébétude to characterize the following:

> Petit Jésus qu'il nous faut être
> Si nous voulons voir Dieu le Père,
> Accordez-nous d'alors renaître
>
> En purs bébés.

Like all those who repeat themselves, Verlaine becomes a bore.
The erotic verse is oddly similar to the religious verse, as is underlined by the fact that some of the titles and terminology are inter-
changeable. Instead of lingering within the half-understood
subtleties of his own sensibility, Verlaine now tends to see himself
from the outside, writing about his life and career. After 1888 or so
he becomes conscious of his own growing notoriety, and his verse
is used to help create the image on which, quite literally, he is living.
As the poems become more explicitly autobiographical there is a
corresponding loss of insight into the nature of his own talent.
Verlaine as bohemian is cast in a conventional mould saved from
complete lifelessness only by a certain coarse vitality, a certain
irrepressible garrulousness, and, in spite of everything, perhaps also
by his sheer professional competence.

For the essence of Verlaine in later life we must look, not at his
work, but at the brilliant drawings of Régamey and Cazals which
show him as a disreputable old man snoozing over an absinthe in the
corner of a café, enjoying a taste of the oblivion he always craved.

NOTE

PAUL VERLAINE, 1844-96, was emotionally unstable, alternately violent and timid. He never really made up his mind whether to be respectable or bohemian. When he was twenty-eight he left his wife and baby to elope with Rimbaud, but the new life was stormy and came to an end a year later when Verlaine shot his friend in the wrist with a pistol he had bought to kill himself. By then he had written four collections of poetry: *Poèmes saturniens* (1866), *Fêtes galantes* (1869), *La Bonne Chanson* (1870), and *Romances sans paroles* (1874). During the ensuing spell in prison he was converted to Catholicism, and the poems of *Sagesse* (1881) show a new religious inspiration. But lapses were frequent, and when his mother died (1886) he became a sort of literary *clochard*. After *Sagesse* his poetry declined, though his output was considerable. Later collections include the uneven *Jadis et naguère* (1884), the Catholic *Amour* (1888), *Bonheur* (1891), and *Liturgies intimes* (1892), and the libertine *Parallèlement* (1889), *Chansons pour Elle* (1891), and *Odes en son honneur* (1893). Verlaine also wrote criticism (*Les Poètes maudits*, 1884) and autobiography (*Confessions*, 1895).

Modern Editions. *Œuvres poétiques complètes* (Pléiade, revised ed. 1962); the *Œuvres complètes* (2 vols., introduction by O. Nadel, Club du meilleur livre, 1959-60) include prose work. Critical editions: *Poèmes saturniens* and *Fêtes galantes* by J.-H. Bornecque (1952 and 1959); *Fêtes galantes / La Bonne Chanson / Romances sans paroles*, in one volume, with notes etc. in French by V. P. Underwood (revised 1963); *Sagesse* by Underwood (1944) and L. Morice (1948). Verlaine's *Selected Poems* are reliably edited with notes in English by R. C. D. Perman (1965).

Criticism. Useful general introductions: P. Martino, *Verlaine* (new ed., 1951) and A. Adam, *Verlaine, l'homme et l'œuvre* (new ed., 1965). J.-P. Richard's essay on Verlaine in *Poésie et profondeur* (1955) is subtle, while Martin Turnell's article in *Scrutiny* (vol. ix, 1940-1) will stimulate some readers to fruitful disagreement. See also the fascinating *Documents iconographiques* published by F. Ruchon (1947) and, for an attack on the tradition which Verlaine represents, if not on the poet himself, J. Benda, *La France byzantine* (1945). Among the most recent studies of Verlaine, mention should be made of A. E. Carter, *Verlaine, a Study in Parallels* (1969), A. K. Diederichs-Maurer, *Le Thème de l'angoisse chez Verlaine* (1971), J. Richardson, *Verlaine* (1971), C. Chadwick, *Verlaine* (1973).

7. Rimbaud

THROUGHOUT his life Rimbaud's attitude was that of a rebel, whether in matters of religion, morals, politics, poetry, or in the day-to-day affairs of ordinary life. Even during his childhood years, when, to all outward appearances, he was the docile and willing pupil who carried off most of the prizes at school, a feeling of revolt seems to have been simmering within him, judging by his auto-biographical poem 'Les Poètes de sept ans'. The reasons for this rebellious attitude can only be guessed at, but it seems more than probable that the notoriously harsh discipline exercised over her children by Mme Rimbaud (no doubt related, in its turn, to the fact that her husband, an officer in the French army, had deserted her after a mere half-dozen years of marriage, leaving her with four children to bring up) was in a large measure responsible.

The first outward sign of Rimbaud's revolt came in the autumn of 1870 when he twice ran away from home, once to Paris and once to Brussels, followed by a third attempt, to Paris for the second time, in February 1871. These repeated failures—on each occasion he was forced to return home after two or three weeks—only served to increase and extend his rebellious mood. It was during these months that he wrote the sarcastic political sonnets, 'L'Éclatante Victoire de Sarrebruck' and 'Rages de Césars', directed against Napoleon III, whose regime was already toppling at the time. He also launched out into social satire in 'A la musique' and the final lines of 'Les Pauvres à l'église' where he poured scorn on the wealthier citizens of Charleville. Further, he ridiculed specific people who had been unwise enough to exercise authority over him, such as the local librarian in 'Les Assis', the customs officers on the nearby Franco-Belgian frontier in 'Les Douaniers', and, in 'Les Poètes de sept ans', Mme Rimbaud herself, 'la bouche d'ombre' as he irreverently called her in a letter written in April 1871.

The most important and lasting aspect of Rimbaud's revolt, however, was the bitterly anti-Christian attitude he adopted. This arose
in part from his political leanings and from a sense of resentment
against a church which seemed to him more interested in wealth
than in the welfare of mankind and in the rich rather than the poor,
as is obvious from the vicious sarcasm of the last lines of 'Les
Pauvres à l'église':

> . . . Les Dames des quartiers
> Distingués, — ô Jésus! — les malades du foie
> Font baiser leurs longs doigts jaunes aux bénitiers.

But it was also based on moral grounds and sprang from a profound
feeling that the Christian religion—as it was doubtless preached by
Mme Rimbaud at least—failed to take account of the sensual side
of man's nature. As early as May 1870 in 'Soleil et chair' (whose
original title, 'Credo in unam', significantly changes the opening
words of the Nicene creed) Rimbaud wrote an invocation to Venus
which seems more than a Parnassian exercise:

> Je crois en toi! je crois en toi! Divine mère,
> Aphrodité marine! — Oh! la route est amère
> Depuis que l'autre Dieu nous attelle à sa croix.

A year later he returned to this theme in 'Les premières communions', treating the same problem from a woman's point
of view:

> J'étais bien jeune, et Christ a souillé mes haleines.
> Il me bonda jusqu'à la gorge de dégoûts!
> Tu baisais mes cheveux profonds comme les laines
> Et je me laissais faire . . . ah! va, c'est bon pour vous,
>
> Hommes! qui songez peu que la plus amoureuse
> Est, sous sa conscience aux ignobles terreurs,
> La plus prostituée et la plus douloureuse,
> Et que tous nos élans vers vous sont des erreurs!
>
> Car ma communion première est bien passée.
> Tes baisers, je ne puis jamais les avoir sus:
> Et mon cœur et ma chair par ta chair embrassée
> Fourmillent du baiser putride de Jésus!

These lines are assumed to have been inspired by the first communion of his sister Isabelle, but the feelings of guilt and confusion they express must obviously be Rimbaud's own, as must the characteristically violent language he uses to argue that Christianity inhibits emotional relationships on the human plane.

Associated with this spirit of revolt against the various constraints, both major and minor, imposed on him by the world around him, there was the desire to escape from it and to attain a state of absolute liberty. This found expression not only in life, in his repeated attempts to run away from home, but also in literature. Poems such as 'Sensation', 'Ophélie', 'Ma Bohème', 'Les Poètes de sept ans', and 'Le Cœur volé' are all concerned wholly or in part with this theme, as is 'Le Bateau ivre', the last poem Rimbaud wrote in Charleville before his successful attempt to escape in September 1871. In a sense, therefore, this is the last poem of Rimbaud's childhood with its theme that once one has tasted freedom, though there may be a lingering tinge of regret at leaving a stable and sheltered existence, however constricting it may have been—

> Fileur éternel des immobilités bleues,
> Je regrette l'Europe aux anciens parapets

—no guidance, control, and surveillance can any longer be tolerated:

> Je ne puis plus, baigné de vos langueurs, ô lames,
> Enlever leurs sillages aux porteurs de cotons,
> Ni traverser l'orgueil des drapeaux et des flammes,
> Ni nager sous les yeux horribles des pontons.

The spirit of revolt and desire for freedom expressed in these poems is often matched by an unconventional quality in their vocabulary. Rimbaud shows a marked fondness for neologisms, provincialisms, and scientific terms at this period and he has no hesitation in using words of a distinctly popular flavour—'merde à ces chiens-là', for example, is the defiant and unusually realistic cry of the blacksmith in 'Le Forgeron', the children in 'Les Effarés' are described as crouching down 'leurs culs en rond', and the choir in 'Les Pauvres à l'église' is defined as 'vingt gueules gueulant des cantiques pieux'. Furthermore, Rimbaud is as frank and unconventional in his imagery as he is in his vocabulary—the same posture as that of the children in 'Les Effarés' is adopted by one of the soldiers in 'L'Éclatante Victoire de Sarrebruck', but this time as an insulting gesture towards Napoleon III, and Rimbaud's teacher Izambard is known to have toned down the last line of 'A la musique': 'Et mes désirs brutaux s'accrochent à leurs lèvres', and to have substituted for it the insipidly romantic line: 'Et je sens des baisers qui me viennent aux lèvres'.

Yet despite the impatience with various kinds of restraint that these poems reveal, as regards their versification they remain cast very much in the classical mould, three-quarters of them being written in alexandrines, one-third of them adopting the form of the sonnet, and all of them observing strictly the alternation of masculine and feminine rhymes. It was not until the famous 'lettre du voyant', written on 15 May 1871, two days after another, shorter letter along the same lines, that Rimbaud tried to spread his rebellion to matters of form in poetry. Not only did he insist in these letters that the true poet must be a seer, capable of looking beyond the real world, and that this could not be achieved by any orderly, intellectual means, but only by the 'long, immense et raisonné dérèglement de tous les sens', he also contended that the poet's function is simply to note down the sensations he thus experiences without intervening to exercise any conscious control. He is not personally involved, since it is a mere accident that he happens to possess this faculty for receiving and transmitting visions of another world: 'JE est un autre. Si le cuivre s'éveille clairon il n'y a rien de sa faute. Cela m'est évident: j'assiste à l'éclosion de ma pensée: je la regarde, je l'écoute.' Rimbaud was, therefore (and in this he is of course the forerunner of the surrealist movement), determined to abandon in poetry the world of ordered reality and its careful presentation, so as to give free play instead to the tumultuous world of the imagination. 'Les inventions d'inconnu', he wrote, 'réclament des formes nouvelles', and he condemned Lamartine as being 'étranglé par la forme vieille', scornfully dismissed Musset's poetry as 'de la peinture à l'émail, de la poésie solide', and even reprimanded Baudelaire, whom he otherwise admired as 'le premier voyant', for the form of his poetry.

Rimbaud's own first attempts, enclosed in the 'lettre du voyant', at giving free rein to his poetic imagination are, however, largely failures because he paradoxically stuck firmly to traditionally rigid patterns of rhyme and rhythm so that the words he uses are dictated to a considerable extent by these two factors. This at least seems to be the explanation of such nonsense verses as:

> Nous nous aimions à cette époque,
>   Bleu laideron!
> On mangeait des œufs à la coque
>   Et du mouron,

and of lines where Rimbaud seems to have wanted above all to maintain his set pattern of rhyme and rhythm without paying much regard to other factors:

> Au gouvernail on voit des fresques
> Ithyphalliques et pioupiesques
> O flots abracadabrantesques . . .

Perhaps not surprisingly, therefore, he returned, in 'Les Sœurs de charité', 'Les Premières Communions', 'Le Bateau ivre', and other poems written in the summer of 1871, to a more carefully and more consciously organized kind of poetry where the themes are obviously handled in an orderly and rational manner that scarcely corresponds to the demand in the 'lettre du voyant' that the poet should indulge in a 'long, immense et raisonné dérèglement de tous les sens'. As regards the matter of 'Le Bateau ivre', however, rather than its manner, this is precisely what the poem is about, so that it too is a plea in favour of the poet subjecting himself to every kind of experience, just as the drunken boat deliberately and knowingly lets itself be carried away on its wild voyage. The time therefore did seem ripe for Rimbaud to launch out into a new and freer kind of poetry, more suited to his concept of the 'poète voyant', if he could be given some help and encouragement. This was provided by Verlaine, to whom Rimbaud wrote in September 1871 and in response to whose invitation he went to Paris.

The effect on Rimbaud's poetry of this meeting with a poet ten years his senior was immediate and startling. He abandoned the sonnet form completely, unless one dates 'Voyelles' from this period, which there is good reason for doing in that Rimbaud adopts a technique new to him, but not to Verlaine, of making all the rhymes, except the last, feminine. 'Qu'est-ce pour nous, mon cœur' has the same technical feature the other way round so that almost all the rhymes are masculine, while 'Mémoire' is in exclusively feminine rhymes, and these two poems, along with 'Voyelles', are the only ones in alexandrines. Several poems are in 'vers impairs', the virtues of which Verlaine was soon to praise in his 'Art poétique', having already made use of this unusual rhythm on a number of occasions, whereas Rimbaud had never done so, and of these poems most are in the short five- or seven-syllable line favoured by Verlaine. But although the older poet undoubtedly and naturally influenced Rimbaud's versification when they first met, the latter's greater boldness and stronger revolutionary spirit soon took him far beyond the relatively timid innovations of Verlaine.

> Tel, j'eusse été mauvaise enseigne d'auberge.
> Puis l'orage changea le ciel, jusqu'au soir.
> Ce furent des pays noirs, des lacs, des perches,
> Des colonnades sous la nuit bleue, des gares.
>
> L'eau des bois se perdait sur des sables vierges,
> Le vent, du ciel, jetait des glaçons aux mares . . .
> Or! tel qu'un pêcheur d'or ou de coquillages,
> Dire que je n'ai pas eu souci de boire!

In these verses from 'Larme', as in other poems from the middle of 1872, Rimbaud is already using assonance and alliteration as substitutes for rhyme in the strict sense of the term and on occasions, in 'Bannières de mai' for example, he abandons it altogether in favour of blank verse. On other occasions, though the use of rhyme is more or less maintained, consistent rhythm is discarded, as in 'Bonne pensée du matin' where the length of the lines follows a decidedly irregular pattern:

> A quatre heures du matin, l'été,
> Le sommeil d'amour dure encore.
> Sous les bosquets l'aube évapore
>   L'odeur du soir fêté.

Mais là-bas dans l'immense chantier
Vers le soleil des Hespérides,
En bras de chemise, les charpentiers
 Déjà s'agitent.

The next step for Rimbaud to take was obviously to break all links
with versification and to write poems in prose. There is no doubt
that he did in fact take this step since Verlaine, in a letter dated
November 1872, refers to letters by Rimbaud 'contenant des vers
et des poèmes en prose' and, in a letter dated May 1873, Rimbaud
himself refers to 'quelques fragments en prose' he has written.
There is, however, some doubt as to whether or not these prose
poems are the same as the group of passages known as the *Illuminations*. The confusion arises from the fact that the latter were nowhere
dated by Rimbaud, were left in manuscript by him, and were finally
published, due to the efforts of others, chiefly Verlaine, only in
1886, when their author had long since lost all interest in his
brief career as a poet and had settled in East Africa. Although
some of the *Illuminations* unquestionably date from the latter
part of 1872 and the early part of 1873, there is no positive and
entirely convincing evidence either to date all of them from these
months or to extend their period of composition to 1874 and even
beyond. The internal evidence too is contradictory, despite the
attempts of numerous critics to prove the case one way or the
other by examining handwriting, style, Anglicisms, literary echoes,
personal allusions, geographical references, and various other
factors.

But although there may be some doubt about the precise period
of time during which the *Illuminations* were written, there is no
doubt that they form the next stage, whether long or short, in the
evolution of Rimbaud's poetry. Some of them indeed still retain
vestiges of traditional techniques. In 'Veillées' the use of rhyme
is more or less maintained, though consistent rhythm is discarded,
with the lines varying enormously in length; in 'Départ' the rhyming
elements are transferred to the beginning of the lines, which again
are of varying length; in 'Marine' and 'Mouvement' both rhyme
and rhythm are abandoned, though they are set out not as prose but
as free verse; 'Barbare', too, is set out not as a continuous piece of

prose but as a number of elements varying considerably in length, of which the second one is repeated as a refrain; 'Solde' achieves a similar rhythmic effect by the constant repetition of 'A vendre'; and 'Fleurs' clearly makes use of irregular assonance and alliteration:

D'un gradin d'or, — parmi les cordons de soie, les gazes grises, les velours verts et les disques de cristal qui noircissent comme du bronze au soleil, — je vois la digitale s'ouvrir sur un tapis de filigranes d'argent, d'yeux et de chevelures . . .

This gradual breaking of the last links with versification does not, however, mean that Rimbaud moved instead towards the formal, well-constructed kind of prose that Baudelaire had used in *Le Spleen de Paris*. On the contrary, the well-turned phrase, the balanced sentence, the ample paragraph were anathema to Rimbaud, who tended instead to pile brilliant images pell-mell one on top of the other in short sentences:

Ce sont des villes! C'est un peuple pour qui se sont montés ces Alleghanys et ces Libans de rêve! Des chalets de cristal et de bois qui se meuvent sur des rails et des poulies invisibles. Les vieux cratères ceints de colosses et de palmiers de cuivre rugissent mélodieusement dans les feux. Des fêtes amoureuses sonnent sur les canaux pendus derrière les chalets. La chasse des carillons crie dans les gorges. Des corporations de chanteurs géants accourent dans des vêtements et des oriflammes éclatants comme la lumière des cimes . . .

These opening lines from 'Villes' and other passages such as 'Antique', 'Being Beauteous', 'Les Ponts', 'Ornières', and 'Métropolitain' attain a density and dynamism greater even than that achieved by the rapid succession of images in 'Le Bateau ivre', contained as the latter are within the framework of versification and a relatively complex sentence structure.

Not only does the form of the *Illuminations* thus show the development of the poet's ideas; so, too, do their themes. Rimbaud is still the rebel and the seeker after freedom that he had been in the verse poems of 1871, but in a slightly different way. The same anger as in 'Les Assis' and 'Les Pauvres à l'église', though now it is of a more

widely destructive nature, rages in 'Conte', 'Soir historique', and
these lines from 'Après le déluge':

Sourds, étang,—Écume, roule sur le pont et par-dessus les bois;
—draps noirs et orgues,—éclairs et tonnerre,—montez et roulez;
—Eaux et tristesses, montez et relevez les Déluges . . .

The same desire for escape as in 'Sensation' and 'Ma Bohème',
though now it is more urgent and compelling, is expressed in
'Génie' and 'Départ':

Assez vu. La vision s'est rencontrée à tous les airs.
Assez eu. Rumeurs des villes, le soir, et au soleil, et toujours.
Assez connu. Les arrêts de la vie. — O Rumeurs et Visions!
Départ dans l'affection et le bruit neufs!

The same visionary scenes as in 'Les Poètes de sept ans' and 'Le
Bateau ivre', though now of landscapes and cities rather than seas
and ships, are evoked in 'Aube', 'Fleurs', 'Mystique', 'Ornières',
'Villes', 'Métropolitain', and 'Promontoire':

L'aube d'or et la soirée frissonnante trouvent notre brick en large en
face de cette villa et de ses dépendances, qui forment un promontoire
aussi étendu que l'Épire et le Péloponnèse, ou que la grande île du Japon,
ou que l'Arabie! Des fanums qu'éclaire la rentrée des théories;
d'immenses vues de la défense des côtes modernes; des dunes illustrées
de chaudes fleurs et de bacchanales; de grands canaux de Carthage et
des Embankments d'une Venise louche; de molles éruptions d'Etnas . . .

Most important of all, however, is the fact that Rimbaud continues
and extends his revolt against Christian morality. The vague longings of 'Credo in unam' and the bitter protests of 'Les premières
communions' are replaced in 'Matinée d'ivresse' by a confident
promise to 'enterrer dans l'ombre l'arbre du bien et du mal . . . afin
que nous amenions notre très pur amour'. But this love beyond
good and evil, which is to be the result of the 'étonnantes révolutions
de l'amour' foreseen in 'Conte', and which is described in 'Génie'
as a 'mesure parfaite et réinventée' and in 'A une raison' as a
'nouvel amour', now refers to the homosexual relationship which,
beyond all reasonable doubt, existed between Verlaine and Rimbaud during the months they spent together in Paris and London

between the end of 1871 and the middle of 1873. Although Verlaine
had recently married, his sexual behaviour throughout his life was
notoriously ambivalent, and if Rimbaud wanted to flout the moral
constraints of Christianity in a typically extreme fashion, then a
homosexual relationship, towards which his troubled and fatherless
childhood could well have inclined him in any case, was a way of
doing this.

He did not, however, succeed in adopting his new morality, or
rather his new amorality, by any means as easily as he had hoped.
'Matinée d'ivresse' is perhaps the most optimistic and enthu-
siastic of the *Illuminations*, but even here a note of doubt creeps in:
'ne pouvant nous saisir sur-le-champ de cette eternité'. Similarly
in 'Royauté' the symbolic marriage of a king and queen who no
doubt represent Rimbaud and Verlaine fails to last, and 'Veillées',
after evoking a moment of perfect harmony between two lovers,
also ends on a note of disappointment:

> C'est le repos éclairé, ni fièvre, ni langueur, sur le lit ou sur le pré.
> C'est l'ami ni ardent ni faible. L'ami.
> C'est l'aimée ni tourmentante ni tourmentée. L'aimée.
> L'air et le monde point cherchés. La vie.
> —Était-ce donc ceci?
> —Et le rêve fraîchit.

Other poems admit much more frankly and even brutally that
Rimbaud's high hopes of abolishing the concept of good and evil
have not been realized. The opening line of 'Vagabonds': 'Pitoy-
able frère! Que d'atroces veillées je lui dus!', is an allusion to
Verlaine whom Rimbaud had failed to restore to his 'état primitif
de fils du soleil', and the rest of the passage makes it clear that
although Rimbaud himself was still 'pressé de trouver le lieu et la
formule', Verlaine had proved unequal to the task of creating a new
way of life. The break-up of their relationship seems to be indicated,
too, in the last line of 'Ouvriers': 'Je veux que ce bras durci ne
traîne plus une chère image', and in the profound feeling of anguish
conveyed by the images of fire and flame and the repeated cry of
'Douceurs!' in 'Barbare'.

But although the failure of Rimbaud's attempt to break away, with the help of Verlaine, from the constraints of the world in which he lived is implicit in the *Illuminations*, it is not until *Une Saison en enfer*, begun in April 1873, some three months before the final quarrel with Verlaine, and finished about a month afterwards in August of the same year, that it becomes explicit. The very title of this short prose work, which should perhaps be described as a long prose poem since its vivid, staccato style is similar to that of some of the *Illuminations*, is virtually an admission that what Rimbaud had envisaged would be a life of bliss has turned out to be a brief spell of anguish and unhappiness. The same is true of the title given to one of the sub-chapters, 'Vierge folle, l'époux infernal', which is the negation of a hoped-for union between a 'vierge sage' and an 'époux divin' leading to a new and better life.

The reason for this failure to achieve 'la conversion au bien et au bonheur' is repeated time and again, in one way or another, throughout *Une Saison en enfer*—Rimbaud has been unable to free himself from the shackles of his Christian upbringing: 'Je suis esclave de mon baptême . . . L'enfer ne peut attaquer les païens.' And not only has he been unable to still the voice of his conscience, he has been unable to live his new pattern of life within the framework of the old world. Despite his protests that he does not belong by nature to this world—'Prêtres, professeurs, maîtres, vous vous trompez en me livrant à la justice. Je n'ai jamais été de ce peuple-ci; je n'ai jamais été chrétien; je suis de la race qui chantait dans le supplice; je ne comprends pas les lois; je n'ai pas le sens moral, je suis une brute: vous vous trompez'—he is forced to admit that 'il faut se soumettre au baptême, s'habiller, travailler', and recognizes that 'mes malaises viennent de ne m'être pas figuré assez tôt que nous sommes à l'Occident'.

But although the kind of society in which he had been brought up and in which he lived was too strong for Rimbaud to succeed either in eradicating its principles from his mind or in disregarding them in his way of life, this does not mean that he conceded that society was right in its ideas and that he was wrong. He was a defeated rebel, but not a repentant rebel. Unlike his 'compagnon d'enfer', Verlaine, who, a few months later, was converted, or re-converted, to the

Catholic faith in which he, like Rimbaud, had been brought up, the latter stubbornly refused to surrender and persisted in believing that life could be changed for the better, even if he himself had failed to bring about this change: 'Quand irons-nous, par-delà les grèves et les monts, saluer la naissance du travail nouveau, la sagesse nouvelle, la fuite des tyrans et des démons, la fin de la superstition, adorer—les premiers!—Noël sur la terre!' Consequently, in the last chapter of *Une Saison en enfer* Rimbaud can admit his defeat: 'Moi! moi qui me suis dit mage ou ange, dispensé de toute morale, je suis rendu au sol', and yet, paradoxically, he can claim a few lines further on that 'la victoire m'est acquise'. The attitude he intends to adopt might be called that of passive resistance; he no longer intends to launch a crusade against the values of the Christian western world, but simply to bide his time, convinced that one day a new and better way of life will emerge: 'Et à l'aurore, armés d'une ardente patience, nous entrerons aux splendides villes.' Strengthened by this conviction, he no longer feels the need for the support of others, and *Une Saison en enfer* ends with Rimbaud's resolve to keep his beliefs to himself and not to risk a renewal of his unhappy experience with Verlaine by trying to share them with others: 'Il me sera loisible de *posséder la vérité dans une âme et un corps.*'

Une Saison en enfer not only marks the failure of Rimbaud's moral, religious, and social rebellion, it also marks the failure of his poetic rebellion. The two had always been closely linked in his mind as parallel and complementary ways of changing the established order of things and the longest chapter of *Une Saison en enfer*, significantly entitled 'Délires', is in fact divided into two sections. The first one, 'Vierge folle, l'époux infernal', deals with the collapse of what Rimbaud bitterly calls, in the final line, the 'drôle de ménage', and the second one, 'Alchimie du verbe', with what he calls, in the opening line, 'l'histoire d'une de mes folies'. He specifically condemns the experimental verse he had written in 1872 and, in more general terms, seems to deride the prose poems of the *Illuminations*. 'Je m'habituai à l'hallucination simple,' he explains, 'je voyais très franchement une mosquée à la place d'une usine . . . Je finis par trouver sacré le désordre de mon esprit.'

But now, although the same kind of hallucinatory effect as in some of the *Illuminations* is often achieved in the 'hideux feuillets de mon carnet de damné' that go to make up *Une Saison en enfer*, accompanied by a similar lack of orderly construction in the way parts are written, Rimbaud is determined to give up this kind of writing: 'Je hais maintenant les élans mystiques et les bizarreries de style', he wrote in a first draft of *Une Saison en enfer*.

He added however: 'Maintenant je puis dire que l'art est une sottise', which seems to suggest that he was ready not only to abandon his pursuit of a revolutionary form of poetry, but also to give up literary activity of whatever kind. Although he may have delayed actually carrying out this decision—if the critics who maintain that some of the *Illuminations* date from 1874 are to be believed —there is little doubt, except in the minds of those who cherish the hope of finding hundreds of poems hidden away somewhere in East Africa, that Rimbaud gave up all interest in creative writing either immediately after or shortly after *Une Saison en enfer*. In other words, his new kind of poetry had failed, but rather than go back to the old, conventional kind of verse he preferred to stop writing altogether. Similarly, his new concept of society had failed, but rather than go back to the old conventional kind of existence he preferred to live a wandering life of his own, mostly beyond the frontiers of western civilization. Silence and solitide are in fact the hallmarks of the last fifteen years of Rimbaud's life. His letters to his family are singularly laconic and factual, and although he inevitably came into contact with a number of Europeans in East Africa, he seems always to have remained an essentially lonely figure.

Whether Rimbaud retained this now sullenly rebellious spirit to the bitter end is a point that it is difficult to decide. His sister Isabelle, who was with him during the last few weeks of his life, wrote to their mother that Rimbaud had agreed to see a priest a fortnight before his death and that the latter had said to her: 'Votre frère a la foi, mon enfant . . . Il a la foi, et je n'ai même jamais vu de foi de cette qualité.' Such a final surrender may perhaps seem out of keeping with Rimbaud's character, but it should be borne in mind that despite the violence and tumult of most of his work, a quieter, gentler note persistently makes itself felt.

> Pitié! Ces enfants seuls étaient ses familiers
> Qui, chétifs, fronts nus, œil déteignant sur la joue,
> Cachant de maigres doigts jaunes et noirs de boue
> Sous des habits puant la foire et tout vieillots,
> Conversaient avec la douceur des idiots!

This feeling of pity for others in 'Les Poètes de sept ans' is present in other early poems such as 'Les Étrennes des orphelins', 'Les Effarés', and 'Le Dormeur du val', turning to self-pity in 'Ma Bohème', 'Les Sœurs de charité', 'Le Cœur volé', and above all perhaps the final lines of 'Les Chercheuses de poux':

> L'enfant se sent, selon la lenteur des caresses,
> Sourdre et mourir sans cesse un désir de pleurer.

In the later work too, poems such as 'Larme', 'L'Éternité', and 'O Saisons, ô châteaux', and passages from the *Illuminations* such as 'Veillées' and 'Aube', reveal a softer side to Rimbaud's nature. His death-bed conversion should not perhaps be too summarily dismissed therefore as the result of his illness or as a piece of wishful thinking on the part of his sister Isabelle. It would on the contrary be quite consistent with an inner tenderness which Rimbaud so often concealed beneath an outer shell of anger and revolt.

NOTE

ARTHUR RIMBAUD, 1854–91, was of outstanding intellectual ability from an early age, and wrote his first poems before he was sixteen. In September 1871, just before his seventeenth birthday, he left home, after several abortive attempts to run away during the previous twelve months, though he continued to return to Charleville periodically during the next few years. He became the close companion of the poet Paul Verlaine, first in Paris, and later in London, until their relationship ended in a violent quarrel in Brussels in July 1873. Rimbaud then began to wander further afield, first over Europe, then to the Middle East, and finally into the interior of Abyssinia, as it then was, having long since lost all interest in poetry. After ten years as a trader, explorer, and gun-runner, he fell ill with cancer in February 1891, was brought down to the coast, and sailed to

Marseilles, where his leg was amputated and where, after having returned home for a few months, he died in November 1891 at the age of thirty-seven.

Works. Four principal stages can be distinguished in Rimbaud's meteoric literary career: first, the early poetry, largely conventional in its form, written in 1870 and 1871; secondly, the much less conventional verse of 1872; thirdly, the group of prose poems known as the *Illuminations*, the date of which is disputed; and finally, in 1873, a prose work, *Une Saison en enfer*, the only one of these four items to have been published by Rimbaud, and even then only in the sense that it was printed, though it was never put on sale by the publishers.

Editions. Suzanne Bernard's edition of Rimbaud's *Œuvres* (1960) in the Classiques Garnier is very well annotated and includes the 'lettre du voyant' and a few other important letters. The major part of Rimbaud's correspondence is included in the Pléiade edition of the *Œuvres complètes*, first published in 1946 and reprinted, with additions and revisions, in 1954 and 1963. Some sixty additional letters dating from the last three years of Rimbaud's life were published by Gallimard in 1965.

Criticism. In 1952 R. Etiemble began the publication of a vast critical bibliography, as yet uncompleted, *Le Mythe de Rimbaud*, of which the first volume, *La Genèse du mythe*, lists the enormous number of books and articles that have been devoted to Rimbaud, while the second volume, *La Structure du mythe* (reprinted, with minor revisions, in 1961), usefully summarizes the various ways in which Rimbaud has been interpreted. The poet's adventurous life has attracted numerous biographers, among whom the most dependable are Enid Starkie whose *Rimbaud*, first published in 1938, was reprinted, with various revisions, in 1947 and again in 1961, and H. Matarasso and P. Petitfils who jointly published a *Vie de Rimbaud* in 1962. C. A. Hackett has published *Le Lyrisme de Rimbaud* (1938), *Rimbaud l'enfant* (1948), and *Rimbaud* (1957). More recent studies of Rimbaud's poetry include C. Chadwick's *Études sur Rimbaud* (1960), J. P. Houston's *The Design of Rimbaud's Poetry* (1963), W. M. Frohock's *Rimbaud's Poetic Practice* (1963), M. A. Ruff's *Rimbaud* (1968), M.-J. Whitaker's *La Structure du monde imaginaire de Rimbaud* (1972), R. G. Cohn's *The Poetry of Rimbaud* (1973), and M. Perrier, *Rimbaud: chemin de la création* (1973). Mention should also be made of P. Gascar, *Rimbaud et la Commune* (1971).

8. Maupassant

IN spite of its continuous popularity and historical importance, Maupassant's work bears, in fairly obvious ways, the stamp of a minor author. To turn to his literary undertaking from those of Flaubert and Zola is to move from high literary idealism (though in Zola's case conducted in a very businesslike way) to a more workaday professionalism. While Flaubert slaved maniacally at his art and Zola carried through a vast life's work in the service of a new literary doctrine, Maupassant wrote regularly for a popular paper whose demands dictated not only the length of his stories but also, one suspects, some of their more lubricious subject-matter. His scanty theoretical writings are similarly lacking in militancy, and the easy-going catholicity of his essay *Le Roman*, prefixed to his novel *Pierre et Jean*, is in marked (and rather pleasant) contrast to the general run of French literary manifestoes. If he is an unambitious writer, he is also a derivative one. His apprenticeship to Flaubert gave him some at least of the master's aristocratic subordination of humanity to art; and, though he soon renounced his loose affiliations with Zola's naturalism, *la bête humaine* remains a fairly appropriate description of his conception of human nature. To contemporary critics the dual lineage was immediately apparent: Henry James, in a mainly appreciative essay, sees in Maupassant the same range of intensely rendered but limited human interests, noting also 'a certain absence of love, a sort of bird's-eye view contempt' as a dominant characteristic; and finding in the emphasis on man as a creature of the senses—though it is a salutary corrective to our English evasions—a 'wonderful want of correspondence' with our own less exclusive vision of reality.

Up to a point, then, Maupassant's stories are chips off an existing vision. But the very lack of a sustained literary idealism, and the adoption of the short-story form itself, favour the development of qualities not present in his two superiors. The absence of artistic pretension, of a systematic aesthetic, leaves an opening to the spontaneity, the unexpectedly ready reference to a personal scale of values, which we find in the stories. And the choice of the form means that Maupassant is never constricted within a philosophical scheme to his own artistic disadvantage. The dominant theme of *Madame Bovary* necessarily pushed to the margin the Justins, the Larivières, the Catherine Leroux, about whom some readers have wished they could hear more. If such figures do not occupy the centre of the stage in Maupassant's work as a whole, they can at least do so within the unit of the single story. His reigning mood does not have to be subordinated to a larger and more permanent conception; he can give himself over temporarily (if not always with the happiest results) to the sentimental, the nostalgic, the mysterious. As a result his picture of life is perhaps more variegated, less suspect of the doctrinaire, than that of his great contemporaries. Even the arch-enemy of naturalism, Brunetière, recognized the breadth of his sympathies, though this has been denied many times since by critics like Martin Turnell, for whom *La Maison Tellier* shows the recurrent Maupassant qualities, 'his crudity, his facile cynicism, a fundamental lack of intelligence'. In a brief essay there is room only to offer some material for adjudicating this question of Maupassant's range and depth.

Flaubert lived just long enough to praise his disciple's first masterpiece, *Boule de suif*, and the early stories, particularly the longer ones, show the extent to which Maupassant had learnt the satirical lessons of *Madame Bovary*; they also reveal aspects of his own distinctiveness. *En famille*, an ingenious story with the cruelly ironic twist that Maupassant is commonly known for, is also a major piece of Flaubertian construction. The death scene in *Madame Bovary* is notable for the way in which the characters fail to transcend their normal selves; the potentially dramatic circumstance is, for most of them, just another occasion for acting in character. *En famille*, too, is about death, and, in spite of the almost miraculous peripeteia, it has many features of the Flaubertian approach. The opening introduces us to the master's familiar world of lives moving in predestinate grooves, of *idées reçues* and endlessly repeated gestures, conversations, and arguments. We watch the effects on this grey world of a dramatic interruption—the death of the grandmother. And the whole spectrum of reactions is put before us, with the Flaubertian sense of a mediocre sameness underlying and uniting the variegated surface manifestations. In the hero, Caravan, maudlin despair gives way to an apathy which necessitates the artificial stimulation of his grief, and finally to the childish pleasure of scoring a victory over his chief by taking a legitimate day off. The wife is calculating and hypocritical from the start; for the doctor it is an occasion for a free meal, a confident display of diagnostic powers, and the dispensing of homespun consolations. The picture is completed by the morbid curiosity of the neighbours and the mimes of the children—already an unsavoury foretaste of adult hypocrisy. And while we get a complete conspectus of this narrow society, there is no sense of artificial manipulation. The successive reactions, over a period of about a day, flow naturally from the narrative. The resuscitation of the grandmother evokes another set of hurried and undignified improvisations, embarrassments, and exasperations, and finally—the tables turned on Caravan for his irreverent expectations—fear, in the culminating line: 'Qu'est-ce que je dirai à mon chef?' A gamut of undistinguished responses to the potentially distinguished situation; here, underpinning the immediate interest afforded by the plot, is the Flaubertian recipe for the stylish and patterned presentation of an irretrievably unstylish reality.

But while there is much that is (in a creditable sense) derivative here, there are also more individual elements—in this particular case perhaps not especially attractive ones. While a Flaubert allows the mournful ordinariness of life to emerge obliquely from such spectacles as Charles eating or the visit to the mill, Maupassant comes more into the open with his characterization. His slightly contemptuous pity is uninhibitedly expressed in his presentation of the 'pauvres diables râpés qui végètent dans une chétive maison de plâtre'. His hatreds are equally overt. Spurning the delicate irony, the subtle devaluations of the *style indirect*, he boldly characterizes Caravan's son as a 'vilain mioche avec un visage de crétin', his wife as 'laide maintenant, de petite taille et maigrelette', with a 'maladie chronique de lavage'. Sometimes this vigour can lead (as in the introduction of the dramatis personae of *Boule de suif*) to characterizations of dazzling virtuosity; here the effect is emphatic to the point of rawness. Again, Flaubert lends his aristocratic disdain in some measure to Emma Bovary herself, she has a certain dignity which will not waste words on Charles, and she brushes him off with monosyllables which leave the artistic surface of the narrative unruffled. In Maupassant, too, the level of response rarely rises above—to use a recurrent word of his—*exaspération*. But it is an exasperation without dignity, and Maupassant delights in portraying it. After the grandmother's revival her daughter and daughter-in-law belabour one another out of an aimless feeling of rage at having been cheated by life, after the momentary glimpse of the inheritance. Maupassant can, on occasion, as in the almost fully tragic *Monsieur Parent*, embody this rage in moving and powerful scenes; but more often he prefers to draw attention to the apoplectic surface, the ugliness of the action is barely redeemed by its remote connection with Maupassant's own metaphysical discontent.

Though *En famille* is a considerable success, it points to the risk that Maupassant continually runs—of exposing a crude misanthropy unshaped by art. Too often the stories are thinly disguised outpourings of his own not particularly edifying personal hates. If he is misanthropic in general, his particular hatred is for women: his pages are filled with the stupid, mercenary young, or—like Madame Caravan—the avaricious and wilfully self-neglecting middle-aged. The bachelors' club in *Le Verrou* has its table linen inscribed with the legend 'Mulier perpetuus infans', and it is clear that Maupassant himself is a member. In general, for him, woman is, in the verse of Louis Bouilhet praised by another of his characters, at best 'un instrument banal sous mon archet vainqueur'. It is the superiority of the narrator which is distasteful here, the failure to include himself in the scene of mediocrity and mutual exploitation. Unlike Baudelaire, whose

> femme esclave vile
> Sans rire s'adorant et s'aimant sans dégoût

is part of a comprehensive, self-accusing vision, Maupassant reserves a privileged status for a rather undeserving élite who are patently his spokesmen—the cynical old *viveurs* who narrate so many of the stories. Hence the objections which one may feel for a story such as *Découverte*. Here the narrator recounts how he married an English girl whose broken French was part of her charm, and how her complete banality was shown up by gradual increase in linguistic proficiency. Such a situation could be a fruitful one for the relation of a bitter *éducation sentimentale*, of the inevitable falling-off between promise and reality; as the bright idea stands, however, in its rather emphatic, undigested form, we may feel that James was not unfair in dismissing it as simply a 'little growl of Anglophobia'.

But if Maupassant sometimes lacks what Flaubert brings to his despair—the patience to frame it in a large scheme, to give it a dignity and coherence which at least make it a proposition to reckon with—his openness and spontaneity also have their positive qualities. Disillusion and disgust, often bitter and cruel, are the central reality of his work, but the squalor of life is not set against the sole and supreme value of art. The joys of the countryside and the Seine, physical activity and the camaraderie of youth, the comedy as well as the ugliness of human relations—all these are vividly present in his work and provide a positive measure by which the rejection of the bourgeois world gains its justification. Though the ideal is almost always set in the past it can be warmly recalled, as in stories like *Mouche*. And the strength of his nostalgia allows Maupassant to view with some sympathy even the most grotesque attempts to achieve a similar fulfilment. The family in *Une Partie de campagne* are observed on the whole with the same satirical gaze that we saw at work in *En famille*. Physically awkward, routine in their admirations, pretending to a *savoir-faire* that they don't possess, they are obviously figures of fun to the good-humoured young oarsmen who undertake their entertainment. But Maupassant has the generosity to attribute to the bourgeois some of his own enjoyment. The sympathy, perhaps, derives partly from the fact that they are the supporting cast in a venture of seduction, they are temporarily involved in Maupassant's own favoured pleasures. The scene between the girl and her partner in the heat of the summer afternoon is beautifully described, but even the mother and her young man ('qui avait dû voir des choses bien drôles') are treated with good humour. She comes crashing out of the undergrowth like a huge animal, 'l'œil très brillant et la poitrine orageuse', to return to the world of shopkeeper reality. Maupassant has given his goodwill to its temporary suspension, in the heightened atmosphere of heat and alcoholic well-being, but now it returns in full force, with the husband sobered up and impatient, the grandmother querulous, the young fiancé unromantically needing something to eat before leaving. As the postscript makes us cast our minds back over the evocation of the afternooon, we feel that the satire of this young man, now the girl's husband, is based on something more substantial than arbitrary anti-bourgeois prejudice; and as his yawning, humdrum self sums up the whole stultifying monotony of the shopkeeper's life, we are left reflecting on the pathetic enthusiasm of the family for their outing, and their fleeting achievement of success in Maupassant's terms, rather than feeling ourselves accomplices in a triumphant piece of satire. At any rate the characters are just a little more than the 'instrument banal' of Maupassant's literary pleasures.

The more nearly Maupassant can project onto or recognize in the bourgeois his own brand of pleasures and ideals, the more sympathetically he will portray him, the more freely he will admit that being locked in *idées reçues* does not constitute an automatic disqualification from humanity. To see him as the vindicator of the 'little man' would be to suggest a sentimentality into which he only rarely falls. But in the face of huge metaphysical doubts and human disgusts he refuses to discount the small solitary, stoical pleasures and virtues, and gives their momentary realization or nostalgic recall its full poignancy. To make a comparison with another pair of writers, each possessed of ample grounds for total rejection of the everyday world, Maupassant might be called the Camus to Flaubert's Sartre. The result can run to humour or to tragedy.

In *Deux Amis* it is tragedy. The story recounts how two former fishing friends meet during the siege of Paris and, emboldened by the effects of alcohol on their starving stomachs, risk an expedition to the river. After a brief idyll, reality returns in the form of a

E

TRINITY COLLEGE
LIBRARY

German officer who accuses them of spying and shoots them un-
ceremoniously before going on to eat their catch. The story of their
death is told with such perfect restraint that even the postscript
indicating the officer's brutality ('C'est le tour des poissons maintenant') seems by comparison a little over-pointed. Nevertheless,
like *Une Partie de campagne*, the story is a triumph of structure, perfectly embodying the author's conception of the possibilities and
limitations of life: the beginning in the hostile everyday world,
giving way to a briefly and precariously sustained idyll, which in
turn is interrupted and then put into a perspective as momentary
and inevitably doomed. The two fishermen are as firmly circum-
scribed by their *idées reçues* as any inhabitants of Flaubert's world,
but they have the virtue of being men of few words, and their
truisms gain stature as the bourgeois expression of stoic resignation.

In *Le Trou* the *décor* is similar, but the tone is comic: a Sunday
fisherman on a charge of murder recounts the intolerable provoca-
tions he and his wife were subjected to on finding their favourite
spot invaded, against all agreed decencies, by another couple. The
device of the trial is a favourite one of Maupassant's. It allows him
to make his moral judgements at one remove, through a judge of
quirky and humane disposition, unbridled by conventional preconceptions; and it reflects his interest in the reality behind the
apparently easily classifiable *fait divers*, his willingness to enter
into the passions of those who have at least a link with his own
values and who come to grief because of it. Many of these trial
stories are comedies of Norman peasant life, with the robust
dialect engagingly transcribed; and perhaps the pure hilarity of
Une Vente and *Le Cas de Madame Luneau* does not require serious
comment, except to say that, like *Le Trou*, they show that, next to
silence, openness and plain speaking command Maupassant's
strongest sympathy. But the trial, and the dialect, can also be used
to serious and pathetic purpose, as in the beautifully conducted
Rosalie Prudent, where a girl, charged with infanticide, tells how she
had prepared to look after one illegitimate child but panicked when,
alone in her garret, she delivered herself of twins. Here Maupassant
combines a full exploitation of the bizarreness of the situation with
social awareness and genuine pathos, so that when we reach the

point where, questioned on the whereabouts of the second body, she has to ask where they found the first:

> 'Lequel que vous avez?'
> 'Mais . . . celui . . . celui qui était dans les artichauts.'
> 'Ah bien! L'autre est dans les fraisiers, au bord du puits',

it is the discomfort of the judges that we share rather than any complicity with a patronizing comic observer.

Other stories have a different sort of framework and many of them, through the device of a narrator, are set in the quite distant past. This feature is seen as ideologically significant by Sartre in the very critical pages he devotes to Maupassant in *Qu'est-ce que la littérature?* He picks on the figure of the *viveur* as typical narrator to make a point which continues the Marxist critique of the French realists—that for all their ostensible hostility to the bourgeois world, they are essentially complacent spectators or parasites, presenting life from a defeatist, aesthetic point of view as static and incapable of change. Sartre suggests that, even when this is not literally the case, all the stories have the *air* of being related by the *viveur* type, who has not even the redeeming feature of a coherent pessimism, but tends to recount the lessons life has taught him somewhat arrogantly, claiming to have created a modest order out of chaos—usually thanks to his economic freedom.

It would be unprofitable to dispute the main charge of political indifference, the more so as Maupassant, more clearly than Zola, makes no claims to be a reformer. This is, of course, to make no concessions as regards a more narrowly interpreted literary value, since the adequacy of the technique to rendering the vision is not in question. What could be argued is that Sartre overstates the degree to which the *viveur* spirit is in charge, and hence the degree to which the stories are 'consoling' to the reactionary or the aesthete. They can in fact be very disturbing, though the disturbance might seem to the revolutionary to be of an unproductive brand.

The appropriateness of the method to the vision can hardly be in doubt. For Maupassant, the good days, if they existed, must always be in the past, expectations for the future based on the past must always be disappointed. Maupassant's world, with something of the simplicity of Anouilh's, is one which is worthless once it has been penetrated, once one has been let down and has seen 'les dessous de la vie'. Knowledge offers only the alternatives of compromise or resignation. Hence the form of the stories is often the recall of a moment of revelation, a definitive insight into life. In *Garçon, un bock!* the narrator tells of an incident apparently well in the past, but which continues to affect him. He went into a café, sat down by a decayed-looking drinker, and found it was a former well-to-do school friend. Punctuating his account with calls for beer, the man tells how he had seen his parents fighting when he was young; having been introduced to 'l'autre face des choses, la mauvaise', he turned his back on the world and retired to measure out his life with interminable *bocks*. There is a sense of reproach for the narrator's only moderately worldly existence. The old man's hands tremble as he tells his story and he drops his pipe; and his own firmly established values are displayed as he curses that it will take him a month to break in a new one. We wonder whether, like Camus's pea-counter, he has perhaps found the only solution to the horror of life. At any rate the narrator's case for 'real' life works only as a momentary interruption, and the story ends with his chastened departure, while the *bockeur*, making the required minute adjustment to his ritual, 'lança à travers la vaste salle, pleine maintenant de fumée et de buveurs, son éternel cri: "Garçon, un bock — et une pipe neuve!"'.

Though the loss of true happiness is final, the characters often manage to accommodate the revelatory experience and find a stoic substitute for happiness which allows them to put the past in a wry or even comic perspective. Such is the case with *Le Père Mongilet* and in the dialect story *Boitelle*. The local *vidangeur*, with his fourteen children and unpleasant but remunerative job, turns out on interrogation to be a drop-out from life, his feats of earning and procreation no more than a mechanical postscript to the great drama of his youth. He tells how he fell in love with a colourfully dressed negress and tried to persuade his parents to approve their marriage; he anticipates their criticisms, breaks down their prejudices, and her domestication nearly wins them over—but not quite: 'Mon pauv'e gars, alle est trop noire. Seulement un p'tieu moins je ne m'opposerais pas, mais c'est trop. On dirait Satan.' As a filial peasant he knows there can be no arguing, but from that time on 'j'ai eu de cœur à rien. Aucun métier ne m'allait pu, et je sieus devenu ce que je sieus, un ordureux.' The mood is not of tragedy but of a good-humoured but uncompromising recognition of the imperfections of life: 'J' peux pas dire que ma femme m'a déplu, pisque j'y ai fait quatorze éfants, mais c' n'est point l'autre . . . L'autre, voyez-vous, ma négresse, elle n'avait qu'à me regarder, je me sentais comme transporté . . .'

The implications of the narrative form, then, can be more disturbing or more humane than Sartre's generalization suggests; what the interlocutors learn can even lead them (as in *Mon Oncle Jules*) to positive action of a philanthropic sort, though clearly this sort of outcome would not satisfy the revolutionary's definition of the positive. However, strictly ideological considerations apart, Sartre's objection to the *viveurs* does pinpoint a weakness in Maupassant that we have already touched on. For, judged by whatever criteria, the impact of the stories is undoubtedly strengthened or harmed by the personality of the fictional narrator or protagonist. Maupassant's sense of a falling-off between youth and adulthood makes the theme of the meeting with a long-lost friend one of his favourites. And the modest character of the narrator in *L'Ami Patience* gives force to the satire of successful man, his bafflement makes Patience's shameless revelation of the source of his wealth the more brash and offensive. But similar stories are often related by the bored, the hypersensitive, the idly curious. The related theme of a visit to an unknown illegitimate child illustrates the consequences of this. In *Duchoux* the 'curiosité égoïste' of an ageing aristocrat is rewarded by finding the son of his youth a self-satisfied, garlic-saturated Provençal. It is the occasion for some accomplished satire of squalid domesticity, but we have a lurking feeling, as the son apologizes for the mess, that the baron's gaze may be unduly reproving. We finish somewhat divided between taking the baron's attitude as a valid comment on the ugliness of everyday life, and seeing his discomfort as a product of his excessive delicacy and a proper punishment for his curiosity. The ambiguity might be an added value; but it remains suspect—an unsatisfactoriness confirmed by a similar story, *Le Fils*, in which an even more bizarre contrast is enclosed in an even more complacent framework; and the straggling, over-emphatic form of which shows up Maupassant's here ill-judged insistence on extracting the fullest profit from a rather unsavoury little *fait divers*.

Much more successful is *L'Abandonné*, which is on the same theme as *Duchoux*, but with a different sort of framework. For the incident can only be satisfactorily 'framed' by the insensitive husband, who begins by predicting a sunstroke as a result of the mother's outing, and ends by congratulating himself on the accuracy of his prediction. For the two other main characters the incident is more difficult to put into final perspective, and the story gains its power precisely through this lack of a neat finality. There is no question, as in *Duchoux*, of satire here. The peasant son and his family are simply seen as going about their normal life, and the mother, by the time she comes face to face with them, is in no state to make a conscious critical observation. She, with her sentimentality and garrulousness, has no clearly defined moral stature. The course of the story simply consists in the drying up of that garrulousness under the reality of emotion—an emotion too strong, and too strongly rendered, for its evocation to be merely a preliminary to moral adjudication among the parties. As the couple walk back along the dusty road we reflect more generally on the vast gulf between people and ways of life, on the irrevocability of the past and the final, necessary disappointment of long-cherished illusions. In reference to Maupassant's limitations in the portrayal of character Henry James maintained that he 'simply skipped the whole reflective part' of human life in favour of the mechanical and sensual; and he noted that even in this story, which he admired, we learn little of the characters' thoughts. But the limited aims of the short story are perhaps best served by suppressing the probable banalities of the characters' conscious thoughts and using the situation itself to prolong the reader's own reflective activity.

It is in fact this rendering of strong but ill-defined emotion in not very distinguished characters that is the mark of Maupassant's most powerful stories; this emotion is the most heightened form of that *exaspération* which is the more usual reaction of the bitter, un-comprehending, satirically observed victims of the tricks of a monotonous but still unpredictable world. One would not want to force too many stories into this scheme—especially the comic ones. But perhaps the famous *La Ficelle*, in addition to the attractions of dialect and rustic observation, owes its stature among the Norman stories to its concern with this central theme. The story is of the economical peasant who picks up a piece of string on the way to market and, with a vestige of shame at his own meanness, hides it furtively when he sees that his action has been noticed. The same day a wallet is lost and, though it is returned, he never quite clears himself of the charge of having stolen it. No moral or tragic point about justice is made; nor yet about the possibility of a particular injustice containing a more general justice (though it is admitted in passing that Hauchecorne would by character have been quite capable of the theft). Maupassant simply concentrates on the rage and frustration of a man who in a particular case is right but unable to prove it. The character, the predicament, are very much those of Molière's George Dandin; the treatment, too, echoes classical comedy, as the victim, driven to decline and early death, mutters repetitively to the last: 'Une 'tite ficelle . . . une 'tite ficelle . . . t'nez, la voilà, m'sieu le Maire.'

In other stories the emotional drama, though still colloquially presented, has a very different tone. *Le Port*, like *La Ficelle*, describes a dramatic episode arising out of a scene of colourful, extrovert activity. Célestin, the returning sailor, connoisseur of the pleasures of the port, acts as confident guide to his friends, only to find at the end of the evening that he has spent it with his own sister, now grown up and reduced by misery to prostitution. The theme is dangerously melodramatic, but it is managed with the extra-ordinary tact which we saw in *Rosalie Prudent*. Célestin's shattered 'J'avons fait de la belle besogne' is complemented by his sister's naïve explanation of how she failed to recognize him: 'Je vois tant d'hommes qu'ils me semblent tous pareils.' Maupassant immo-bilizes the scene as Célestin stares at his sister, still in her playful, mercenary posture astride his knees in the noisy café; and we share with him 'une émotion confuse et si forte qu'il avait envie de crier comme un petit garçon qu'on bat'. There is no attempt to enter into the sailor's conscience, still less to suggest a moral or a reclamation. Maupassant stops at the emotion, which is prolonged in the final tableau as the uncomprehending companions, thinking him drunk, carry him off 'jusqu'à la chambre de la femme qui l'avait reçu tout à l'heure, et qui demeura sur une chaise, en pleurant autant que lui, jusqu'au matin'. A somewhat reverberant, Flaubertian final period for Maupassant, but we feel on this occasion he has earned the right to the indulgence. And in general the compression and simplicity of the story make it compare favourably with the more ambitious treatment of discovery in the midst of festivity which is attempted in, for example, *La Femme de Paul*.

The stories considered so far suggest that James's complaint of the hard, bird's-eye view of humanity can at least be modified to some degree. The hardness is in fact most apparent in the Norman stories, but it is justified by the fact that these deal with a hard world in which murder, or at least accelerated death, are so common-place that they seem amenable to purely comic treatment (as in *Le Diable* or *Le Petit Fût*). We may conclude our discussion of individual stories by looking at one which certainly escapes James's charges, while at the same time not deserting that more salutary hardness which saves Maupassant from declining into senti-mentality. Of the stories with a 'domestic' background, *Hautot père et fils* perhaps best demonstrates the scope and limits of Maupassant's positive values, as well as the art with which he chooses his subject-matter and circumscribes his treatment of it in order to go just as far as he wants and no further along the road of sentiment. As has been said already, Maupassant by no means dis-qualifies the bourgeois from a share in the qualities he admires. But he does not go as far as to show these qualities more than fleetingly embodied in a stable domestic situation. The scenes which excite his good humour and indulgence are rather in the category of the final festivity in *La Maison Tellier*; or else there are stories of moments of sexual renewal in a worn-out marriage, like *La Serre* and *Au Bois*. But these are only good-humoured bits of *gauloiserie*, with none of the pretensions of Lawrence's recurrent treatment in his stories of thematically comparable moves from 'death' to 'life'.

Hautot *père et fils* are well-off farmers, widower and son. Fatally wounded in a shooting accident, the father entrusts his son with the task of conveying the news to a long-standing mistress and making financial provision for her and her small son. Hautot *fils* apprehensively makes the visit, is moved by the existence of this illicit but orderly household, eats the dinner prepared for his father, and postpones his business till the following week. His loneliness makes him look forward to the next visit and the story ends with the pair hesitantly making another rendezvous, and the implication that the boy will replace his father in the regular *jeudis*.

Considering his own personality, Maupassant is surprisingly delicate in the portrayal of the timid young man (we find the same quality, though perhaps in over-sentimental measure, in *La Martine* and *Le Petit Soldat*). And the story is rich in other notations of feeling: the girl's horror and modesty, the gradual dawning of trust and affection, the boy's loneliness as he wanders through the autumn fields, expecting every moment to see again the 'grande figure gesticulante de son père'. At the same time, sympathetically as the domestic scene is drawn, Maupassant's central interest is the strong, silent relationship of the boy with his father. It is the girl's role to prolong the memory of this relationship, as it is the mementoes of his father—the pipe, the bread with the crust cut off because of his bad teeth—that first endear the boy to her little room. For all the sentimental colouring, this is anything but a praise of ordered domesticity. Indeed it is the optional nature of the attachment which first recommends it to Hautot, 'une famille qu'il pouvait prendre ou laisser à sa guise, mais qui lui rappelait son père'. They are appendages to the stoic world. And—another link with Maupassant's more permanent, sceptical moral attitudes— he takes a pleasure in attributing the birth of Hautot's affection to the contrast the girl presents with his puritanical preconceptions about the 'kept woman'. Finally, the story stops short at the birth of affection and makes no suggestions about its permanence. 'I am much mistaken', James commented on Maupassant's portrayal of the relations between the sexes, 'if he has once portrayed a gentleman in the English sense of the term.' Hautot *fils* seems to have the makings of one, but the girl's *mioche* has some affinities with Caravan's. The domestic idyll is precarious, and Hautot may well be driven later to join the ranks of the hard-hearted *viveurs*. In the meantime, without in the least committing himself to any conventional code, Maupassant has given us an attractive presentation of human values satisfactorily if only temporarily embodied.

To have taken a dominantly thematic approach to Maupassant requires some apology; but his technical powers have already received generous praise and analysis. Moreover, the examination of technique frequently takes us back to, or makes complete sense only in the light of, consideration of the content and the under-lying ideology. The narrative framework in which so many of the stories are set is a technique for arousing interest, for establishing a direct, conversational relationship with the reader; it is also, as we have seen, a way of conveying a view of life—used either to pin-point a significant moment of disillusion or simply, in more relaxed stories, to communicate the standpoint of a man who places him-self outside acceptance of everyday life and whose chief pleasure and consolation is to recall its incoherence, its oddities, and its transitory pleasures. Similarly the laconic endings for which the stories are so famous are valuable primarily for their contribution to the rendering of a vision, for the way they put into perspective what has gone before, sometimes by giving us the comment of the un-comprehending observer who has missed the sense of the drama. By taking us back to the everyday they put into sharper focus the reality which lies beneath the surface.

It is difficult to summarize a survey which has been concerned more with demonstrating variety than unity. Maupassant's gaze has been compared to that of the lawyer, and the image is in some ways apt. His aim is not *tout comprendre*. He takes up his characters at an interesting stage in their lives and relinquishes them without much compunction. But he also has the humane lawyer's virtues, an indulgent familiarity with the *inédit*, a calm assumption that the reality is very different from the respectable surface of life. He has his severities, often more scathing than Flaubert's. But when he

actually brings his characters to court it is usually to acquit them—
and acquittal was a rare moral judgement in the literary climate in
which he was working. If the lawyer's approach represents an
altogether too contingent relationship with humanity to provide the
basis for fiction of the highest order, it also ensures the absorbing
readability of the second rank.

NOTE

GUY DE MAUPASSANT, 1850-93, enjoyed a carefree upbringing in Normandy
—later to be the scene of many of his stories. After law studies and military
service he became a clerk in the Naval Ministry, another milieu which he exploited
in his stories. His mother was a sister of Flaubert's great friend Alfred Le Poittevin
and he submitted his first literary exercises to Flaubert for criticism. Flaubert in
turn introduced him to Zola and his circle and Maupassant's first published story,
Boule de suif, appeared in Zola's collection *Les Soirées de Médan* (1880). During
the next decade he wrote some three hundred stories, many for publication in the
newspapers *Gil Blas* and *Le Gaulois*. Though physically active and apparently
robust he had contracted syphilis in youth and died prematurely after a period of
insanity.

Editions. The standard edition of the complete works is the Conard edition in 29
volumes (1908-10). The most complete and convenient edition of the short
stories is *Contes et nouvelles*, ed. Albert-Marie Schmidt (2 vols., 1956-7). A
further volume contains the complete *Romans* (1959). Selections of Maupassant's
short stories include *Quinze contes*, ed. F. C. Green (1943), *Choix de contes*,
ed. F. C. Green (1945), and *Selected Short Stories*, ed. J. H. Matthews (1959).

Criticism. R. Dumesnil, *Guy de Maupassant* (revised ed. 1947), and F. Steeg-
muller, *Maupassant* (1949), are biographical in approach. Interesting contemporary reactions to Maupassant are those of Henry James, included in *The
House of Fiction* (1957), and F. Brunetière in *Le Roman naturaliste* (1891).
E. Sullivan, *Maupassant: the Short Stories* (1962), is a useful and suggestive study.
A. Vial, *Guy de Maupassant et l'art du roman* (1954), contains interesting
references to the stories, though they are not its chief concern. See also the relevant
parts of S. O'Faolain, *The Short Story* (1948), and M. Turnell, *The Art of French
Fiction* (1959).

9. Symbolism and Mallarmé

ONLY since the last century has it been generally accepted that the human mind relies as much on symbols as on ideas and images. Goethe and the early Romantics first suggested this in poetry, but it was not exploited systematically until the late nineteenth century. Since then, as commonly happens in the history of ideas, symbolic explanations have become essential to fields as varied as anthropology, psychiatry, and advertising, thus perhaps vindicating the symbolists' belief that their 'invention' was an instrument of discovery. Yet the very success of symbolism in literature has made it a rather confused notion. In English the term is often applied rashly to the whole of French poetry from late romanticism to the surrealists, whereas it was originally the banner of a small literary group flourishing in Paris between 1885 and 1900: shallow, inbred, and pretentious, but with technical and idealistic aims that may seem to sum up the ambitions of nineteenth-century poetry.

The much abused term 'symbol' needs first to be carefully defined in relation to the artist's activity before we try to relate the symbolist movement to the particular social and literary context in which it appeared. We shall finally illustrate it with reference to the one poet without whom the group would be indistinguishable from the rival 'fin de siècle' trivialities: Mallarmé.

In Greek *symbolon* was an object (often a ring) cut into two, and constituting a means of recognition when the pieces were reassembled by the carriers to make a unified whole. The early Church, and secret societies such as freemasonry, applied the word first to test-phrases, of which two people spoke half each; then later to formulae or names used to gain admittance to a meeting. The latter were correctly called *symbols* by the initiate, whom these broken-off parts of sacred formulae, once assembled, brought into comradeship; but for an outsider they were mere pass-words, or *signs*. A sign is part of an arbitrary code, whereas there is a natural correlation, albeit tenous and metaphorical, between a symbol and the completed reality it stands for. What we call 'road signs' are often merely images: given certain cultural simplifications according to which a 'pin-man' represents a human being and wavy lines stand for movement, it is easy to understand the picture of a pedestrian crossing the road. Others are *signs* in the correct sense: no one who had not read or been taught the highway code could guess that a triangle stands for danger. Other notices, now usually become signs through usage, probably originated confusedly as *symbols*: red lights (connected with fire, blood, danger) or green light (suggesting, to Europeans, Nature and freedom of movement) at first caused these associations to be applied to the situation where they were seen.

The notion of 'symbol', if widened, can become very close to that of 'image', since a picture of an object is, in the observing mind, almost inseparable from the object itself. The privilege of the symbol lies in its immediacy for the grasping intellect, and the fact that the link is made unconsciously. No reflective process goes into the appreciation of a skull and crossbones on the label of a bottle—and yet this is not merely a code used by manufacturers of poison; the symbol would evoke some associative and cohesive meaning in any situation. This purpose would certainly not be served as well by spelling out for ignorant consumers the word 'poison'. Illiterate people or foreigners would not understand it: language is normally a series of signs.

The uses of language, however, vary. The function of words usually varies between that of images (onomatopoeic words) and that of signs: in both cases, once said and understood they may be forgotten and are no longer necessary to the idea or object referred to. In poetry, however, they need not merely refer the reader to an idea, only to fade out; their sound or appearance can make them objects in their own right. This is particularly true of Mallarmé's poetry:

> Le vierge, le vivace et le bel aujourd'hui
> Va-t-il nous déchirer avec un coup d'aile ivre
> Ce lac dur oublié que hante sous le givre
> Le transparent glacier des vols qui n'ont pas fui!

Un cygne d'autrefois se souvient que c'est lui
Magnifique mais qui sans espoir se délivre
Pour n'avoir pas chanté la région où vivre
Quand du stérile hiver a resplendi l'ennui.

Tout son col secouera cette blanche agonie
Par l'espace infligée à l'oiseau qui le nie,
Mais non l'horreur du sol où le plumage est pris.

Fantôme qu'à ce lieu son pur éclat assigne,
Il s'immobilise au songe froid de mépris
Que vêt parmi l'exil inutile le Cygne.

The first intention of the word 'Cygne' in the last line is to remind us of the swan already mentioned before (conventional use of language as a code). True, this swan is unusually significant: the atmosphere of graceful sterility, coldness, and despair conveyed by the whiteness running through the sonnet leads us to associate the bird metaphorically with Mallarmé's pervading anxiety over his paralysis as a writer. In a first sense the swan is a symbol in that it suggests a privileged link to which the poet, by not spelling it out as an extended metaphor, lends a greater impact. Any standard romantic piece about the author's projection of his feelings on to Nature could be similarly abbreviated. This poem constitutes evidence that the swan left an impression in the poet's mind, arranged so as to suggest that there is also something poet-like in the swan. A kind of cohesive circle is formed for the reader.

There is, however, a second, more interesting side to this symbol. The idea suggested by the various elements in the poem is that the poet-swan would like to be an inspired translator of ideal experience into everyday language (his 'songe' would become a 'chanson', by a 'coup d'aile'), but that he can only write a contradictory lament on sterility. He would like to become a living symbol, but remains a living sign, whose place in the natural order obviously exists, but expressed in an unknown code: an idea ironically underlined by the word 'cygne', homophonous with 'signe'. This pun deprives the word of its transparency, makes of it an object in its own right. Indeed, as the poet changes from symbol into sign, the word 'cygne—signe' becomes a symbol. This is largely because of its importance in the complex of sounds making up the poem: the sound *i* appears in all the rhymes and dominates the syllabic pattern in stanzas 1, 2, and 4. Thus 'cygne' echoes the natural setting and the feelings derived from it (confirming the suggestion that there is a sign to be read here), but does so in an essentially meaningless way (justifying the poet's despair), since there is nothing particularly significant about the sound *i*.

Another sonnet of Mallarmé's exemplifies a second way in which written words can become part of a symbolic entity.

> Ses purs ongles très haut dédiant leur onyx,
> L'Angoisse, ce minuit, soutient, lampadophore,
> Maint rêve vespéral brûlé par le Phénix
> Que ne recueille pas de cinéraire amphore
>
> Sur les crédences, au salon vide: nul ptyx,
> Aboli bibelot d'inanité sonore,
> (Car le Maître est allé puiser des pleurs au Styx
> Avec ce seul objet dont le Néant s'honore).
>
> Mais proche la croisée au nord vacante, un or
> Agonise selon peut-être le décor
> Des licornes ruant du feu contre une nixe,
>
> Elle, défunte nue en le miroir, encor
> Que, dans l'oubli fermé par le cadre, se fixe
> De scintillations sitôt le septuor.

This is one of Mallarmé's most difficult poems if one wishes to find exact meanings, but its very point lies in blurring the precise identity of objects (either by their absence or the fact that they are seen through a mirror). Conversely, the words become opaque. Thus in line 6 the word 'bibelot' *means* 'knick-knack', and in prose the reader might not be aware of its further suggestiveness. Admittedly, one interpretation of this sonnet stresses the dictionary meaning: a 'bibelot' as a hollow horn, and this points to a metaphorical interpretation. A horn can be an instrument of expression or discovery. But 'bibelot' is used for the expressiveness of the word itself as much as for the suggestiveness of the object it refers to. Its sound is knotty and fragmentary, perfectly suited to the small, hard, carefully designed uselessness and multiplicity of knick-knacks. The appearance of the printed word 'bibelot', with its regular upstrokes forming compartments for unrelated, trifling vowels, also conveys their cheap swagger. The poet has stressed this representation by juxtaposing the word 'aboli'—again a word with a possible literal meaning within the poem (the horn has been removed from the sideboard in Mallarmé's lounge), but mainly there to support 'bibelot'. As well as doubling, with an extra 'b' and 'l', the number of consonant compartments, it parodies in a switched order the vowel sounds of 'bibelot', so that the final effect 'a-o-i, i-e-o' is indeed inane as well as noisy. The words are used both in sound and in appearance, as symbols in themselves. Poets have always made some effort to use sounds and integrate them into the sense; here, however, an attempt is made to replace the meaning of words as signs by another equally cohesive relationship between them, apprehensible with an immediacy and generality that characterizes symbols.

The use of words as symbols in their own right relates the symbolists most directly to Edgar Allan Poe and Baudelaire. From Poe, translated by Mallarmé and interpreted by Baudelaire, they learnt to exploit the suggestiveness of language systematically. There is a commentary by Mallarmé on his own poem 'L'Azur' that can be compared with profit to Poe's commentary on 'The Raven' in 'The Philosophy of Composition'. In Les Fleurs du mal the symbolists found an obsessive and fairly elaborate demonstration of the various 'correspondances' between the sound and the meaning of words and the five senses, which would stimulate the symbolic process in the reader; Verlaine's 'Art poétique' and Rimbaud's sonnet 'Voyelles' further illustrated how rhythms, sounds, and impressions were notes to be played in search of a tripartite incantatory harmony symbolizing Reality. It was a commonplace of the time, neatly summed up in England by Walter Pater, that all art, and poetry in particular, aspired to the condition of music.

The wish to give back to poetry a place amongst the plastic arts by using its full resources of expression stems from some experiments in artistic transposition first conducted by the Parnasse.

Gautier had written a clever poem on the sound 'blanc' and the idea of whiteness, and playfully called it 'Symphonie en Blanc Majeur'. The symbolists made an aesthetic principle of this metaphor. More widely, they considered poetry, music, drama, ballet, and sculpture as avenues leading the artist and his public towards one perfect beauty; if 'art transpositions' reached further than single arts, the absolute might be achieved when someone succeeded in combining their several virtues into a single charm. This feeling was not confined to the symbolist group; Wagner probably helped most of all to give general currency to the belief that the future would see a synthesizing art, which he personally thought would consist in music, poetry, and 'abstract' movement fused into grand opera. Even the 'decadents' shared this ideal, but as an instrument for enjoyment rather than a means of discovery: caricatures of the time picture the Decadent with an empty Baudelairean perfume bottle in his hand experiencing Real Awe reading Goethe's poetry to the strains of Wagner's music amid voluptuous statues in an exotic garden. The symbolists of course chose poetry as the essential tool, but tried to incorporate other arts by analogy. Mallarmé's most ambitious work, 'Un Coup de dés jamais n'abolira le hasard', was not just literature: it incorporated typography as orchestration into the symbolic pattern, with words of various sizes and shapes performing a ballet-like movement within the black and white harmony of the printed page. A great deal of his so-called obscurity is due to his substituting a new synthetic pattern for the normal syntactic logic that readers, brought up on romanticism, expected of poetry. One of the main events of symbolism was the performance in 1894 of a musical 'tone poem' by Debussy, inspired by Mallarmé's poem 'L'après-midi d'un faune': Debussy's piece was in its turn produced as a ballet by Diaghilev in 1912. In the early nineties the *avant-garde* Théâtre d'Art (later the Théâtre de l'Œuvre), which launched Maeterlinck, produced, under Paul Fort, stage versions of poems by Laforgue, Mallarmé, and Poe. These attempts met with little success, but the ideal of a unified art was still alive in the days of Stravinsky and Brecht.

In showing how words can be symbols and not signs, we have

described the language, but not the aims of symbolism. Now words, however concrete or particular, naturally take us towards the abstract or general. A word in a symbolic poem may do this in a more complex way, but its function is essentially the same. Goethe said that a symbol 'seeps forth a particular without independently thinking of or referring to a universal, but in grasping the particular in its living characteristics it implicitly apprehends the universal along with it'. This definition might apply to any word, except that in a symbol the process appears to work both ways—the word being at once an image and an abstraction—and we return here to our idea of a circle reconstituted.

In this privileged function, the symbol is a kind of solution to the ancient and medieval philosophic quarrel between the supporters of the real flower and of the ideal flower. Some people think that the idea is a representation of the object: they point out that in reality 'flowers in general' do not exist, but only roses, violets, and cultivated weeds, so that it is only a convention to use the category 'flower' in speech and thought. Others take the opposite view and hold that a flower would be difficult to distinguish from its surroundings (bush, roots, vase) to someone with no preconceived idea of what he was looking for. This philosophic problem of 'abstraction' is raised by Mallarmé when he writes of the language of poetry in a Platonic vein: 'Je dis: une fleur! et, hors de l'oubli où ma voix relègue aucun contour, en temps que quelque chose d'autre que les calices sus, musicalement se lève, idée même et suave, l'absente de tous bouquets.' Plato, and many dualistic philosophers such as Schopenhauer, consider reality a poor relation, a representation of the essential world of Ideas. For Plato the philosopher alone dares turn his back on the projection screen and contemplate the sources of light themselves. Mallarmé substitutes the poet for the philosopher, and claims it his mission to study 'le Rêve' or 'l'Idéal', or what his contemporary Gustave Kahn called by a more Baudelairean word, 'les limbes'. But he does not despise reality. His role is to understand and apply the universal laws of Analogy, or laws of symbolism, which form esoteric bridges between the 'Ideal' and the everyday world.

Thus the word 'cygne', within that particular sonnet, symbolized an aspect of the Ideal not normally or easily expressible in words. Or else, to satisfy the substantialists, one could merely use the verb 'symbolize' in its passive form. In this, symbolism is the ultimate flowering of an idea inherent in romanticism from the start, though often lost under the profusion of self-expansion and socio-moral didacticism of the earlier poets: that poetry is not merely an instrument of refined or vigorous expression, but also a means of penetrating and exploring a whole world protected from the normal gaze by a painted veil. Hugo, echoing Lamartine, had written in the 1822 preface to his *Odes et ballades*: 'La poésie, c'est tout ce qu'il y a d'intime dans tout', and repeated often enough that the poetic 'verbe' was creative, but hardly demonstrated how until the 1850s when his analogies were indeed still mainly of a moral kind. [The romantic predilection for expressing inner states of mind through images taken from Nature, and the subsequent tendency towards the 'pathetic fallacy' which leads one to see Nature itself as a projection of larger forces beyond, was the breeding-ground of symbolism.]

Parnassian poetry encourages the 'pathetic fallacy' by describing only the objective realities of Nature, and using the tensions of the poem to suggest that there is life beyond the surface of things. But, as we have pointed out above, there is nothing to prove that the only reality lies in or beyond Nature, and that Man does not search in Nature for symbols to express the reality of his own mind. In these opposed uses of Nature's zoo lies the essential difference between the Parnassians and the symbolists, and particularly between Leconte de Lisle and Mallarmé. Mallarmé's swan symbolizes, brings together Nature and the poet's mind; Leconte de Lisle's very real tigers and elephants suggest some mystical reality that neither poet nor reader knows.

The symbolists' conception of the poet, however, reminds us that they grew from the Parnassian movement and that all had at one time or another contributed to *Le Parnasse contemporain*. Like the decadents, they tried to break down the official alexandrine, an act clamoured for by Hugo in alexandrines and only really begun by Banville. They imitated the fluid style of Verlaine and tended, like Laforgue, towards free verse. But the decadent style of poetry, slack towards the recognized tradition, experimenting with popular turns of phrase and generally lacking in poetic tension though not in inventiveness, was expressive of a moral attitude. This explains the scorn shown for the decadents by what Verlaine in turn called 'cymbalisme'. Foreigners visiting Paris for a bit of irregular life may have found Verlaine and his companions the Hirsutes and the Zutistes, in their haunts in Montmartre and the Latin Quarter, entertaining and picturesque; but this latter-day romanticism bordering on vice, expressing what we would call today a 'sick' view of life, went against the grain of many a middle-class reader who subscribed to the *Revue des deux mondes* and looked to literature for the idealism clarioned by Vigny and Hugo. Symbolism, as *l'art pour l'art* had been a generation before, was a new attempt to lift poetry to a high ideal. Its followers were, according to Henri de Régnier, 'les chevaliers servants de la poésie'. It could indeed be argued that it was better placed to succeed. The Parnasse had refused to exploit the easy romantic themes of adventure and gesture, but had been exposed to the danger of apparently trivial subjects. Symbolism, as well as preferring self-compulsion to self-consciousness, was more flattering to the powers of the mind. To the banner of 'art for art's sake' the symbolists could add a metaphysical idealism.

Symbolism thus takes from earlier romanticism its interest in the 'pathetic fallacy', or the less tendentious relationships between the objective and the abstract world; and inherits the high moral stand though reversing the philosophy of the Parnasse. We must now separate clearly Mallarmé and the symbolists who flourished as a school, from Baudelaire, Rimbaud, and the later Hugo.

First, it is all too easy to transfer the pathetic fallacy from the 'significance' of Nature to the prophetic function of the poet himself. If the flowers and the trees are signs of a supernatural world beyond, then the poet is the symbol, and the next step is all too easy: he and his audience assume that he is a living analogy, placed somehow 'in and beyond' Reality, thus able to express supernatural truths symbolically through the objects known to men. As a result, Hugo visualized the poet as a giant with his head in the clouds. Rimbaud, Nerval, and possibly Lautréamont are also vivid examples of this barely literary position: they appeared, through semi-madness or a state of quasi-hypnotic enthusiasm, to have 'jumped' the process of metaphoric analogy, and experienced directly, in hallucinations and dreams, incursions of real life into the Ideal. The subsequent image of the poet as a madman/genius can only appear to an idealist such as Mallarmé as an utter misconception. The world of ideas is too far from that of objects for one man to bridge the gap by direct vision. Only in the economy of a poem, with active participation by the reader, can the symbol be achieved.

Secondly, if the poet uses words as symbols for the inner reality he wishes to express, he tends towards a private language, to which he initiates the reader by first using complex metaphors (swan-white-sterile-poet) and then cutting out links (swan = poet). Such was the path followed by Hugo and Baudelaire. The danger appears when a symbol is referred to outside the pattern of the poem where its value was created. In the same book, well and good; by the same poet in another work, still acceptable. But when certain objects begin to be accepted as more 'poetic' in themselves than certain others because Baudelaire or Verlaine or Mallarmé have used them successfully, the symbols have become signs, poetry has become a code for the initiate only. This depreciation, by which poetic language becomes a technique used by a craftsman to whip up the symbolic process in the reader, takes place as any movement develops but is usually confined to theme and verse form. It happened very soon to Baudelairean words such as 'ennui', 'encens', 'chevelure'; Hugo conducted a self-depreciation of his favourite 'gouffre' and 'ciel'. This, unfortunately, is also what characterizes most of the poets who called themselves 'symbolists': Gustave Kahn wrote little more than depressed *pastiches* of Baudelaire and Verlaine; Viélé-Griffin drew heavily on the later manner of Hugo. Even Verlaine had tended towards self-parody, and the use of words whose 'poetic' virtue he knew in advance.

Mallarmé avoided both these poetic fallacies.

There could hardly be a better foil to the Lives of the Great Romantics than the drab existence of Stéphane Mallarmé. Following those aristocrats who even in their democratic flights retained the conviction that they were made to lead men, and contrasting with the *poètes maudits* whose accursed existence opened into the unknown, here was a teacher from an uninteresting middle-class family, leading a normal eventless life, disappointed by the reality within his reach but not grasping beyond it. He may have had a mistress, and his son died young; a more expansive poet might have made capital out of these two episodes. But his personal hopes and achievements, his domestic life, and his political beliefs are to his reader as a dark incoherent room whose only function is to offset the wonderful brilliance shining through the window and his attempts to gaze at the Ideal outside.

His first poems were directly influenced by *Les Fleurs du mal*. They practise Baudelairean transpositions, develop correspondences between women and scenery, talk of 'accablement' and 'ennui'. But he criticizes Baudelaire in his letters for being too conscious of the decay of the flesh and the despair of the soul and not aware of the Ideal that permeates everything. His poems begin to lay less stress on his own physical and moral situation, and though they reveal the temptation of nihilism they also aspire towards mystical presences hinted at by such things as blue sky, open windows, the sound of bells, a woman's hair, ships leaving port. The poet appears in various guises: a mournful Hamlet-like patient in a hospital, horrified by everyday existence; or a desperate clown on the point of abandoning the Dream of Art for animal survival; or a man suddenly catching a glimpse of the Ideal as in a mirror, through the memory of a beautiful woman.

During the next ten years he went through a crisis questioning the value and form of poetry. He was known to be working on 'L'Après-midi d'un faune' and on a verse drama, *Hérodiade*; the second remained in fragments. In this second crucial period we see him worried by the tension between the sensual appeal of the outside world and a thirst after the inner absolute. The poem 'L'Azur' had already suggested that reality could have a symbolic meaning; but Mallarmé had been conscious of the shortcomings in the pathetic fallacy since he could not interpret the blueness of the sky, though it haunted him. Now Salome in *Hérodiade* refuses the outside world entirely, and seeks the absolute in a pale internal night of her own making, represented by her obsessive chastity; though the faun in 'L'Après-midi d'un faune' has indulged in the sensuous pleasures of the world, he now doubts whether this experience was imagined or not, and sees how unreliable reality is. Even desire exists on an ambiguous half-real and half-memorized plane. The poem depicts his delight at the memories and rather dismisses the real experience. 'Igitur', a very curious prose piece discovered recently, also belongs to this period. The poet still appears as a kind of poetic Zarathustra; the text, a 'dramatic sketch' in very intricate prose, is an allegorical record of a crisis in the spiritual progress of the poet, who turns out to be the hero of a pre-ordained Fate. In gradually stripping himself of chance traits in search of the creative Absolute where Chance does not exist, he indulges so much in subjective lucidity that when he finally understands it he is identified with it and cannot contemplate the Ideal objectively. In other words, he is part of that Ideal. He has killed the romantic illusion that poetry is dictated to the poet by chance (he has staked his life on the non-existence of Chance), but realizes that though it is an inner quest based on painful analysis and not inspiration, it finally uncovers unavoidable and universal truths. 'Toast funèbre', written to commemorate the death of Gautier and thereby to define a grandiose conception of the poet's place in the universe, forms a conclusion to this dilemma of internal absence and external transience: Mallarmé, like Keats, Proust, and the few other great artists, reaches the belief that the poet survives through his work, the only thing assured of permanence—in this case because it continues even after his death to reflect the privileged vision of the Ideal that he built for himself while writing it. The sonnet 'Le vierge, le vivace . . .', which we have already commented on, is best understood at this point in his quest: he had realized that symbols are created by the poet's search, and that while the poem lends them its reality, the poet does not necessarily understand them.

Having arrived so to speak at artistic maturity there only remained to accomplish the life's work that would achieve permanence and perhaps knowledge of the Beyond. Had Mallarmé succeeded fully, we would by now be building churches to him. Looking back on the pseudo-scientific mysticism on which he intended to base his

TRINITY COLLEGE
LIBRARY

exploration of the Ideal, his failure was perhaps inevitable. But the grandiose hope as well as the poetic talent remain and make the few poems he produced during the last period glistening shards of a superhuman project. After 'Toast funèbre' Mallarmé composed some fifty pieces of which half are no more than circumstantial verse, written with a refined and delicate touch that Musset only achieved in his finest moments, but really no more than curiosities; apart from some essays collected in *Divagations*, and various prose pieces retrieved by scholars from the pages of reviews, there remains his notoriously difficult poetry, an enigmatic *ars poetica*, 'Prose pour des Esseintes', and two dozen sonnets that are the sum of Mallarmé at his most powerful, but were only written as trial runs while he was trying to produce his *Grand Œuvre*.

The *Grand Œuvre* was to revolutionize literature. It was to consist of twenty volumes which the reader would first peruse without cutting the pages, thus reading only two pages in every eight. Having thus gathered the 'exoteric' meaning of the whole, he would turn to the 'esoteric' explanation inside. Its whole structure would be architectural and not subject to the inspirations of the moment— here as in many ways Mallarmé expresses the secret ambition of every poet to be read as a whole and not as a mere dabbler whether in images, metaphors, or symbols. He only published a fragment, 'Un Coup de dés jamais n'abolira le hasard', which develops, allusively, the theme of 'Igitur'. The book was never finished, and Mallarmé instructed his family to burn what remained of it in his papers. As with Nerval and Rimbaud, though in a less demonstrative way, his plan for an Orphic insight into the Ideal had failed.

It is obvious that Mallarmé was sorely tempted, as were his predecessors, by the easy way of resolving the poetic fallacy: considering himself as a prophet, outside and beyond Reality. In his Baudelairean period he only displays his own feelings reluctantly, sympathizing with other people in similar situations rather than pushing himself forward. An early poem, 'Le Guignon', savages the *poètes maudits*, or 'mendieurs d'azur', for their dangerous amateurism and their belief that they are favourites of the gods; it seems to suggest that though poetry is a quest, it can be carried out equally well by reticent, law-abiding intellectuals. Symbolism was for him a way of remaining true to this advice in his central, complex poetry. 'L'Après-midi d'un faune' can be interpreted as a metaphoric account of Mallarmé's dilemma, but it is equally possible to read it as a graphic or plastic description of its outward subject, the thought of the faun, or, if one is conscious of the ambiguity of the man–beast symbol, on a more general level. The sonnets that follow his crisis are free from personal figuration, though their material symbolizes the poet's inner and outer experience.

It is, however, too much to expect that in a century obsessed by the artistic personality cult, Mallarmé should have been entirely free from literary spotlighting. When his symbolist disciples began to carry their belief in the existence of an ideal world past the field of literary expression into mystical conjecture, Mallarmé failed to object to their meeting as a brotherhood, on Tuesday afternoons in his flat in the rue de Rome, to listen to hermetic phrases issuing from his lips as if from a high priest or a medium. Some notes on his *Grand Œuvre* suggest that it would be read in religious ceremony by an operator using permutations of loose sheets and a set of pigeon-holes. His followers, with the usual reticence of true converts, have only hinted at the proceedings at the famous 'mardis', but it is clear that poetry was to become a religion, or at least, until the Truth was fully revealed, a freemasonry: at one time Mallarmé planned to create a nation-wide lodge for the profession.

These sincere but misguided practices cannot be ignored completely. Without exactly suffering from clinical delusions, Mallarmé carried literary dandyism as far as seriously suggesting that he might be one of the godlike beings called 'Elohim' in the Scriptures. His attitude is, however, largely different from that of the *poètes maudits* with their personalized version of the pathetic fallacy. For him it is a reaction against the romantic image of the poet leading crowds. A youthful essay of his entitled 'L'Art pour tous' complains that literature has become so universally readable that even poetry is no longer a cloistered adoration of the Beautiful, but is being taught in schools as a technique. The poet, he says, should retain high ambitions and follow the example of religions which preserve their value by retreating into mysterious cults and restricted admission. His language should ultimately be as mysterious to the layman as musical notation, like that of old documents whose hieroglyphs are as suggestive as they are unapproachable. Accordingly, Mallarmé avoided the general frivolous public for whom poetry was an amusement, by making his work difficult to understand; indeed, only as a concession did he ever publish it. He and his disciples countered the ever-growing circulations of the Zolas and the Maupassants with private editions or texts for circulation amongst the initiate only.

This desire for privacy is easily understood. The economic boom of literature from 1880 onwards did undoubtedly create a need for a more secluded form of writing. The rapid accumulation of wealth throughout Europe, the enormous growth of towns and communications together with the extension of the franchise and of secondary but not higher education, made for a tremendous increase in the demand for middle-brow reading material—hence a relative vulgarization of formerly respectable genres. The nineties, a golden age for theatres, concert halls, and publishing houses, were producing, along with a few masterpieces, some of the most trivial writing Europe had known.

Yet in spite of the professed objections to positivism and the naturalist novel, symbolism, like all the literature of the time, was strikingly permeated with para-scientific ideals. Mallarmé may have scorned the realists' analysis of superficial realities, but his attitude towards the exploration and codification of the symbolic world between them and the Ideal is almost a replica of that of science. In the 1890s it was still possible to argue cogently against the universal validity of the laws of matter. In a century wholly obsessed by the risk of ignoring important tools of Knowledge, there was a slight possibility that poetry, the esoteric study of language, might provide the answer. The symbolist brotherhood believed itself to be a higher and possibly all-revealing spiritual state, particularly well placed to exploit the word as a mystical link between the superficial everyday world and its Ideal Meaning. René Ghil's *Traité du verbe* (prefaced by Mallarmé), and Mallarmé's 'Petite Philologie à l'usage des classes et des gens du monde', exploit the old belief, still unrefuted at the time by anthropology, that the specific mean-

ings and connotations of certain sounds or groups of sounds are
remnants of the 'pure' language given to mankind by the gods.
Though he suggested that only the initiate understood words properly, Mallarmé thus avoids the fallacy of a 'poetic language'. When
he emphasizes certain words, he is really implying that poetry,
based on a Platonic view of the world and with ontological and pan-
artistic ambitions, derives its creativeness from the symbols we
handle unwittingly every day: it is also a science of words.

It is impossible to delay any more a consideration of the question
that every reader of Mallarmé must ask himself: can the 'experience' recorded in the poem be shared by the reader? There are three
possible answers.

Many historians of literature consider implicitly that it cannot be:
the Mallarmean poem is a puzzle with a solution, and its bizarre
words and involuted style and associations have one definite meaning, which the normal reader cannot appreciate. The motto for this
view could be Mallarmé's own dictum: 'Nommer un objet, c'est
supprimer les trois quarts de la jouissance du poème, qui est faite
de deviner peu à peu — le suggérer, voilà le rêve.' Indeed, some of
his poems centre on the connotations and relationships of an object
that is not explicitly mentioned. If we read in an annotated edition
the poem 'Ses purs ongles très haut . . .' and learn that 'L'Angoisse
. . . lampadophore' is an ornate statuette on the sideboard, that the
'cinéraire amphore' (and also 'ptyx, Aboli bibelot') is an ashtray,
that the 'licornes' are part of an ornate mirror, and that the 'septuor'
is the seven stars of the Great Bear seen through the mirror, we may
be able to 'understand' the poem in the sense in which we understand a newspaper article.

Mallarmé himself encouraged this attitude by tending to deni-
grate his own achievements. To an admirer who was praising him
for concentrating the ideal universe into a single poem, he is said
to have answered, 'Not at all, it's a description of my kitchen
dresser.' Yet he also made fun of those who sought the 'real' meaning when he wrote to a reader, 'Cherchez bien et à la fin vous
trouverez une pornographie — ce sera votre récompense.' However, in the manner of the true prophet, he wrote little enough for

the mystique that grew around him to benefit from infinite conjecture. It has been upheld, for instance, that his 'real' meaning is
to be found by looking up the definitions of his keywords in the
Littré dictionary. It is also said that by a study of his vocabulary
one can deduce central meanings such as 'poem' for 'guirlande',
'sterility' for 'blancheur', and then replace these words in their context in order to clarify it.

Giving reasons for this approach, Mallarmé's disciple Valéry
shows how his desire for literary privacy led him to avoid the poetic
vernacular, preferring to build ascetic protective devices around his
poems, whose shiny facets conceal the inner content from all but
the prudent, self-disciplined reader. Reading and writing are thus
both restored as an ambitious intellectual exercise. We are supposed
to recapture the rare pleasure enjoyed of old by the reader of
Thucydides and largely lost since the immense vulgarization of
printing and the large-scale invasion of literature by prose, with its
attendant laxity.

There is certainly truth in this view. Not only does it agree with
many of Mallarmé's writings, but it explains perfectly the deliberate
blurring he carried out, particularly in his first period. He expects
the reader to be as scornful of the first steps of the poetic process as
he is; this can be illustrated by comparing an early poem such as 'Le
Pitre châtié' with a pièce by Baudelaire. It does, however, fail to
explain why the mature Mallarmé is better than the early Mallarmé.
In fact it is not a judgement of objective value at all, merely an act of
faith in 'difficult literature', which could be very bad literature and
still provide the intellectual pleasure of discovering the right
answer.

Also, one should beware of the assumption that a symbolic poem
can be solved if one knows the key to a code—this is confusing a
symbol with a sign, and neglecting the separateness of the real
symbol from any precise expression as from any exact meaning.
The very fact that 'guirlande' means both 'poem', 'festoon', or in a
certain context 'wreath' or even 'stars', gives it its symbolic value.
Besides, if the reading of a poem is a kind of intellectual crossword
game, at which some people are better than others because they
happen to be equipped with an edition with footnotes, if a critical

apparatus is needed even to begin to understand the meaning, then one should seriously question its literary worth. It would become vulnerable to the objections always levelled against preciosity.

The second approach is the one most commonly adopted by the symbolists themselves, who emphasized that in a good poem the symbols were plurivalent, and had a literal meaning for the shallow reader, a 'secret' meaning for the poet, and in between a whole array of meanings, some of which the poet may not have thought of. Rémy de Gourmont compared such a poem to the emperor's coat— invisible but appearing differently to each courtier. Mallarmé certainly shared this feeling, reacting with his contemporaries against romantic rhetoric, which, like the architecture and music of the time, tended to seek its effects in an accumulation of details. Several of his poems dealing with the theme of absence, such as the following, are indeed plurivalent.

> Une dentelle s'abolit
> Dans le doute du Jeu suprême
> A n'entr'ouvrir comme un blasphème
> Qu'absence éternelle de lit.

> Cet unanime blanc conflit
> D'une guirlande avec la même,
> Enfoui contre la vitre blême
> Flotte plus qu'il n'ensevelit.

> Mais, chez qui du rêve se dore
> Tristement dort une mandore
> Au creux néant musicien

> Telle que vers quelque fenêtre
> Selon nul ventre que le sien,
> Filial on aurait pu naître.

The symbolic word 'dentelle' here acts as a turn-table that can direct us towards several possible meanings, all interrelated through it. It could, literally, be a lace window curtain, disappearing against the white dawn seen through the 'vitre blême'; or it could suggest a bed curtain or lace sheet (together with 'unanime conflit' and 'nul ventre que le sien') in the place for love (the supreme game), and possibly creation with woman; or else a winding-sheet, with the idea of death and absence (see 'enfoui', 'ensevelit', 'guirlande'); or, if 'dentelle' can refer to a poem (and this one has the worked intricacy of lace), we have the supreme game of Poetry, a window opening out on to the ideal world. There could be further links with the same or different words in the poem, and it may be that not all were in Mallarmé's mind. The poem is a non-representative object similar to a Persian carpet, consisting of words arranged suggestively to make the reader see patterns in them for himself. Mallarmé it was who wrote

> Le sens trop précis rature
> Ta vague littérature.

This kind of explanation has the advantage of stressing the part played by the reader, but it has two weaknesses. First, it still suggests that to appreciate a poem fully one needs to put together all the possible reactions of various readers likely to enrich one reader's appreciation—hence another critical apparatus, less dogmatic than the first kind but still not proving the literary value of the poem. Secondly, though Mallarmé believed in challenging his reader, to stop at this point would be to misunderstand the idea running through his poetry—that the Poet, as the most self-conscious representative of man's intellect, is able to impose or view a new order in the accidents of the outside world.

Whatever the value of intellectual gymnastics, one is inevitably led to the third approach to symbolism. Mallarmé stated it clearly enough, but his ascetic life and the unique themes of sterility and emptiness which are essential to his metaphysical quest tend to throw his mature poetic achievements into the shade. From 'L'Après-midi d'un faune' onwards it is trivial to see his value in the elusiveness of his verse. Every poem of his is a symbol of (i.e. a step towards as well as an expression of) the emergence of transcendental realities into the immanent world through the poet's intercession. Anything, even as prosaic as a kitchen dresser or as sensuous as a woman making love, can provoke it; but these supports are then blurred, leaving a fluid result with as little relationship with what caused it as there is between the proverbial pearl and its grain of sand. Real identities and appearances are as unimportant as the name of a railway junction or the shape of the branches between which a spider spins his web. If they do remain, they have acquired a symbolic charge, as they henceforth reflect the universe into a private microcosm, where the reader penetrates to find that things exist more truly through their absence. Obscured and divested of their objectivity, they have left only the echoes of their essential suggestiveness in the transcendental scene on which the poem is set. A piece of marble, a fan, a swan, flowers, an ashtray, a woman's hair, a bare room at dawn, are made by the 'accident' of the poet's attention recipients of some of Man's questions about the meaning of his life. Mallarmé never describes. He refuses the accidental universe that existed outside his mind to start with, preferring the difficult new world that he called the Ideal, and made of strange similarities and familiar contrasts which coexist without the hierarchy implied by metaphoric poetry; a world with a new and powerful order bound by human symbols. Whether it belongs to the mind of the author who engenders it, or to the mind of the reader who reconstructs it for himself, possibly with different stresses, hardly matters. The very polish of the form, for Mallarmé has a masterly knowledge of the intimate harmonies and rhythms of French, excludes any firm meaning such as traditional prosaic syntax implies. The only thing that is certain is that words, though recipients of the accumulated ideas and intentions of mankind, are not used here as mere carriers of meaning. *They* are the objects: 'le monde existe pour aboutir à un livre.'

The slenderness of his poetic works and the inevitable quixotic failure of his overrated occult ambitions should not prevent us from appreciating Mallarmé's originality and the stature of his thought. His constant theme, so frequently belittled and misunderstood, is the reverse of Pascal's: the power of the human intellect. In this he stands apart from the literary tradition of a period so immersed in the accidents of the material or personal world. More important, he stands alone in the development of French poetry: after 1866 he underwent practically no outside influence, and no one has achieved

the same since. There have been outwardly hermetic poets in this
century, but always with an anthropological, esoteric, or scientific
cipher. The strangeness of Mallarmé's poems, the measure of their
power, has not lessened over the past eighty years. New fashions
have not altered their significance, nor new analyses blunted their
meaninglessness. The greatest mistake is to hope that time and
historico-scientific modes of inquiry will elucidate these defiant
human structures—and here lies both the vindication and the
vulnerability of his admirers.

NOTE

Symbolism began with a manifesto published by Jean Moréas in 1886 as an
answer to the founding of the review *La Décadence* by René Ghil. A group of
poets joined Moréas under this banner: the main ones were Gustave Kahn,
Francis Viélé-Griffin, Henri de Régnier, Édouard Dujardin. They wrote in *Le
Symboliste*, *La Plume*, *La Revue Blanche*, *Le Mercure de France*. After a time the
symbolist and decadent groups drifted together, but the symbolists were linked
by scorn for decadent styles, represented by Verlaine, Laforgue, Banville; by
admiration for high ideals in poetry represented by Gautier, Leconte de Lisle,
Villiers de l'Isle Adam; and by Mallarmé's *salons* held every Tuesday at his flat
in the rue de Rome.

STÉPHANE MALLARMÉ, 1842-98, taught English in Tournon, Besançon,
Avignon, and finally Paris. He had been brought up in literary circles and helped
to direct several literary journals; he published seventeen short poems in various
magazines between 1862 and 1866. From 1880 he started running his 'literary
afternoons'. After a long gap his *Poésies* appeared in 1887. From then until his
death he was an acknowledged leader of a self-styled 'élite' among young French
poets.

Mallarmé's poetic and prose works were almost all collected for the first time
by H. Mondor and G. Jean-Aubry in *Œuvres complètes* (Pléiade, 1945). This
includes his translations of Edgar Allan Poe, a treatise on English translation,
a full list of editions, and a comprehensive list of secondary works, with some
English items. Several articles first collected here are essential. But Mallarmé is
accessible through the current edition of the N.R.F. collection of *Poésies* (1913,
etc.) which only excludes minor material, and that of *Divagations* (Charpentier,
1897, etc.), a collection of articles and lectures. A good number of the major
pieces are exceptionally well commented on in *Mallarmé: Pages choisies* (ed.
G. Delfel, Classiques Hachette, 1956). The fruits of more recent scholarship
may be studied in C. P. Barbier (ed.), *Documents Stéphane Mallarmé* (1968-   ).

Mallarmé's influence on the symbolists can be best judged through the remini-
scences and aesthetic theories of his disciple Paul Valéry: more particularly in

the nine essays on him collected by Valéry in *Variété* (vols. 2 and 3, 1929 and 1936; Pléiade, 1957). The two standard studies on Mallarmé are still A. Thibaudet, *La Poésie de Stéphane Mallarmé* (1926), and H. Mondor, *Vie de Mallarmé* (1941). To these it is worth adding P. Beausire, *Mallarmé. Plaisir et poétique* (1949), and R. G. Cohn, *Towards the Poems of Mallarmé* (1965). Examples of individual approaches to the understanding of his poetry can be found in E. Noulet, *Dix poèmes de Stéphane Mallarmé* (1948); C. Mauron, *Introduction à la psychanalyse de Mallarmé* (1950); C. Chassé, *Les Clés de Mallarmé* (1954); L. Cellier, *Mallarmé ou la morte qui parle* (1959); J.-P. Richard, *L'Univers imaginaire de Mallarmé* (1961); C. Chadwick, *Mallarmé: sa pensée dans sa poésie* (1962); W. Fowlie, *Mallarmé* (1962); and C. Abastado, *Expérience et théorie de la création poétique chez Mallarmé* (1970).

F

10. Zola

'CE matérialisme m'indigne . . . Tas de farceurs qui veulent se faire accroire et nous faire accroire qu'ils ont découvert la Méditerranée.' The vigour with which Flaubert dismisses the theoretical claims of naturalism has been generally echoed by subsequent critics. And so, too, especially in recent years, has the substance of his generous praise for the novels themselves: 'Et je maintiens que vous êtes un joli romantique. C'est même à cause de cela que je vous admire et vous aime.' Having pardoned the virulence with which Zola himself attacked Hugo, critics are now willing to give him credit for his own Hugolian virtues, to recognize the power of the mythic and poetic qualities of his work.

These judgements are to a large extent justified. The fallacies and pretensions of naturalist doctrine have frequently been exposed. It need only be repeated here that, even if we accept the materialistic assumptions about human behaviour, the parallel between the 'experimental' novel and the activities of the chemist or pathologist is an absurdity. The writer can only 'discover' in his characters what he puts there himself; and while an inspirational view of writing might conceivably envisage an author setting up his characters and sitting back to watch them interact, a scientific theory could not possibly do so. In any case it seems that Zola himself regarded the more extravagant claims of the theory as publicity for his cause rather than as a description of his working method; and his frequent use of the word 'poème' in his preparatory notes for his novels (*Au bonheur des dames* is to be 'le poème de l'activité moderne', *La Terre* 'le poème vivant de la terre') suggests that the sort of praise he has received does justice to at least one aspect of his work.

Nevertheless it would be a distortion if Zola's scientific aims were completely discounted. Though difficult to define they were real and lasting. It was they that sustained him in his long and systematic labour—the labour which left him, in Henry James's words after their first meeting, 'fairly bristling with the betrayal that nothing whatever had happened to him in life but to write *Les Rougon-Macquart*'. The scientific aim cannot be watered down into a more traditional concern for *vraisemblance*, tightness of motivation, 'inevitability' as a literary virtue rather than a philosophical proposition. And beside this persistent aim of sociological *truth*, as against the hypocrisies of traditional psychology and social morality, Balzac's programme can be made to seem a predominantly aesthetic one—that of establishing the parity of the bourgeois world with the royal and the mythological as raw material for tragedy. Zola's confident generalizing use of the definite article in his notes on his characters ('le type du père goguenard, bourgeois républicain', 'le prêtre amoureux de la créature', and many more), as well as the recurrence of the words 'étudier', 'analyser', 'montrer', shows that the novels were conceived of primarily as demonstrations. And it is on the force and quality of the demonstration that their value as artistic wholes largely depends.

But demonstration is a difficult business in fiction, especially when the genetic rather than the environmental is in question. There are plenty of circular demonstrations in Zola—murders accounted for by irresistible homicidal urges, and the like. It is therefore perhaps not surprising that Zola is most incontrovertibly successful when demonstrating, or illustrating, what nowadays can be accepted as a moral or social truism. It is for this reason that the working-class novels seem the finest and truest. The naturalist theory of total conditioning seems least controversial here, though we should not underestimate Zola's courage and originality in putting it forward in a world which—witness the Victorian distinction between the deserving and the feckless poor—still clung to the ideal of moral absolutes.

There seems, then, no need to revise the traditional valuation of Zola's novels, whereby *L'Assommoir* (1877) and *Germinal* (1885) are considered to be the major achievements. Great claims have been made for *La Débâcle* (1892) (not strictly working-class, of course); but it seems to me not fully to solve the problem of writing

about confusion without being confusing and repetitive itself. Zola
significantly admired Flaubert's attempt in *L'Éducation sentimentale*
to deal with a similar problem, that of writing about boringness
without being boring; perhaps today we feel that the futility of the
detail of war needs less exhaustive illustration, that the Flaubertian
sense of form is the least we require to mitigate the aimlessness of
the subject-matter. As for *La Terre* (1887), it has a rich variety of
tone and scene, with the theme of filial ingratitude, the beauty of the
natural descriptions, the mixture of the horrific and the—for Zola
—rare, almost Rabelaisian humour. But as a whole it suffers
perhaps from certain features recurrent in Zola, to which we shall
have to return later.

L'Assommoir has strong claims to be considered the model of the
naturalist novel and the finest product of Zola's genius. And chiefly
because, while Zola exploits here to the full the talents for which he
is now in danger of being praised exclusively, it is more than a
panorama, it never slackens into a mere collection of working-class
sketches, essays in urban impressionism and symbolism. It is the
story of an individual fate, or rather of an individual 'case', a successful sequel to what the Goncourts had attempted in *Germinie
Lacerteux*, the first 'naturalist' novel: namely the full-length study
of a character in which the traditional moral and psychological
approach is replaced by the sociological, the scientific, the medical,
the behaviouristic; and in which these are used in the service of a
more humanitarian and relativistic judgement of conduct. *L'Assommoir* fulfils the naturalist prescription: by the end we feel that we
know all we need to know, that things could not have been other
than they were. At the same time—and here *Germinie Lacerteux*
had been less completely successful—it obeys what appear to be
the prerequisites of the novel. Whatever the ultimate truth about the
physiological and environmental basis of behaviour, there can be
little doubt that medical and scientific terminology are inimical to
the novel. As Sartre maintained in his well-known criticism of
Mauriac, whether we are free or not the novel can only live on the
appearance of freedom.

On the technical level at least, Zola solves the problem of reconciling freedom and necessity by making the book's proposition wholly

unexceptionable, indeed tautological. The parallel with *Germinie Lacerteux* in fact needs qualifying. Zola's aim is in a sense more modest. In spite of the novel's comprehensive air, Gervaise's is not, by comparison with Germinie's, the fully documented case, sealed with final social and physiological exculpation. We first meet Gervaise in mid-career; she is admitted to have severe inherent defects: she is a reclaimed drinker, capable of hard work but basically weak and easy-going. The approach to the character is completely undogmatic, the sources and status of these weaknesses are not exhaustively investigated. And Zola avoids not only the dangers of special pleading, but also those of excessive reliance on the symbolic and impressionistic; wisely, since the portrayal of the mine as devouring monster or the distilling machine as malignant devil may well provoke the hostile moralist's objection that the individual will cannot be victim of such things, that this is an example of the pathetic fallacy at its most pernicious. But here the impressionism does not simply work symbolically: Gervaise *is* afraid of big buildings and easily lulled by smells. The book in fact succeeds because it operates within a relatively narrow and homogeneous area: Zola sets down Gervaise in a society which has precisely her own qualities. Life is the irresistible force which defeats her, but she herself is the easily movable object. Thus there is little to 'prove' about the case, no tricky apportioning of responsibility for the reader to be made to subscribe to; and Zola can devote himself to the task of *illustrating* the broader proposition—the total interdependence of the individual and the social and moral environment in this particular situation. It is the detailed and—to a Flaubertian degree—artistic working-out of that proposition that constitutes the achievement of *L'Assommoir*.

The novel is distinguished from Zola's others by the originality and perfection of its structure. It is, in some degree, a series of set-pieces—F. W. Hemmings remarks how easily we could find descriptive titles for the chapters; we are reminded of Flaubert's use of the well-shaped, detachable episode in *Madame Bovary* (the wedding, the *comices*, and so on). The same critic comments on the simple, classical line of the story, the unwavering parabola which it traces of Gervaise's rise and fall; the comparison here might be with

Balzac's *Grandeur et décadence de César Birotteau*. Both these points are true in their way—but *L'Assommoir* is something more besides.

It *is* a magnificent series of set pieces, but they are always subservient to the whole. There *is* a tracing of the rise and fall of Gervaise, but the commercial adventure story never obscures the central sociological theme. The character of Gervaise never breaks free from the pattern in which Zola has placed her. For, even in the early part of the book, every chapter gives us as it were a dual vision of her progress: we see her as apparently autonomous, making concrete social progress, temporarily, it seems, triumphing over life. But the triumph is never complete, she never achieves quite the status of the Balzacian commercial hero; the seeds of disaster are present from the beginning, invisible to Gervaise only because of her robust, unreflecting temperament. The reader becomes aware of a pattern more significant than—and cutting across—Gervaise's rise in fortune. Each chapter begins on the simple, forward-looking note appropriate to a character for whom every day is a new sally against life, who is too pressed to make a synthesis of the portents or a calculation of the statistical probabilities. Each chapter ends on fear or the symptoms (whether symbolic or realistic) of disintegration, which are, as it were, superseded and forgotten in the next opening. The reader is thus engaged in the apparent autonomy and reality of Gervaise's struggle, and at the same time registers the probabilities, the more permanent realities. *Her* very blindness to those realities is the guarantee, in terms of fictional convincingness, of the inevitability of her downfall; that inevitability is not *claimed* by her (or, when it is, the formulation is clearly shown to be partial and self-pitying); it is *shown* by the dwarfing of the individual will, the invasion of the individual purpose, which the massively constructed chapters body forth. (A measure of Zola's success is that his rare authorial comments seem unnecessary in their emphasis: as when, in the much-admired scene in the laundry where Gervaise weakly allows her drunken husband to kiss her, Zola adds the gloss: 'Et le gros baiser . . . était comme une première chute, dans le lent avachissement de leur vie.')

It is this ability to hold the meaning always present, to inform an apparently descriptive scene with it, which constitutes the strength of what can look at times like a self-indulgent pictorial art. Zola's predilection for scenes of festivity, for instance, is not just a descriptive trait, by Brueghel out of the *Madame Bovary* wedding-scene. The social event serves him both artistically and philosophically. Artistically because, while aiming at anthropological accuracy, he likes to portray what is exciting and colourful; and the celebration is the one aspect of working-class life which has a bit of colour, which frees him from the self-imposed drabness of his subject-matter. But there is a further purpose. The aim of social festivity, as most of us, and Zola's characters, understand it, is to escape from the real, to transcend it by a ritual which suspends personal suffering and social contingencies. The realism of Zola's portrayal consists in the demonstration that the transcendence, the escape, are impossible. The magnificent scene of the birthday dinner in *L'Assommoir*, for all its purely artistic virtuosity, illustrates this perfectly. It conforms structurally to the pattern just discussed, moving from the practical, forward-looking opening to an ending fraught for the reader with tokens of danger and disintegration— the re-entry of Gervaise's former lover under the cover of the reigning *bonhomie*, the general dissolution of will-power through alcohol. It is a high-point in a sense, the seal is set on Gervaise's position in the *quartier*, old enmities seem to be reconciled. But the episode's central position in the book, its marking of the top of the curve, does not blind us to the constants that it contains. Coupeau, Gervaise's already heavy-drinking husband, is missing when the festivities begin, and these have only been made possible by her first resort to the pawnshop. Harmony is established, but a precarious harmony still interrupted by mildly dissatisfied guests and old maman Coupeau admonishing père Bru: '. . . j'ai l'air d'être heureuse, n'est-ce pas? eh bien! je pleure plus d'une fois . . . Non, ne souhaitez pas d'avoir des enfants.'

Transcendence is achieved only momentarily, through alcohol. Alcohol is an artistic *trouvaille* for Zola, enabling him to transmute his scene beyond the bounds that sober realism would dictate for a dinner in a rather sordid tenement; and at the same time to show just how unreal the victories are, how they are only won at the expense of a weakening of individual autonomy. The society's 'sacrée envie de nocer' is itself the best proof of the dependence of the individual. For it is made abundantly clear, by that original use of the *style indirect libre* which sets the moral tone of *L'Assommoir*, that the party is, sociologically, a necessity, the only thing that makes life tolerable in such a society. Hence the consequences of the party, the re-entry of Lantier and the setting-up of the *ménage à trois*, are directly related to what is possible and necessary, by general consensus, in the world in which Gervaise lives. Gervaise is enthroned, almost canonized by the *quartier*, but that canonization itself, coming from so suspect a source, is also a token of her inevitable doom. In this chapter Zola, with extraordinary success, fuses the realistic and the symbolic. Gervaise is, literally, invaded; the pressures of life actually burst into and disrupt the artificially created security of the feast. The artistic operation, however, is completely unobtrusive, felt but hardly consciously registered by the reader beneath the din of the closing choruses of a successful evening.

Zola was to use this technique again, on a smaller scale, in *Germinal*. The scene of the *ducasse* has been analysed in part by Auerbach, who shows how different this is from a gratuitous and aesthetic approach to low-life, how every detail takes us back to the limitations of the miners' existence. The analysis could be taken further. The unstated aim of social events—that they should have no repercussions when ordinary life is resumed—is not achieved. Far from putting life aside in order to return to it invigorated, the characters plunge themselves deeper into life in the very midst of the feast. Again alcohol produces an artificial *bonhomie*, a lassitude in which irrevocable decisions are made and acts performed. Étienne decides to go to live with the Maheus, La Maheude reconciles herself to her son's marriage, children take their first steps in delinquency—and 'il dut se faire beaucoup d'enfants cette nuit-là'. And a particular theme of the novel, the relation of political purpose to the mass situation, itself gets treatment—of a pretty pessimistic kind. The dwarfing of the individual is again displayed, as Étienne incongruously tries to elaborate his plans for action amid the hubbub of music and the comings and goings of his listeners, who are more interested in enjoying one of their rare days off.

The end of the scene is sharply ironic: the reconciliation between Étienne and Chaval is mediated only through drink, and the
claim that in the fight against the bourgeois they would give all—'la
boisson et les filles'—rings hollow. The terrible closed plight of the
miners is revealed: the apparent purposiveness is little more than
impotence in festive disguise; and because it springs from an event,
the *ducasse*, which is so totally justifiable and 'necessary' in sociological terms, we have a sense, under the temporary optimism, of the
basic, desperate realities. This is the society at its best and its worst,
and we see that the attempt to pull itself up, to transcend itself,
represents an almost impossible hope.

These two scenes—and the structure of *L'Assommoir* as a whole
—are total artistic successes; but successes on the assumption that
we give a high value to what might be called the novel of defeat.
Their achievement lies in asserting and making concrete and undeniable the limitations under which the characters act. Such an
undertaking seems totally acceptable to us today, in relation to the
under-privileged of the nineteenth century; it was a protest that
needed to be made, which could afford to postpone questions of
responsibility and prognosis. But it was not acceptable at the time,
and the protests of Marxists, moralists, and trade-unionists are still
at least intelligible to us. The Marxist criticism of Zola is well
known—that he plays down or denies the existence of genuinely
dynamic elements in society; that he portrays detachedly, and ultimately complacently, tiny, tied men against a great backdrop of
realistic apparatus; that his world is static, pessimistically conceived, deterministic in the least constructive sense. This is a
variant of the simpler contemporary objection that the workers are
being calumniated, and not unconnected with the purely moral
objection that, while there obviously are people in social situations
so extreme that moral judgements become nonsense, they are not
an improving topic for fiction.

Some of the objections posed by the Marxists can arise even from
a sympathetic reading of *Germinal*; and it seems worth looking at
several of these points. They may at least clarify for us the implications of the novel of defeat and remind us of the terms on which we
accept it. They may also point to genuine conflicts of purpose in

Zola, as between social satire, determinism, and radicalism, which *could* justify a partly critical verdict, if not on moral or philosophical grounds, at least on grounds of literary incoherence.

First of all, then, there is the question of the ending. It is ambiguous, but how intentionally so? It is the kind of ending that the book needs if it is to justify the promise of its title, but does not the body of the novel in some sense cry out against it? Étienne strides away over the horizon like the hero in some ancient film; but his springing tread is as much the result of his escape from the mining community as of rational optimism; he thinks he hears the sound of picks prophesying victory—but they are the picks of men driven back to work after their strike has failed, victims of an apparently insuperable economic system. Apart from the particular question of Zola's temperamental timidity about the prospect of revolution, there does seem to be a genuine conflict between his radical and his scientific aspirations. The naturalist doctrine led him to categorize, to see all men and things as products, as the end-term rather than the first or the intermediate. It was difficult in these circumstances, even if he intended to, to introduce a really dynamic and autonomous *agent* into the scheme, to suggest ways in which ideas and action might affect the course of history. The disbelief in the dynamic may correspond with our own beliefs. But, if nothing more, we might want to make a purely literary point about the characterization of Étienne: does not Zola, perhaps, seem just a little over-hasty in turning him into a type, an example of the way that agitators go, offering through him a general and not very flattering anatomy of the idealist who inevitably succumbs to pride and personal ambition? It is dangerous of course to talk about an author being 'unfair' to a character of his own creation. The charge can only be meaningful if we feel we detect Zola pointing out Étienne's weaknesses before we have noticed them ourselves, giving us the impression that in real life he, Zola, would be predisposed to see what is caricatural, repetitive, typical in character, at the expense of what is personal and individual.

In other words the allegation might be that Zola's actual observation of reality was distorted by an Olympian, Flaubertian approach, which would be at odds with any serious political intention his better self might have had; and that the dynamic last page is a belated and unconvincing attempt to redress the balance. How far such a charge can be sustained could be examined by looking at the famous episode in which the strikers' cry for bread is counterpointed by the agony of the manager Hennebeau, who has discovered his wife's infidelity and, in an impassioned tirade to the unhearing crowd, castigates the folly of those who first saw happiness in economic and educational equality, and envies the miners their sexual *mores* and the lack of reflective consciousness which goes with them.

Zola, it seems to me, rejects Hennebeau, and the words 'le cri du ventre domina' represent the moral as well as the physical primacy of the workers' case. If so, Zola's avowed intention to 'mettre au-dessus de l'éternelle injustice des classes l'éternelle douleur des passions' is justified as an added complexity and is not merely a bit of hedging. Nevertheless, the incident hovers dangerously between the appearance of a genuinely embracing compassion and that of a more aesthetic pleasure in ironic juxtaposition for its own sake. It is a typical and powerful Zola confrontation, but ultimately slightly obscure, and not completely answering the question whether, even if we know that man cannot live by bread alone, this is precisely the moment in a seemingly radical novel to bring it up.

Two other points in *Germinal* which might interest our Marxist are the love story of Étienne and Catherine and the violent murder of Cécile by old Bonnemort. The consummation in the flooded mine is again a very powerful and characteristic Zola scene. But the whole horrific idyll, with its climax among the tokens of death, and precipitated only by the imminence of death, is, at the very least, profoundly alien to any public theme connected with progress. It is distantly related to other Zola idylls, in more congenial surroundings—and there are many of them, some mystical and sugary, others charming, like that of the children in *Le Ventre de Paris* (1873) who disport themselves among the chicken pluckings in the market. Such scenes seem to proceed from deep preoccupations of Zola's— visions of innocence and fears of corruption which are personal and poetic rather than scientific and observational. The crime of

Bonnemort, and the homicidal tendencies of Étienne himself, are the obverse side of this dual vision.

The purpose of these remarks is not to chip away at the stature of an undeniable masterpiece; I want to use them as pointers towards characteristics of other Zola novels, which are rightly less admired, though still for the most part immensely readable. For the retreat into Flaubertian irony and juxtaposition, the recurrence of the violent, often in its most unnatural forms, the idyllic in the face of defeat and death, the lyrical optimism based on pantheistic faith rather than political idealism—these are frequent and sometimes directing features of Zola's novels, they are what tends to take over when he breaks free from, or runs out of, documents. Their irruption in the documentary itself is significant. Zola hesitated over the death of Cécile and this suggests that he saw the danger of using as a symbol of pent-up social resentments a gesture which could all too easily be interpreted as a token of a more permanent human bestiality and irrationality. That he finally decided to use it shows how readily the mythopoeic takes over from the sober sociological imagination.

It was in fact not only bourgeois outrage which made Zola's contemporaries—and which makes us—feel that the novels describing bourgeois and upper-class life are less factually truthful than the working-class ones, makes us rejoin that life is not as bad, as uniform, as mechanically brutish as that. These novels are in fact more openly symbolical. Zola knew less, at any rate by the time of *Nana* (1880) and *Pot-Bouille* (1882), about domestic life in the upper levels of society than he did about the lower, with which years of youthful poverty had familiarized him. When documents failed, the myth-maker took over; the desire to give shape to private fears and visions was given its scope; while the political or social analysis is relegated to a minor role. Essentially these novels are extended images of evil, having only fitful connections with the ostensible satirical object, the corruptions of the Second Empire. There is a shrillness, an apocalyptic quality about the language which make us feel that it is more than the end of a regime that Zola is prophesying.

Significant in particular is Zola's evident assumption that Nana would be a suitable instrument for his political and social theme.

Nana, the daughter of Gervaise, and now a high-class prostitute, runs like a scourge through society and avenges the injustices done to her own class by creating a trail of misery, bankruptcy, and humiliation. It is a justified revenge, but we feel that what characterizes the book is Zola's interest in the means of the revenge, the sort of grandiose prurience with which he treats the manifestations of Nana's sexuality. This is a creature before whom her creator as well as her victims trembles; 'la bête d'or' stands for something more alluring and more dreadful than any of the wrongs that she sets out to avenge. Zola can only scotch her by a terrible death, which has little to do with either her profession or the society that produced her.

The same sort of vast elaborated image is to be found in *Pot-Bouille*. Again there is a powerful central idea—though one which has become rather hackneyed subsequently: Zola as it were takes the lid off one of the opulent, respectable apartment houses which were products of the re-building of Paris and tokens of the prosperity of the Empire, and shows the squalor, misery, and pleasureless promiscuity which the façade conceals. A class point is being made and, perhaps to the same degree as in *Madame Bovary*, an educational, an anti-convent point. But the scene is more horrific, more concentrated than life. Zola gets absorbed by the vision of the whited sepulchre, which he emphasizes by a striking recurrent scene: across the back court, away from the ornate façade, the servants, with inventive crudity, shout the latest scandal about their superiors, as they throw the garbage—reflection of the moral *ordures* of their masters—contemptuously down into the yard below. Caught up unexpectedly in one of these storms of vituperation and detritus, Octave and Berthe reflect not on the servant problem, or on the class problem, but on the corruption of the flesh.

As Lionel Trilling remarks, we read the book not as realistic social criticism but for its 'fierce energy, for the strange pleasure we habitually derive from the indictment of the human kind'. It is, he goes on, in the tradition of the 'massive comic morality' (it is in parts a very funny book); and the terms of comparison are Brueghel and Ben Jonson, Hogarth and Swift. In so far as it makes statistical implications and precise class references the book might still be accused of distorting social reality. But after reading *Pot-Bouille* we feel that the charge, if it is to be made, needs rephrasing in terms of a profounder disagreement with Zola's vision of life.

Jules Lemaître called the *Rougon-Macquart* series 'une épopée pessimiste de l'animalité humaine'. On the evidence of the whole work political pessimism certainly seems undeniable; the Marxists were right in doubting Zola's belief in the validity of political motivations or the reality of political arguments. The nearest we come to a serious presentation of such problems is in *Germinal*, and nowhere else is politics anything but caricaturally portrayed; indeed political discussion, as in *La Terre*, often takes place under the influence of drink. In *Le Ventre de Paris* we watch through the frosted glass of the revolutionaries' café the grotesque gesticulations of Florent's republican associates; and their words, equally, are parody versions of well-known positions. The central image of this book, the struggle between the fat and the thin, already suggests, by its Darwinian undertones, how easily Zola slips from the particular to the general, from satire to myth, from anti-Empire criticism to the illustration of a sort of evolutionary pessimism (for the fit are also the corrupt) which must be the despair of the Marxist. It need not, however, be our despair. *Le Ventre de Paris* is one of Zola's most humane works, as well as one of his most professional performances. The values of the losing side—the market-gardener Mme Françoise with her distrust of 'ce diable de Paris', Florent the born victim, the artist Claude who exploits the markets as beautiful spectacle, the children for whom it is a colourful playground—these are finely realized; and in spite of the mythic conception of the subject the satire of glutted materialism remains fairly specific. There is real force of social truth in the picture of the bourgeois closing their ranks when Florent needs protection. Here, at least, an uncomfortably precise point is being made, and we feel that Claude's final comment, 'Quels gredins que les honnêtes gens!', has been justified in fictional terms.

The visions of corruption and innocence, then, coexist, but corruption is quantitatively dominant; and Zola systematizes one aspect of this vision in a late novel, *La Bête humaine* (1890), which explicitly sets the dream of progress against the unalter-

able realities of the beast in man. The setting this time is the
railways:

> Montrer toujours le flot de voyageurs circulant [Zola notes in his
> *ébauche*], . . . l'échange des idées, la transformation des nations, le mélange
> des races, la marche vers une unification universelle. Les idées qui se
> répandent, se pénètrent et s'unifient. Et sur ce fond, sur ce roulement
> mécanique des trains, sur ce résultat intellectuel et social, montrer le
> statu quo du sentiment, la sauvagerie qui est au fond de l'homme, par
> mon drame mystérieux et poignant. Voilà l'hérédité de la bête, le mari
> qui se rue sur l'amant, Étienne qui tue par atavisme : le lointain homme
> primitif . . .

Yet in spite of the clear thesis there perhaps remains in the novel a
trace of Zola's deepest confusions and contradictions. For there is
still a sort of radical intention. The story is an attack on corruption
in high places. But Zola, significantly, thought that he could marry
his satire with a portrayal of the deeper and more permanent corruption in the heart of man, that it was fictionally safe to embody
that corruption in the victims of society rather than in the per-
secutors. As this broader theme takes over, the exact status and
purpose of the detail of railway organization becomes problematical;
it seems rather an artificial elaboration. It might have been more
fully justified if Zola had run a minor theme, illustrating perhaps
the disintegrating social effects of the new system. Certainly there is
a hint of this—the engine-driver with a wife in every terminus is an
authentic naturalist phenomenon. Zola toys with this theme, but it
becomes submerged in a horror story as compulsive for Zola as for
the characters themselves.

The conflict of intention comes up more overtly in another strange
and impressive novel, *La Joie de vivre* (1884). Here Zola's two
great preoccupations, the radical, positivist belief in science and
progress, and the physiological view of human conduct, come into
almost head-on collision. Lazare, as Zola's notes show, is meant to
be an attack on the new generation of pessimists, imbued with
Schopenhauer, whom he saw as endangering progress. In the
setting of the decaying house on the misty, windswept Brittany
coast Zola builds up a Chekhovian atmosphere of boredom and
doom; but also of physical illness and malaise, which makes a firm

satirical purpose virtually impossible. Lazare's inertia and fears
may be intended as a critical warning, but they are so persistently
described in neurological terms that we become increasingly uncertain whether we are in the presence of a clash of philosophical
systems or a fatalistic impression of things as they genetically are.
The forces of balance and sanity represented by Pauline are likewise genetically determined. It may be lack of positivist faith that
stops Lazare carrying out his projects; but Pauline's oddly detached
charitable activities, born of a calm good nature so imperturbable
as almost to qualify as amoral, can hardly relate to any practical
social programme. Give us the genes and we'll get on with the job—
this seems the only moral we can extract from the novel. Virtue and
life in fact are defeated: Lazare's mother suffers an appalling death,
the old servant hangs herself, the father is mutilated by gout, even
the dog dies after tracing out its path with the drippings of an inces-
sant haemorrhage. What are we to make of the final comment of
Chanteau? As his little grandson takes his first steps towards him
he hears the news of the servant's suicide, and this wreck of a man
comments incredulously: 'Faut-il être bête pour se tuer!' There
may be some irony here at his expense, in that he keeps alive only
because his gluttony makes it worth his while, worth while even to
suffer the agony which transgression of his diet brings on. But it is
not just ironical; if nothing else the insistence of the endings of so
many of the other novels makes this clear. *Germinal*, *La Terre*,
L'Argent, and *La Débâcle* end on what is essentially an irrational
praise of life, of the goodness of nature. The question remains—
what are the sources of this optimism, and are they adequately and
concretely embodied in the novels? In the last novel of the series
Dr. Pascal witnesses the violent extinction of several of his hereditarily depraved and degenerate family. Again Zola spares us
nothing in horror: the paralysed centenarian foundress of the line,
Tante Dide, dies after a last spasm of life, having watched her
haemophiliac great-great-grandson bleed to death unaided at her
feet. Pascal himself doubts of science and ponders the family tree
in vain to find an answer to the way things are tending. Yet the book
then turns straight from horror to idyll, and the union of Pascal
with his niece Clothilde—genetically unpromising, one might have

thought—produces a child in whom the hopes of Pascal, now placed in love and work rather than science, seem destined to be fulfilled.

The conclusion must be that, while the duality of his outlook was genuine, Zola's attempt to express it in his work does not entirely escape an appearance of arbitrariness. The move towards an optimistic resolution is likewise authentic: the ending of *Le Docteur Pascal* (1893) was no doubt dictated in large part by the new happiness Zola found, after many years of childless marriage, in his fruitful liaison with Jeanne Rozerot. This happiness certainly helped him to embark, with his unique energy, after finishing the twenty-year task of the *Rougon-Macquart*, on *Les Trois Villes* (1894-8) and later on the *Quatre Évangiles* (1899-1903), in which he was to sing more overtly the praises of work, fecundity, and social justice. But the weakening of imaginative power in the last works suggests that the former tensions, whatever their adverse effects, were essential to the creative process.

Poetic and affective qualities apart, then, the working-class novels remain the greatest achievement, as raising the least obtrusive problems, affording the most comprehensive and satisfactory demonstrations. If the others are to be criticized, however, it should be not so much in relation to a programme or a previous expectation, as on grounds of internal contradictions and shortcomings. If we criticize Zola's recurrent violence or obsession with the sexual it will be not so much because it is pessimistic or portrays society unrealistically, as because it is sometimes suspect of becoming a routine artistic convenience. Zola may have believed in the physiological drives as the most important, but he also knew that he was bad anyway at portraying complex types. There is a story of a conversation in which Zola repeatedly tried to make Flaubert agree that the sexual impulse was all there is to love: 'N'est-ce pas, au total, qu'il n'y a que ça?' But Flaubert in malicious mood would go no further than: 'Oui, oui, il y a de ça.' We detect here perhaps not only a philosophical question but a plea for aesthetic justification, Zola's hope that the depersonalized *mâle* and *femelle* into which his characters fitfully turn would not be ruled artistically out of court. The real specifically literary vice is to indulge one's own clichés, to narrow one's vision of the world to suit one's artistic shortcomings. There is, it has been suggested, some suspicion of this wilful simplification in the characterization of Étienne in *Germinal*. And it is in this sense, and in this sense only, that the common reader, whom Angus Wilson answers in his discussion of *La Terre*, can be justified in complaining that, especially after he has accepted Palmyre's incest out of pity with her hair-lipped cretinous brother, two rapes in one field, in a single afternoon, is overdoing it a bit.

If we criticize the pessimism itself, it must again be on grounds of literary incoherence—when Zola seems to promise us one thing and give us another, to be unaware of the implications of his method; to promise ideas and give us fatality, to counsel hope with the evidence for despair. At the seat of these confusions is his very choice of the Rougon-Macquart family as the bearers of his meaning. The hereditarily depraved family seemed both a perfect instrument for demonstrating the genetic laws and a convenient symbol for a satirical attack on the Empire from a liberal standpoint. But the device was more powerful than Zola suspected, its choice sprang from deeper psychic sources than he knew. Whichever way he turned it, it refused to serve him exactly as he hoped. When he attempted constructive satire it often produced what looked like a closed symbolic world of total corruption, in which no progress could be hoped for. If he introduced positive ideas, they sorted oddly with the human raw materials, so that he was driven more and more into trying to correct the balance by introducing fragments of faith and goodness, which he can admire and believe in but can see no systematic way of propagating.

Yet if we get outside the strictly literary critical approach, Zola's is an appealing and understandable predicament. It is part of the wider nineteenth-century crisis about science. Belief in science seemed to Zola the only way forward from superstitition and tyranny. Yet science threatened to deny our freedom to initiate the very progress he wanted. If belief in science was salutary in itself we might be put in the position of being saved only by believing ourselves damned: it was perhaps the first time that a purely secular philosophy had threatened men with such a paradox. But it is a common one of the century, and Zola embodies it in an array

of the most striking and original images. His waverings were
genuine; and when, in the *ébauche* for *L'Argent*, he noted 'je
voudrais, dans ce roman, ne pas conclure au dégoût de la vie', he
was not just reminding himself to give the public variety—though
as a good professional he recognized the need for that. Perhaps
salvation *would* come from enlightened capitalism, perhaps the
laissez-faire sophistries of the end of the novel ('l'argent . . . le
ferment de toute végétation sociale, le terreau nécessaire aux
grands travaux') *were* true. Zola could not decide, nor could he
finally read the riddle of the genes. The nineteenth-century doubter:
as such he reminds us—a final paradox—of the perfect English
gentleman who attacked him so contemptuously:

> Rip your brothers' vices open, strip your own foul passions bare;
> Down with Reticence, down with Reverence—forward—naked—let
>   them stare . . .

> Set the maiden fancies wallowing in the troughs of Zolaism,
> Forward, forward, ay and backward, downward too into the abysm.

So Tennyson wrote, execrably, in *Locksley Hall Sixty Years After*.
But the speculative parts of his own *In Memoriam* strangely resemble
those last-page meditations in which Zola and his characters put
their trust in some 'but lointain et obscur', in 'la terre . . . qui refait
continuellement de la vie pour son but ignoré, même avec nos
abominations et nos misères'. For Tennyson, too, science brought
no certain comfort, the natural world was red in tooth and claw, a
thousand types were gone and belief in progress could be no more
than an act of faith:

> And yet we trust that somehow good
> Will be the final goal of ill,
> To pangs of nature, sins of will,
> Defects of doubt, and taints of blood.

Taints of blood: Tennyson did not know just how much it was safe
to hope for in regard to those taints of blood; and neither, except at
times in the facile final period, did Zola. Perhaps, in the present
state of literary and historical fashion, it would be a fitting com-
pliment to honour him as a great Victorian.

NOTE

ÉMILE ZOLA, 1840-1902, was brought up at Aix-en-Provence (the 'Plassans' of his novels). His father, an engineer, died when he was six, and his beginnings in the literary world of Paris were hampered by poverty. Once established, he settled down to an ordered and immensely productive professional life. Various literary and scientific influences of the sixties led him to the conception of his novel series *Les Rougon-Macquart: histoire naturelle et sociale d'une famille sous le Second Empire*, the twenty volumes of which were completed in the years 1871–93. Zola also attempted theatre and short stories, was a prolific journalist, and acted as leader and spokesman of the naturalist group of writers (his most important theoretical work was *Le Roman expérimental*, 1880). Zola's novels frequently outraged public opinion, but on the whole his life was uneventful until his intervention in the Dreyfus affair (1897-8), when his pro-Dreyfus article *J'accuse* brought him many enemies. He died of asphyxia, under rather mysterious circumstances, and the theory of assassination is periodically revived.

Editions. Zola's novels are easily accessible: all the *Rougon-Macquart* novels as well as *Thérèse Raquin*, their most important predecessor, have been reprinted by Le Livre de Poche. The first critical edition of the works was by Zola's son-in-law, Maurice Le Blond (1928-9), but this has been improved upon by the five-volume Bibliothèque de la Pléiade edition of the *Rougon-Macquart* (1960-7) by A. Lanoux and H. Mitterand.

Criticism. A succinct history of the naturalist movement may be found in P. Martino, *Le Naturalisme français* (1923). The most scholarly and comprehensive general study of Zola is F. W. J. Hemmings, *Émile Zola* (2nd ed., 1966), which also contains a valuable bibliography. Other useful introductions are G. Robert, *Émile Zola. Principes et caractères généraux de son œuvre* (1952), Angus Wilson, *Émile Zola* (1952), the relevant part of H. Levin, *The Gates of Horn* (1963), E. M. Grant, *Émile Zola* (1966), J. C. Lapp, *Les Racines du naturalisme: Zola avant les Rougon-Macquart* (1972), and A. Dezalay, *Lectures de Zola* (1973). J. H. Matthews, in *Les deux Zola* (1957), studies the combination of the scientific and the subjective in Zola's work. H. Barbusse, *Zola* (1932), is highly individualistic, but contains an interesting critique of Zola's political attitudes. A more academically expressed Marxist viewpoint is that of G. Lukács in *Studies in European Realism* (English translation, 1950). Hostile contemporary reaction may be studied in F. Brunetière, *Le Roman naturaliste* (1891), and Henry James's more favourable response in the essays collected under the title *The House of Fiction* (1957). E. Auerbach, in Chapter 19 of *Mimesis* (English translation, 1957), analyses passages from *Germinal*; my argument on *L'Assommoir* may be found in greater detail in I. Gregor and B. Nicholas, *The Moral and the Story* (1962).

11. Literature and Ideology: 1880–1914

On 9 December 1893 a home-made bomb exploded in the Chamber of Deputies. Thrown by a poverty-stricken anarchist, Auguste Vaillant, it killed no one, although in the confusion several deputies claimed to be mortally wounded. As the uproar subsided the voice of the Chamber's president M. Dupuy was heard: 'Messieurs, la séance continue.' Together, Vaillant's bomb and Dupuy's sense of continuity appeared to symbolize *fin-de-siècle* France, a period of violent change, excitement, and diversion in which old familiar issues were perpetuated with stubborn conviction.

The popular newspapers of the 1890s point to the more sensational aspects of change. The first motor cars and bicycles and the new fashions in sea bathing gave columnists and cartoonists their spectacular vocabulary and holiday humour, while by comparison Debussy's impressionist setting of Mallarmé's 'Prélude à l'après-midi d'un faune' in 1892 and the discovery in 1898 of radium by Pierre and Marie Curie received little publicity. In December 1895, however, most shades of opinion were arrested by news of the first moving pictures. Invented by the brothers Lumière of Lyon, a cinematographic device was set up on the Boulevard des Capucines in a showman's booth. Within a week the future pioneer of the French cinema, Georges Méliès, had offered to buy the invention. He was refused—the device, said the Lumière brothers, had no commercial value—but by 1900 he had established his own film studio at Montreuil. Under Méliès and, later, Gaumont and Pathé, the new art and industry mirrored its own nature by the speed of its development, and movement became a cultural term. The car, the cinema, and later the aeroplane rivalled the primitivism of Gauguin, the expressionism of Van Gogh, and the architectural modulations of Cézanne as inspiration for the pre-war art world.

More fundamental, if less spectacular, was social mobility. 'Les villes tentaculaires', in Verhaeren's poetic image, were realities answering the steady 3 per cent drift from the country decade by decade since 1848. In the nineties this urbanization was further propelled by a minor industrial revolution. Between 1892 and 1902 the application of power to industrial establishments increased by over 400 per cent, bringing France into more realistic competition with Germany and Britain. Behind Méline's protective tariffs of 1892, industrial output expanded to give confidence to a republican regime shaken by a series of financial scandals and political crises. In response to this forceful drive by capital, labour organized itself more effectively in the C.G.T. (Confédération Générale du Travail), founded in 1895 and pledged to revolutionary action by strikes, boycotts, and industrial sabotage. In practice it enrolled only a minority of workers, but the violence of its syndicalist theory was sufficient to alarm even the most radical of the forces of order: in 1908 Georges Clemenceau became a breaker of strikes.

Conflict can thus be added to movement as a positive value emerging in this period of rapid change. A third value was the activism of youth, perhaps the most significant feature of late-nineteenth-century France. In the 1880s the educational reforms of Jules Ferry and his colleague Paul Bert had made primary schooling compulsory and had extended the quantity and range of secondary and university education. The anticlerical nature of the reforms made the subject one of envenomed controversy. Attention was focused sharply on the role of youth in society, and church and republic competed for the right to inoculate their own particular world views. France was fighting over its young, and for the first time youth became a major social and political force. It was flattered by political leaders and religious authorities and its own vigour and idealism became the norm of political behaviour and religious commitment. This vigour society endorsed, but it remained punitive towards adolescent crimes, which rose steeply during the nineties, and it was horrified by the fact that the two famous anarchists of 1894, Émile Henry, who threw a bomb into the crowded Café Terminus, and

Jeronimo Santo Caserio, who assassinated President Carnot, were aged eighteen and twenty-one respectively.

In 1900 much of the spirit of change, movement, and activism was embodied in the Paris International Exhibition. France proclaimed itself finally rejuvenated, modernized, and confident after the military defeat of 1870, the succession of crises, and a long economic slump in the 1880s. The visiting business world was received by Millerand, the first socialist minister in Europe, and to the assertive Tour Eiffel had been added another impressive steel construction, the Pont Alexandre III, and two monumental buildings of eclectic style, the Grand and the Petit Palais. Designed as permanent museums and exhibition halls they replaced the old Palais de l'Industrie, remembered as the scene of the most macabre exhibition of the century. Calcinated bodies had been brought there after 125 people had been burned alive on 4 May 1897 at the opening of the fashionable Bazar de la Charité, an annual event sponsored by members of Parisian high society whose charitable activities occupied a regular column in *Le Figaro*. It was noted by militant women that only five men were among the victims, by occultists that the Angel Gabriel had foretold the fire through the clairvoyant Henriette Couedon, and by sceptics of progress that the blaze had started in the cinematographic room. A later, more analytic observation was that the fire had decimated the paternalist classes and had contributed, together with debts and the First World War, to the final decline of the French aristocracy.

Throughout these changes of the nineties the issues which had exercised French polemic since the eighteenth century were forcibly restated. In the years 1898-9 the headlines were captured by the conflicts of the Dreyfus Affair, whose issues cut deeply into society. The historian Daniel Halévy was divided from his friend Degas, Anatole France from the younger critic Jules Lemaître, Marcel Proust from the cartoonist Forain, and one half of France from the other. Ostensibly about the guilt or innocence of Alfred Dreyfus, a Jewish officer convicted in 1894 of treason, the Affair produced an embittered debate on the past, present, and future of France. The Dreyfusards appealed to a long republican and revolutionary tradition of justice and the rights of man; the

TRINITY COLLEGE
LIBRARY

anti-Dreyfusards to an even longer memory of authority, hierarchy, and basic Catholic values. Hugo's line was repeated by the protagonists of both sides: 'C'est ici le combat du jour et de la nuit', and the apparent clarity of the issues gave to the Affair the quality of civil war, more verbally acute because armed violence was avoided. In Dupuy's phrase, the séance, on which France had been engaged for over a hundred years, continued.

But the symbol is not an exact one. Dupuy's words and Vaillant's bomb may have been contrasts of continuity and change, but between the vicious debates of the Dreyfus Affair and the changes at the end of the century there is a close interrelationship. Despite the familiarity of the conflicts, the Affair is as much an index of change as the Exhibition of 1900. The very conduct of the Affair had a motorized character: generated by belligerent journalism and powered by angry protests, duels, and accusations of conspiracy, it moved with all the noise and unpredictability of an early Renault.

The most striking synthesis of continuity and change was the new nationalism. Emotionally expressed in the writings of Maurice Barrès and institutionalized in the Ligue de la Patrie Française and later in the movement of the Action Française, it was dedicated to the saints of old France, but based on popular anti-Dreyfusism. In the doggerel of Francœur, one of the League's unknown poets, as in the speeches of Barrès and the League's president Jules Lemaître, an old élitism was united with a new mass appeal:

> Pour sauver ma patrie et l'arracher vivante
> Aux mains de ses bourreaux, s'il en est temps encore,
> Et pendant que Judas trahit et met en vente
> Son honneur et sa foi pour quelques lingots d'or,
> Des Français, grands d'instinct à l'âme magnanime,
> Ardents dans la mêlée au devant du danger
> Se dressent résolus . . .
>
> France! regarde et vois! ton horizon se dore
> De rayons tout nouveaux. En Dieu seul mets ta foi!
> Ta voix redeviendra ce qu'elle était, sonore,
> Pour proclamer encore: Je suis le peuple Roi.

The mixture of traditionalism and demagogic ardour was hardened into a particular doctrine by the vitriolic leader of the Action Française, Charles Maurras, who rejuvenated the dying concepts of aristocratic virtue and monarchical authority. The deafness and provincial origin of this young literary intellectual, combined with his admiration for the culture and politics of Periclean Athens, produced a rancorous hatred for the chaos and conflicts of Paris during the Affair. In a situation of extremism he proposed an extreme solution. 'Pour que vécût la France', he maintained, 'il fallait que revînt le Roi.' This passion for monarchy distinguished Maurras from Barrès, Lemaître, and the League, one of whose branches at Sedan included in its aims: 'De revendiquer les libertés qui sont de l'essence même du régime républicain.' By comparison, Maurras was a defiant reactionary, but his remorseless denunciation of Jews, Protestants, Freemasons, and all established interests of the Dreyfusards was radical in both tone and method. Nationalists, whether monarchist or republican, met on this aggressive platform, and the properties of revolutionary thought and action, for over a century the monopoly of the political Left, were adopted by the forces of tradition. Like working-class syndicalists, the ideologues of the new nationalism became openly subversive.

Barrès, Maurras, and Lemaître in their role as prophets presented nationalism as a spiritual awakening of France. From this it has been argued that French nationalism, like the later phenonemon of Fascism, was a secular religion compensating for a declining Christianity. But at the turn of the century the Church in France was far from moribund. Catholicism had been expected to wither away in the harsh light of positivist analysis, but at the end of a century dominated by scientific and technological advance it moved dramatically on to the offensive. The two decades before the war saw a resurgence of Catholic doctrine and activity which affected even that student matrix of anticlericalism, the École Normale Supérieure. In 1898 the *normaliens* led the vanguard of active Dreyfusism against Army and Church: by 1913 a third of the École Normale was Catholic. The revival was as powerful a compound of old and new as nationalism, but its character was more diffuse. At one extreme the influential literature of Léon Bloy,

J.-K. Huysmans, Paul Bourget, and Paul Claudel (discussed below) idealized the authoritarian hierarchical nature of Catholicism and maintained the virtues of peasant faith against the character of the Republic, pilloried by Bloy as 'athée, rénégate, apostate, sacrilège, parricide, infanticide . . .'. By contrast, a young ex-officer, Marc Sangnier, seen by his wife as Ibsen's Brand, founded 'Le Sillon' in 1898, a movement of popular Catholicism and Socialism, which shocked the *bien-pensants* by supporting the Russian Revolution of 1905 and by displaying the evils of capitalism in a 'Salon de la Misère'. The extremes had one feature in common: an active idealism which responded to the exigencies of the period by a positive reaffirmation of traditional Catholic values. The difference lay in the values selected.

The position of youth in these various movements was a central one. Where the bicycle gave escape from parental control, the aristocratic doctrines of Maurras, the romanticism of the literary Catholics, and the social commitment of Sangnier all provided an escape from the positivistic materialism of the republican fathers. Bourget's novels gained a large public within middle-class youth; the Action Française formed the 'Camelots du Roi', a cohort of young activists; and Marc Sangnier was surrounded by admiring young men, including François Mauriac, who were organized into 'La Jeune Garde' to perform modern acts of chivalry, a vocation recollected in Mauriac's first novel *L'Enfant chargé de chaînes* (1913). The accent throughout was on the dynamic experience of conversion, political or religious. Enthusiasm was self-justifying and moderation condemned as an attempt to compromise with scepticism, or, as particularized by Péguy, 'ne pas faire sourire M. Anatole France'.

Much of the significant creative writing of the eighties and nineties needs to be set within this frame of reference. Many works of fiction and drama reflect, either in the distortions of their formal structure, or in their appeal to transcendental modes of experience, or in the violence of their language, the ideological strains of the period and, more narrowly, its powerful current of irrationalism. This current appears in the literature of the 'Catholic Revival', where a central preoccupation with a revitalized Catholic faith is combined with genuine imaginative force and originality. This kind of Catholicism is characterized by an almost elemental directness of response to the Christian revelation, by trust in unanalysed insights, disdain for the intellect, and contempt for the whole apparatus of popular religious art ('la bondieuserie').

The religious writers who are important in this context (Léon Bloy, J.-K. Huysmans, Paul Claudel, and Charles Péguy) are united by no common aesthetic and while remaining, though not always without strain, within the broad spectrum of Catholic ortho-doxy, they tend in their individual ordering of religious experience to grant a privileged status to quite different theological notions. For example, poverty is crucial to Bloy's view of the Christian life, while Huysmans is deeply concerned with vicarious suffering, and Péguy with the Incarnation of Christ. Nor ought these writers, for whom the simplicities of the Creed are a living reality, to be con-fused with an influential literary precursor like Barbey d'Aurevilly in whose fiction, notably *Un Prêtre marié* (1865) and *Les Dia-boliques* (1874), Catholicism is largely an aesthetic convention and its system of beliefs a source of equivocal metaphysical thrills. A distinction needs further to be maintained between these major religious writers and a conservative novelist like Paul Bourget for whom Catholicism represents a precious instrument of social cohesion and a tested system of morality rather than a blinding revelation transforming the quality of spiritual life. In the same way, though Maurice Barrès and Charles Maurras are beneficiaries of the revival of religious faith, in the sense that it creates a climate of feeling and thought congenial to their own versions of patriotism, they view Catholicism principally as an institutional fact important in accounting for the unity and continuity of French society.

Even within the community of fervent believers, significant dif-ferences of emphasis divide the major writers of the Revival, with their appeal to an almost primitive faith, from 'modernist' theo-logians and young Thomist intellectuals, like Jacques Maritain, whose approach was felt to smack too much of the methods of the 'atheistical' Sorbonne. In much the same spirit, Léon Bloy was never quite able to reconcile himself to aspects of Huysmans's religious observance, which was always marked by intense aesthetic preoccupations. In a consciously 'decadent' novel like *A rebours* (1884) these preoccupations take the form of a loving elaboration of aesthetic surface (exotic furnishings, rare book-bindings, etc.), but they persist, too, in the later novels which chart in fictional terms Huysmans's own conversion to Catholicism. In the Satanism of *Là-bas* (1891) religious themes become assimilated to a literary mode and function like the properties of the novel of terror earlier in the century. Elsewhere, this aestheticism is transposed into a fascination with the detail of church architecture (*La Cathédrale*, 1898) or into elaborate investigations of plain-song, priestly vestments, and the symbolic beauties of the liturgy (*L'Oblat*, 1903). Even the experience of Christian endurance and sacrifice, so strongly present in Huysmans's obsession with vicarious suffering, often tends to be refracted through the medium of art, as in the many references to the crucifixions of Grünewald. These preoccupations, like the richly mannered style and syntax by which they are conveyed, offer the polar opposite of Bloy's direct and impatient faith and provoke the satirical verve of his allusions to the 'école des Rares' and the 'esthétique de la prière'.

The degree to which the literature of the Revival reflects both the mystery of religious faith and the revenge of sensibility and imagination upon the prosaic vision of positivism is illustrated with special vividness in the work of Léon Bloy. In the chaotic novel *Le Désespéré* (1886), Bloy draws upon his own experience for the story of Caïn Marchenoir, his religious conversion and relations with a prostitute, Véronique. In a gesture which is intended to convey her saintly simplicity, Véronique has all her teeth extracted and cuts off her hair in order to destroy Marchenoir's passion for her. Her 'sublime' action simply exacerbates his love, and the relationship persists and is crowned by religious visions in which the divine symbolism of history is revealed to the lovers. Finally, Véronique becomes insane and, on his way back from a visit to the asylum to which she has been committed, Marchenoir is run over and dies without benefit of the sacraments. This plot alone serves to epitomize Bloy's radical break with the themes and preoccupations of the

conventional French novel of the period and to illustrate his
restoration of religious, and even mystical, experience to a centrally
important place in fiction, though this experience is seen in terms
that are eccentric both to institutionalized Catholicism and to
received morality.

One of the dominant metaphors in Bloy's writings is that of
history as a timeless drama in which the sufferings of the world are
a re-enactment of, and participation in, Christ's Passion. This conception reposes on a system of symbolic correspondences which
equates the poor with Christ, and money, the fruit of the suffering
of the poor, with the blood of Christ. Such an insight tends to raise
Bloy's own destitution to the level of a sacred myth and to imply
a radical critique of capitalist society, of the Catholic bourgeoisie
who benefit from it, and of their Church which, to the degree that
it does not condemn their wealth, consecrates their economic status.
The mystique of poverty, already present in *Le Désespéré*, emerges
as the theme which unifies the structure of his second novel, *La
Femme pauvre* (1897), in which the heroine, Clotilde Maréchal,
after experiencing various kinds of moral degradation, contracts a
marriage of dire poverty that is made meaningful for her and her
husband by the constant striving towards sanctity in which they
are engaged.

Bloy's picture of life lived at subsistence level is so authentic, his
sense of the waste-land of modern materialism so acute, and his
insight into human despair so true that they help one to understand, if not always to tolerate, the endemic violence of his work.
In spite of Maritain's defence of it, we are right to be sceptical of
Bloy's 'charity', if only because of the characteristic and odious glee
which colours the entry in his *Journal* about the fire at the Bazar
de la Charité and in which the only regret he expresses for those
'belles dames . . . carbonisées' is that there were too few of them:
'Le petit nombre des victimes . . . limitait ma joie.' Bloy's significance transcends the scatological obsessions which permeate his
work, though these are an index to a more generalized disgust with
the world. It lies mainly in his aspiration towards a more intense
experience of religion and his indictment of a callous and materialistic society. This self-styled 'pilgrim of the Absolute' is fanatically

at odds not only with the principles and forms of a secularized Third Republic but also with a conventional Catholicism which, in his eyes, risks dwindling from a vital faith to the status of a hollow bourgeois ritual.

This power of articulating a whole imaginary universe about the vicissitudes of the spiritual life and of rendering those vicissitudes with the colour and energy of melodrama prefigures something of Claudel's theatre, and, later, of the fiction of Bernanos. In Claudel's plays, the rage against bourgeois materialistic society, which, in Bloy, takes the form of a rather demented anticipation of the imminent end of the world, is transposed into brief apocalyptic flashes, as in the first version of *La Ville* (1890), where the denunciation of bourgeois society is accompanied by the implication that only total destruction of it will allow a truly Christian society to emerge. The same idea recurs in *L'Échange* (1894), where the burning down of the house of the millionaire Thomas Pollock Nageoire clearly functions as a symbolic destruction of capitalist society. The old order needs not so much to change as to collapse, which is symbolically what occurs in *Tête d'Or* (1890) when the king who represents that order is killed by the hero. Here Claudel, on his own admission, has been infected by the anarchist terrorism of the period.

In its ramifying formal structure, Claudel's drama is the image of the complexity of the relationships between human and divine, temporal and eternal within a universe divinely created and sustained. The tragedy of Simon Agnel, the adventurer and model of human energy who is the main agent of *Tête d'Or*, lies precisely in the fact that he is blind to this pattern and believes he can find salvation in himself alone. Even *Partage de midi* (1906), the most incandescent image of erotic passion in Claudel's entire theatre, connects sexual desire with the 'desire and pursuit of the whole', sees human love as a mode of aspiring to the divine, and so sets it within the perspectives of eternity. The relationship of the human to the divine, so central to Claudel's vision, is perhaps most dramatically stated in the miracle which lies at the heart of *L'Annonce faite à Marie* (1912) where Mara's dead child is resurrected by her leper-sister Violaine. Violaine's disease has been contracted through the

kiss she gave in charity and forgiveness to the homeless leper and
builder of churches, Pierre de Craon, and her subsequent death
from an accident engineered by the envious Mara is invested with
a radiance which symbolizes the power of sacrificial innocence to
transcend a corrupt world.

Precisely because his dramátic action always points to that other
dimension in which God is seen to move, and to a providential
design transcending individual human schemes, Claudel's theatre
tends in its religious impulse to lead him beyond the national
boundaries of France (though there are moments of crude chauvinism in his work) and even beyond the limits of Christendom.
Péguy's poetic universe, on the other hand, though also concerned
with suffering, sacrifice, and the workings of divine providence, is
even more strongly identified with French society and a cult of
French national grandeur. His great contemporary, it has been
acutely said, is the Third Republic and he epitomizes in his own
career the reforms which provided universal primary state education with its related republican ideology of 'esprit civique' and
'esprit laïc', though he becomes a severe critic of competitive merit
and its replacement of the 'world of work' by the 'world of talent'.
As poet and polemicist, he achieves a kind of exemplary status for
his generation because he reflects in his own vicissitudes the conflicting ideological currents of the two decades preceding the First
World War.

Brought up in poverty in Orléans by an illiterate grandmother
and a young widowed mother who mended chairs for a living,
Charles Péguy seems to have broken with the Catholic faith of his
forebears round about 1891 and to have embraced a kind of guild
socialism, strengthened by the socialists he met on his entry into
the École Normale Supérieure in 1894 and of whom the most
remarkable were Lucien Herr and Jean Jaurès. Péguy's socialism,
as idiosyncratic as his restored Catholic faith was later to be, is
embodied explicitly in the moral idealism of *Marcel: premier
dialogue de la cité harmonieuse* (1898) which, with its faith in
human perfectibility and its dreams of an economic and social
utopia, expresses a luminous fable of human equality and solidarity
based on the abolition of private property. However, *Marcel* is

fundamentally ambiguous, its egalitarian commonwealth being shot through with intimations of a spiritual life connecting the individual soul, the family, and the community. It is rooted in a concrete sense of the misery of the poor, but it also exhibits a mystical strain. That is why it is easy to reconcile it with Péguy's dramatic trilogy, *Jeanne d'Arc* (1897), where Saint Joan's life is seen in terms of both spiritual and temporal salvation, her human suffering and frailty strongly emphasized and her compassion for the poor combined with revolt against both human and divine injustice. The dedication to *Marcel*, with its reference to those who have lived and died for the cause of good and the founding of the 'Universal Socialist Republic', aptly characterizes the book's underlying tendencies. The Dreyfus Affair intensified Péguy's commitment to socialism and provoked him into disclaiming any ties with Christianity. Subsequently, the whole burden of his thought was to identify the defence of Dreyfus with a uniquely privileged moment of the human conscience and to elevate Dreyfusism to the status of a mystique, using it as a touchstone for political morality and an index to true Republican virtue.

To move from the world of Péguy's *Jeanne d'Arc* (1897) to that of the mystery plays of his later years is to be made aware of a decisive spiritual shift. *Le Mystère de la charité de Jeanne d'Arc* (1910), *Le Porche du mystère de la deuxième vertu* (1911), *Le Mystère des saints innocents* (1912), and the epic poem *Ève* (1913) restate man's quest for salvation in terms so fully mystical as to be incompatible with a secular ideology like socialism. In fact, they reflect Péguy's return to Catholicism, which dates formally from a period of illness in August–September 1908, but which seems to have taken place as early as 1906. Several factors contributed to this change of heart. Fatigue, and disappointment with the failure of his remarkable periodical, *Les Cahiers de la Quinzaine* (founded in January 1900), to reach a larger public must be counted among them. There were also doubts about the validity of purely material solutions to human problems and about the secularists' confidence in continuous and unlimited progress. These misgivings were strengthened by specific acts of political policy. Péguy felt that the alliance between radicals and socialists which followed on the

radicals' convincing victory at the polls in 1902 was fatally compromising to revolutionary purity. He also became progressively
alienated from his former political friends because of the socially
divisive effects of the Combes ministry's anti-clerical legislation
(1902–5) with its wholesale dissolution of religious orders and its
attacks on Catholic schools. To these strains must be added the
dramatic effect produced on him by the Tangier crisis of March–
June 1905 and its humiliating defeat for French power in Morocco.
Tangier helped to convince Péguy that France had been reduced to
impotence and her survival threatened because of Republicans who
had purged and demoralized the army, anti-clericals who had
sacrificed social harmony to the separation of Church and State,
and socialists who preferred class-war to national unity. Tangier,
together with outbreaks of violence abroad (the Turkish massacres
of the Armenians in 1894 and 1896, the Russian 'Bloody Sunday'
of January 1905) which seemed to spell the disintegration of old
civilizations, brought home to Péguy the truth that nations are
mortal. Much of his subsequent work vibrates with a kind of pre-
Spenglerian *frisson*, a passionate concern with continuity, and an
urgent need to redeem what is temporal and doomed through a
religion that offers eternal life.

Notre Patrie (1905) crystallizes all this in its new awareness of
the French historical tradition, its pride in France's civilizing
mission, and its appeal to the soil, to national roots, and the memory
of the dead. Here Péguy rejoins the equivocal poetry of Barrès, but
with none of Barrès's eclecticism and pagan admixture; here, as in
Notre Jeunesse (1910), he aspires to an apolitical unity founded on
the mystique of a shared national past. This nationalistic, not to say
chauvinistic, strain is certainly one of the most distinctive elements
to be found in the three sacred plays and the Christian epic, *Ève*.
Speaking of the betrayed Christ in *Le Mystère de la charité de Jeanne
d'Arc*, Joan proudly affirms: 'Jamais les hommes de ce pays-ci,
jamais des saints de ce pays-ci, jamais des simples chrétiens même
de nos pays ne l'auraient abandonné. Jamais des chevaliers français;
jamais des paysans français; jamais des simples paroissiens des
paroisses françaises . . .' This kind of patriotic fervour passes over
rather too easily into the exalted invocations to those fallen in battle

G

which one meets in *Ève* and which cannot decently survive the
slaughter on the Somme and the Marne:

> Heureux ceux qui sont morts dans les grandes batailles,
> Couchés dessus le sol à la face de Dieu.
> Heureux ceux qui sont morts sur un dernier haut lieu,
> Parmi tout l'appareil des grandes funérailles.

The key to this exaltation, as to the glorification of the death of the
holy innocents in *Le Mystère des saints innocents*, is, no doubt, to be
found in Péguy's growing desire to escape the 'contagion of the
world's slow stain', but its general effect is to bathe some of his
poetry in the light of a patriotic ritual.

On this common ground of a national mystique Péguy and Barrès
meet. However, the world created by Barrès in his early trilogy
(*Sous l'œil des barbares*, 1888; *Un Homme libre*, 1889; *Le Jardin de
Bérénice*, 1891) does not point irresistibly to his future as a purveyor
of nationalistic myths. It is a world of swarming intuitions and
poetic sensibility in which new experiences are avidly explored and
in which the private self is a vacuum waiting to be filled, a source of
unemployed energy, of fugitive emotions, sensations, and thrills.
This self is at odds with the 'Barbarian' who appears under a
variety of guises, but whose essential characteristic is that he
embodies collective values and a belief in universals. These Barrès
sees as in conflict with the claims of the inner life, with the truths
registered on the pulses and the insight that permits one to grasp
the unity of one's own personality.

The appeal here is plainly to the irrational or the instinctive, as
against the reasoning mind with its tendency to universalize and so
deform the concrete and particular truths apprehended by the
unique self through intuitive processes. The instinctual or intuitive
are seen as dialectically opposed to the intellectual and moral values
of the Third Republic, to its emphasis on civic virtue and reliance
on the procedures of science and positivism. This, at least, is consistent. A sense of strain emerges only when this intuitive Barrès
has to be reconciled with the later Barrès and his generalizing, quasi-
political concepts of a national community. In the same way, it is
not easy to square Barrès's narcissistic preoccupation with develop-

ing one's personality (often expressed in the early trilogy in a mannered idiom that pays homage to the aestheticism of the nineties)
with his subsequent enthusiasm for what has been called 'cette
fusion avec l'âme des groupes'.

In fact, Barrès strives to reconcile these conflicting tendencies
through a quasi-mystical experience of his personal relationship to
Lorraine, an experience transcribed in that section of *Un Homme
libre* called 'La soirée d'Haroué' and in which the personification
of his native region addresses him: 'C'est peut-être en ton âme
que moi, Lorraine, je me serai connue le plus complètement.
Jusqu'à toi, je traversais des formes que je créais, pour ainsi dire,
les yeux fermés; j'ignorais la raison selon laquelle je me mouvais;
je ne voyais pas mon mécanisme.' He is possessed by the spirit of
the place; Lorraine comes alive in him and he finds his own identity
through Lorraine, and a sense of his own continuity in the past of
the place. Certain landscapes or cities have a special appeal because
they reflect the dualism of some civilizations, an equilibrium between contradictory natures, such as is symbolized by the figure of
the Hermaphrodite in *La Colline inspirée* (1913). One such city is
Toledo, and Barrès's fascination with it and its amalgam of Moorish
and Christian elements points to his need to reconcile pagan and
Christian elements in the French past and to show how distinctive
is the texture of national life which derives from these double roots
and how much the vitality of a national tradition owes to this con-
fluence of different styles of belief (*Gréco ou le secret de Tolède*,
1911).

This is the emotional and mystical basis of Barrès's nationalism.
Its features find expression in imaginative form in the three
volumes of the *Roman de l'énergie nationale* which cover the period
from Boulanger's abortive quest for power to the Dreyfus Case.
Of these three volumes (*Les Déracinés*, 1897; *L'Appel au soldat*,
1900; *Leurs Figures*, 1902), the first is certainly the most influential,
though all three are united by a mystique of the national 'soul', a
cult of the dead, and an unflagging hostility to what is felt to be the
anarchy of individualism and of the democratic forms which it has
produced. Central to *Les Déracinés* is the notion that the sickness of
the individual and the sickness of French society, as manifested in

its political crises, both derive from a common cause: rootlessness. This concern with the process of being uprooted from one's origins and of losing contact with an organic community vivified by a sense of the past is, of course, based on an economic and social fact of the period: the drift from the countryside to the big towns. In showing its ravages in the lives of seven young Lorrainers, Barrès reveals himself as deeply reactionary because, like Maurras, he fails to come to terms with the fact of industrialism or to envisage social mobility as anything but a dangerous malaise. Indeed, as Professor Brogan has noted, it is characteristic of Barrès that he does not adequately grasp the implications of the great changes that were transforming the France of his day into an increasingly complex urban and industrial society, in much the same way as the Gilchrist–Thomas process, which was to revolutionize the Lorraine steel industry, was already changing the poor rural province of his childhood.

In fact, Barrès's tendency is to attribute the rampant individualism which is a product of the capitalism of the period to the 'official' neo-Kantian ideology of the Third Republic with its emphasis on the autonomy of the moral reason. The schematic plotting of his novels reflects these strongly felt insights with their implication that no individual morality can survive outside the framework of a hallowed moral tradition. Not only does Bouteiller, the philosophy teacher and corrupter of youth, crown his career as a deputy by being involved in the Panama Scandal, but the moral disintegration of his pupils is shown to be a consequence of his teaching. This is dramatized in the pattern of their lives: Racadot is executed for murder; Mouchefrin becomes a spy in the pay of the detested Republican police; Renaudin succumbs to corruption; Saint-Phlin, shattered by Racadot's execution, returns to Lorraine and devotes himself to good works. A mystique of the wholesome rural life is offered as a prophylactic against the poison of the towns and the fever of change.

The irrational, fully accepted by these writers, was also a saleable commodity by which the public was entranced and exploited. On the fringe was the flamboyant occultism of Joséphin Péladan, who wore oriental robes, gave himself the title of Sâr Merodack, and founded a new order of Rosicrucians, but more central were the conspiracy theories of history which proliferated in the ideological conflicts of the period. From all sides came revelations of hidden forces, occult powers, and satanic plots. The Jews, the Freemasons, and the Socialists were seen as the sinister threat to tradition; the Jesuits and Royalists as the mysterious saboteurs of progress; all were accused of undermining society by conspiratorial methods. The polemic against the Jews, led by the writings of Édouard Drumont and the activities of the Ligue Antisémite, found a willing and credulous audience among declining urban artisans, conservative Catholics, and rabid nationalists. Drumont, author of *La France juive* (1886) and editor of *La Libre Parole*, a paper with a circulation of over 500,000 during the Dreyfus Affair, produced stories of Jewish barbarity and established a vogue for crude anti-semitic humour. The Ligue, first under Drumont and then Jules Guérin, actively victimized Jewish businesses and shops and demonstrated against the 'Jewish syndicate', held to be the organization behind the Dreyfusards. In fact, as Bernard Lazare and, later, Péguy and Léon Blum pointed out, most French Jews were too discreetly assimilated to risk themselves for the Dreyfusard cause, but such facts were denounced by *La Libre Parole* as evidence of Jewish cunning. The power of anti-semitism lay in the web of mystery and secrecy which it wove round the world of Judaism, thus allowing the discontent and paranoia of insecurity to create its own facts. This fantasy-building occasioned most of the anti-semitic excesses, particularly in the clerical West where Jews were almost unknown, though it led eventually to an overestimation of anti-semitic strength: for a month in 1899 Guérin resisted arrest by defending his 'fort' in the Rue Chabrol hoping that France would rise to release him. But, as Proust shows in his recreations of salon life and Péguy in *Notre Jeunesse*, the Jews were never fully ostracized by society, and despite a continuum of anti-semitism in modern France, racial aggression is mainly a product of crisis. By 1900 the recent crisis was ebbing and even Drumont was losing his audience.

More inventive than anti-semitism, though less effective, was the campaign against the Freemasons, whose sympathy for radical republicanism and anti-clericalism was openly acknowledged. In 1884 Pope Leo XIII in his encyclical *Humanum Genus* declared the Masons to be working for Satan against church and humanity, a verdict which gave status to the numerous pamphlets claiming to reveal the Satanic rites of the Masonic Lodges. By such tracts the ground was prepared for the massive hoax of Léo Taxil who invented the infamous Diana Vaughan, ex-priestess of the fabricated Masonic Order of Palladism. For two years, 1895-7, she held a Catholic public in thrall by her horrific accusations in *Mémoires d'un expalladiste*, by her prayers and her chronicled fight against the demonic legions, before Taxil finally revealed his cynical intention to an angry meeting of devotees. His interest was not in social pathology but in financial gain, yet he had forcibly emphasized the gullibility of a prejudiced public.

When Taxil returned to a more explicit anti-clericalism he continued to make the same point. Fantasy was not confined to literature against Jews and Freemasons; a substantial market also existed for stories of clerical perversion and secrets of the confessional, a market which Taxil fully exploited with his 'Bibliothèque anti-cléricale'. His titles alone, *Le Fils du Jésuite*, *Les Maîtresses du Pape*, *Les Crimes du Clergé*, amply illustrate the nature of popular anti-clericalism, but the prejudice was not confined to scurrilous pamphleteering. During the Affair the Jesuits were denounced as the agents of army injustice, and a Catholic plot held responsible for anti-semitism by Dreyfusards as scholarly as Joseph Reinach (*Histoire de l'Affaire Dreyfus*, 1901-8) and as scientific as Zola (*La Vérité en marche*, 1901).

These forms of extremism tend to obscure the persistence of less hectic modes of feeling and belief. Even as conservative a figure as the novelist and critic Paul Bourget, so completely in tune with the politics of nationalism, so much the voice of traditional Catholic values on moral and social questions, illustrates in the 'good' characters of his novels the degree to which reason has a place in Catholic belief. However, it is true that the main purpose of these novels is to display the inadequacy of the rational mind alone as a source of the moral life. Though reason can be conscripted to support traditional morality, it cannot meet moral need or create a viable morality of its own. Hence, the 'morality of reason' cannot sustain Julie Monneron in *L'Étape* (1902) when she finds herself pregnant by a cheap seducer. The moral disorder to which she succumbs is seen by Bourget to stem from the criminally inept education given her by her free-thinking father, a typically anti-clerical product of the Third Republic's competitive educational system. In much the same way Adrien Sixte, the dehumanized philosopher of Bourget's influential *Le Disciple* (1889), is made to feel ultimately responsible for the corrosive effects of his own deterministic and positivistic ideas upon Robert Greslou, a student who, though unknown to him personally, has become one of his 'disciples'. Alienated by his intellectual training from what Bourget implies are his 'healthy' plebeian origins, Greslou has to gratify his sense of intellectual superiority by seducing Charlotte, the daughter of a nobleman in whose household he is employed as a tutor. Here sex is both the engine of class revenge and the instrument of a perverted intellectual emancipation. In order to experiment with emotions and test the limits of will-power, Greslou contrives a suicide-pact in which only Charlotte dies. In this death, the traditional virtues of trust and honour are seen to be destroyed by the moral irresponsibility of a Tainian positivism placed in the uncertain hands of a youth who has broken away from his 'natural' place in the social scheme.

It is, of course, wholly consistent with the narrow didacticism of this fiction that a secular morality is never explored with any degree of seriousness but is caricatured and shown to lead inevitably to the most disastrous consequences. The novels fail as works of art precisely because they cannot create a moral experience to match the complexity and ambiguity of life, but their sociological importance is very real. The particular ideological tensions exhibited by *Le Disciple*, and its general intellectual resonance, are best appreciated in the context of the campaign mounted by anti-clerical republicans in favour of a secular ethic. We have only to recall here how the diffusion of neo-Kantian ethical idealism in organs of opinion like Charles Renouvier's *Critique philosophique* (1872-89) fuses imperceptibly with the whole movement for free, compulsory primary education within the framework of a secular and republican ideology and animates not only official reports, like Paul Bert's *Rapport présenté à la Chambre des Députés sur la loi de l'enseignement primaire* (1880), but the textbooks on civic virtue prescribed for use in State schools from 1882 onwards and of which Paul Bert's own *L'Instruction civique à l'école* is an example.

The contributions of thinkers like Renouvier modify traditional morality without, of course, displacing it, and they exemplify the felt need of an assertive republicanism for a systematic secular creed capable of informing the moral life at its crucial points. These influential publicists wanted to invest vague humanistic attitudes with specific content and to establish a coherent social philosophy on a basis other than that of religious sanctions. The awareness, which Renouvier in particular displayed, of the moral vacuity of certain secularist positions and of the need to remedy it reflects a valuable strain in the ideological debates of the period and testifies to the persistence of a strong current of rational and humane idealism. Yet, though rationalism and the secular idea continue to be influential and though the appearance of Renan's *L'Avenir de la science* in 1890, over forty years after it was written, suggests a continuing belief in the validity and unity of science and in the notion of progress as a moral ideal, scientism and rationalist philosophy have already begun to lose by the nineties the confidence they showed a generation earlier.

If one turns to Renan's literary heir, Anatole France, one can detect that the sceptical temper, often serenely affirmative in the older writer, has suffered a failure of nerve. After an initial conflict in the seventies between science, especially Darwinism, and the 'poetry of Christianity', Anatole France's philosophy of life emerges as an urbane scepticism but, increasingly in the novels he wrote after 1907, this modulates into a pessimism verging on nihilism and greatly at variance with the traditions of the Enlightenment to which he seems, superficially, to belong. It is true that his distrust and fear of unreason and blind authority can continue to raise parts of his work to a fine ironic power, the more telling for the humane values implied. Such is the case with *Crainquebille* (1901) in which an honest costermonger is wrongfully condemned to prison by an authoritarian judge on the evidence of an officious policeman. In the four volumes of political satire entitled *L'Histoire contemporaine* (1897-1901) and featuring the keen, deflating irony of a provincial humanist, Professor Bergeret, at the expense of church, royalism, army, and anti-semitism, Anatole France continues to imply a commitment to republican and socialist ideas and to identify both with the spirit of rationalism. The same is true of many of his public speeches (*Vers les temps meilleurs*, 1906) and of his political pamphlets like the anti-clerical *L'Église et la République* (1905). A sharp eye for the irrational characterizes France's exposure of the primitivism implicit in the growing nationalist mystique, though his own patriotism is at least as deeply rooted in the French past as that of Barrès and reflects a more genuine piety for the national tradition than Maurras's abstract and exclusive system-making. In spite of all this, the attentive reader of Anatole France cannot fail to notice the dissonance between the tone and vision of his major imaginative works after about 1907 and the positive, if not always optimistic, inflections of his public utterances. In his public role France may be a socialist, but the whole tendency of *Les Dieux ont soif* (1912), his striking study of fanaticism and the presumption of ideology under the French Revolution, as of *La Révolte des anges* (1914), is to show that revolutions result in tyrannies as oppressive as those they were designed to replace. In much the same way, the dream of universal brotherhood and peace which figures in *Sur la pierre blanche* (1905) is obliterated by the powerfully ironic *L'Île des pingouins* (1908), a satire in which modern industrial society is blown off the face of the earth by embittered workers and in which the history of humankind is seen as a cycle of crimes and follies endlessly repeated. One of the great clinching images of the book must certainly be the apocalypse imagined by Dr. Obnubile: 'Le sage amassera assez de dynamite pour faire sauter cette planète. Quand elle roulera par morceaux à travers l'espace, une amélioration imperceptible sera accomplie dans l'univers et une satisfaction sera donnée à la conscience universelle, qui d'ailleurs n'existe pas.' This is a far cry from the 'smiling scepticism' which distinguished France's earlier work when he was still the sage of a *rentier* public, and it illustrates very well to what degree a cultivated intelligence and sensibility can be shocked out of their normal modes of interpreting experience by the harshness of social and political conflicts.

The rational idealism which lies behind Renan's view of science or Anatole France's political radicalism, at its most expansive and confident moments, finds a finely realized image in Roger Martin du Gard's novel, *Jean Barois* (1913), where it is set in counterpoint to the religious aspirations of the age. In this work, the dialogue between science and religion, faith and reason is sustained in fictional terms and rises to the level of mature seriousness that the theme demands. In Jean Barois's fervent adherence to a secularist ideology and his dying return to the religion of his childhood, as in his wife's simple, unyielding Catholic faith or the philosopher Marc-Élie Luce's serene belief in reason, the intellectual and spiritual temper of *fin-de-siècle* France is reflected with sympathy and fidelity.

NOTE

JORIS-KARL HUYSMANS, 1848-1907. Of Dutch descent, he combined writing with his employment as a civil servant until 1898. He was successively associated with the 'naturalist' and 'decadent' movements of late-nineteenth-century France and later became converted to Catholicism, spending a period (1899-1901) as an oblate in the Benedictine Abbey of Ligugé. Apart from his fiction he wrote art criticism. He died of cancer after a long illness borne with courage.

LÉON BLOY, 1846-1917. Born in Périgueux, he became a Catholic as a result of a meeting with Barbey d'Aurevilly. His whole life was marked by intense experience of religious faith, violent polemics, and extreme poverty which forced him to move constantly from one lodging to another. He was influential in bringing about conversions to Catholicism among young intellectuals of the period, notably Jacques Maritain.

PAUL CLAUDEL, 1868-1955. Born in the Champagne country and educated mainly in Paris, Claudel was converted to Catholicism after a mystical experience in Notre-Dame on Christmas Day 1886. He frequented Symbolist circles and attended Mallarmé's 'Tuesdays' at the rue de Rome from 1887. He entered the French foreign service (1890) and, from 1893 onwards, spent some forty years in consular and diplomatic posts in the U.S.A., South America, China, Japan, and Europe. During this period he wrote prolifically as poet and dramatist, though his drama was so much at odds with the conventional 'well-made play' that it tended not to receive full recognition until years after its first appearance (but increasingly after 1945). His letters reflect a strong polemical vein in defence of his religion.

CHARLES PÉGUY, 1873-1914. Born at Orléans and brought up by his grandmother and widowed mother in a humble home, he won scholarships to the École Normale Supérieure (1894) where he came under the influence of distinguished socialists like Lucien Herr and Jean Jaurès and left without taking his degree (1897), opening a socialist bookshop which, with his passionate involvement on the side of Dreyfus in the Affair, became a centre for pro-Dreyfus intellectuals. In January 1900 he founded a remarkable intellectual review, *Les Cahiers de la Quinzaine*, the influence of which far exceeded its limited circulation and the running of which occupied him to the point of exhaustion for the next fourteen years. Péguy subsequently embraced a mystical and idiosyncratic Catholicism, dating from 1906-8, and died bravely at the first battle of the Marne (5 September 1914).

MAURICE BARRÈS, 1862-1923. Born at Charmes-sur-Moselle (Lorraine), he studied law at Nancy and then went to Paris to try a literary career, which might be said to date from his founding of a short-lived review, *Les Taches d'encre* (1884). Though he began as a dilettante and aesthete, he soon became involved in the politics of the Right and was elected a Boulangist deputy for Nancy in 1889.

PAUL BOURGET, 1852-1935. Born at Amiens, he abandoned medicine and philosophy for literature. Establishing his reputation as a novelist with *Cruelle Énigme* (1885), he continued this vein of psychological analysis in his subsequent novels where it was combined with the exploration of topical moral and sociological problems. He was a friend of Henry James and gained a deserved reputation as a literary critic. In his public life he became increasingly identified with Catholic orthodoxy and royalist politics.

ANATOLE FRANCE, 1844-1924. Son of a Parisian bookseller, he came early under the influence of the world of bibliography and antiquarianism, both in his father's shop and in his twenty years as reviewer, editor, and publisher's reader; and this perhaps accounts for the bookish character of some of his own fiction. After a period as assistant librarian of the Senate (1876-90) he became active in the world of letters under the aegis of a *salon* hostess of the period, Mme Arman de Caillavet, who became his mistress and encouraged his literary production. He sympathized strongly with Dreyfus during the Affair and moved increasingly to the left in politics, becoming a committed socialist in his later years. He was awarded the Nobel Prize for Literature in 1921.

Editions. For Huysmans the best edition is *Œuvres complètes*, ed. L. Descaves (25 vols., 1928-40). In addition, there is important correspondence: with the abbesse de Saint-Cécile de Solesmes (1950); E. de Goncourt (1956); Camille Lemonnier (1957); Jules Destrée (1966).

The definitive edition of Bloy's works is the current *Œuvres*, ed. J. Bollery and J. Petit (1964-   ). There is a separate edition of the *Journal*, ed. J. Bollery (4 vols., 1956-8).

For Claudel the standard collection is the (still incomplete) Œuvres complètes (26 vols., 1950-67), but authoritative and handy are the Pléiade Œuvre poétique (1957), Œuvres en prose (1965), and Théâtre (2 vols., 1947 and 1966). Previously unpublished material is contained in the Cahiers Paul Claudel (6 vols., 1959-66)— in progress. Important correspondence includes that with J. Rivière (1926; reprint 1963); Gide (1949); A. Suarès (1951); and F. Jammes (1952). Illuminating too are Mémoires improvisés, ed. J. Amrouche (1954).

Péguy's work is published by Gallimard: Œuvres complètes (20 vols., 1917-55), but convenient are the Pléiade Œuvres poétiques complètes (1957); Œuvres en prose, 1909-1914 (1957); and Œuvres en prose, 1898-1908 (1959). Interesting correspondence includes that with A. Fournier (1946); André Bourgeois (1947); and Romain Rolland (1955).

A collected edition of Barrès's work is in progress: Œuvres, ed. Ph. Barrès (1965-   ), but convenient reprints exist of his major fiction: Le Culte du moi (1966); Les Déracinés (2 vols., 1959); and La Colline inspirée, ed. J. Barbier (1962). Separately printed are Mes Cahiers (posth., 14 vols., 1929-57), selections from which are available in Mes Cahiers, 1896-1923, ed. G. Dupré (1963).

The so-called Œuvres complètes (9 vols., 1899-1911) assembles the most important texts of Bourget.

The Œuvres complètes illustrées, ed. L. Carias (25 vols., 1925-35), contains the great bulk of the work of Anatole France. It needs to be supplemented by Vers les temps meilleurs : trente ans de vie sociale, ed. C. Aveline (3 vols., 1949-67); La Vie littéraire, 5e série (posthume) (1950); and Les Carnets intimes, ed. L. Carias (1946).

Criticism: Movement of ideas. The most suggestive survey of the literature of the period is H. Clouard, Histoire de la littérature française du symbolisme à nos jours, Tome I: 1885-1914 (1960). Useful studies of the Catholic literary revival include E. Fraser, Le Renouveau religieux d'après le roman français de 1886 à 1914 (1934); R. Griffiths, The Reactionary Revolution: the Catholic Revival in French Literature, 1870-1914 (1966).

Important intellectual tendencies of the period are examined in R. Arbour, H. Bergson et les lettres françaises (1956); M.-C. Bancquart, Les Écrivains et l'histoire (1966); D. W. Brogan, French Personalities and Problems (1946); V. Brombert, The Intellectual Hero: Studies in the French Novel 1880-1955 (1961); H. Bourgin, De Jaurès à Léon Blum: l'École Normale et la politique (1938); C. Digeon, La Crise allemande de la pensée française, 1870-1914 (1959); A. Goldberger, Visions of a New Hero (1965); H. S. Hughes, Consciousness and Society: the Reorientation of European Social Thought 1890-1930 (1958); M. Tison-Braun, La Crise de l'humanisme: le conflit de l'individu et de la société dans la littérature française moderne, I: 1890-1914 (1958); and E. Wilson, To the Finland Station (1940).

Criticism: Authors. The authoritative biography of Huysmans is R. Baldick's The Life of J.-K. Huysmans (1955). Useful studies on aspects of Huysmans dealt with in this chapter include H. Trudgian, *L'Esthétique de J.-K. Huysmans* (1934); H. R. T. Brandreth, *Huysmans* (1963); P. Cogny, *J.-K. Huysmans à la recherche de l'unité* (1953); and H. M. Gallot, *Explication de J.-K. Huysmans* (1954).

The most thorough biography of Bloy is J. Bollery, *Léon Bloy : essai de biographie* (3 vols., 1947-54). Other helpful studies include R. Barbeau, *Léon Bloy, un prophète luciférien* (1957); A. Béguin, *Léon Bloy, mystique de la douleur* (1948); M.-J. Lory, *La Pensée religieuse de Léon Bloy* (1951); and J. Petit, *Léon Bloy* (1966).

For the purposes of this chapter, the most useful critical essays on Claudel are L. Barjon, *Paul Claudel* (1953); L. Chaigne, *Vie de Paul Claudel et genèse de son œuvre* (1961); S. Fumet, *Claudel* (1958); and P.-A. Lesort, *Claudel par lui-même* (1963). On Claudel's theatre, illuminating studies include J. Bastien, *L'Œuvre dramatique de Paul Claudel* (1957), and J. Madaule, *Le Drame de Paul Claudel* (1964).

On Péguy, excellent biographical studies include F. Challaye, *Péguy socialiste* (1954); D. Halévy, *Charles Péguy et les Cahiers de la Quinzaine* (1919); J. Isaac, *Expériences de ma vie, I : Péguy* (1959); R. Rolland, *Péguy* (2 vols., 1944); and M. Villiers, *Charles Péguy: a Study in Integrity* (1965). Good general introductions are B. Guyon, *Péguy* (1960), and J. Delaporte, *Connaissance de Péguy* (new ed., 2 vols., 1959). Useful critical essays include A. Dru, *Péguy* (1956); N. Jussem-Wilson, *Charles Péguy* (1965); and A. Rousseaux, *Le Prophète Péguy* (2 vols., 1946). E. Cahm, *Péguy et le nationalisme français* (1972) contains some important documents and an excellent biography while H. A. Schmitt, *Charles Péguy, the Decline of an Idealist* (1967), offers a valuable dissenting opinion.

For Barrès, most useful are H. Massis, *Barrès et nous, suivi d'une correspondance inédite 1906-1923* (1962); P. de Boisdeffre, *Maurice Barrès* (1962); J.-M. Domenach, *Barrès par lui-même* (1954); J. Godfrin, *Barrès mystique* (1962); P. Ouston, *The Imagination of Maurice Barrès* (1974); and J. Vier, *Barrès et le culte du moi* (1958). A special number of *La Table ronde* (March 1957) was devoted to Barrès, and so was a symposium, *Maurice Barrès: actes du colloque organisé par l'Université de Nancy* (1964).

For Bourget, the most helpful studies are A. Autin, *Le Disciple de Paul Bourget* (1930); A. Feuillerat, *Paul Bourget* (1937); V. Giraud, *Paul Bourget* (1934); and M. Mansuy, *Un Moderne: Paul Bourget de l'enfance au 'Disciple'* (1960).

Good general introductions to Anatole France are E. P. Dargan, *Anatole France, 1844-1896* (1937), and J. Suffel, *Anatole France* (1946). Most useful for relating France to the intellectual and political life of his times are M.-C. Bancquart, *Anatole France polémiste* (1962); H. Chevalier, *The Ironic Temper: Anatole France and His Time* (1932); C. Jefferson, *Anatole France: the Politics of Scepticism* (1965); J. Levaillant, *Les Aventures du scepticisme: essai sur l'évolution intellectuelle d'Anatole France* (1965); and A. Vandegans, *Anatole France: les années de formation* (1954).

TRINITY COLLEGE
LIBRARY

CHRONOLOGY

History	French literature	English literature
Loi Falloux, 1850	Sand, *François le champi* (1850)	Hawthorne, *The Scarlet Letter* (1850) Kingsley, *Alton Locke* (1850)
Coup d'état of Louis-Napoleon, 1851	Labiche, *Un Chapeau de paille d'Italie* (1851) Murger, *Scènes de la vie de Bohème* (1851)	Hawthorne, *The House of the Seven Gables* (1851) Borrow, *Lavengro* (1851) Melville, *Moby Dick* (1851)
Napoleon III proclaimed Emperor, 1852 (beginning of the Second Empire)	Dumas *fils*, *La Dame aux camélias* (1852) Gautier, *Émaux et camées* (1852) Leconte de Lisle, *Poèmes antiques* (1852)	Stowe, *Uncle Tom's Cabin* (1852) Arnold, *Empedocles on Etna* (1852) Thackeray, *The History of Henry Esmond* (1852) Dickens, *Bleak House* (1852–3)
Haussmann begins reconstruction of Paris, 1853	Hugo, *Les Châtiments* (1853) Nerval, *Petits Châteaux de Bohème* (1853)	C. Brontë, *Villette* (1853) Mrs. Gaskell, *Cranford* (1853) Reade, *Peg Woffington* (1853) Kingsley, *Hypatia* (1853) Thackeray, *The Newcomes* (1853–5)
Crimean War, 1854–6	Augier, *Le Gendre de M. Poirier* (1854) Nerval, *Les Filles du feu* (1854)	Dickens, *Bleak House* (1852–3) Thoreau, *Walden* (1854)
	Dumas *fils*, *Le Demi-monde* (1855) Augier, *Le Mariage d'Olympe* (1855) Nerval, *Le Rêve et la vie* (1855)	Kingsley, *Westward Ho!* (1855) Whitman, *Leaves of Grass* (1855) Longfellow, *Hiawatha* (1855)

Painting and music	Criticism and aesthetic theory	Ideas and philosophy
Berlioz, 1803–69 (*L'Enfance du Christ*, 1854; *Les Troyens*, composed 1856–9)	Vinet, *Études sur la littérature française au XIXe siècle* (1849–51)	
Liszt, 1811–86		
Verdi, 1813–1901 (*Rigoletto*, 1851; *La Traviata*, 1853; *Il Trovatore*, 1853; *Aïda*, 1871; *Otello*, 1887; *Falstaff*, 1893)		Cournot, *Essai sur les fondements de nos connaissances* (1851) Spencer, *Social Statics* (1851) Ruskin, *Stones of Venice* (1851–3) Comte, *Système de politique positive* (1851–4)
Wagner, 1813–83 (*Tristan und Isolde*, 1865; *Die Meistersinger*, 1868; *Das Rheingold*, 1869; *Die Walküre*, 1870; *Parzifal*, 1882)		Marx, *Der achtzehnte Brumaire des Louis Napoleon* (1852) Comte, *Catéchisme positiviste* (1852)
	Taine, *Essai sur les Fables de La Fontaine* (1853)	Cousin, *Du Vrai, du beau et du bien* (1853)
Millet, 1814–75 ('Les Glaneuses', 1857; 'L'Angélus', 1859)		Gobineau, *Essai sur l'inégalité des races humaines* (1853–5)
Franz, 1815–92	Pontmartin, *Causeries littéraires* (1854–6)	Kierkegaard, *The Attack on 'Christendom'* (1854–5) Mommsen, *Römische Geschichte* (1854–6)
Daubigny, 1817–78		Renouvier, *Essais de critique générale* (1854–61)
Watts, 1817–1904	Chernyshevsky, *The Aesthetic Relations of Art to Reality* (1855)	

H

History	French literature	English literature
	Champfleury, *Les Bourgeois de Molinchart* (1855)	Trollope, *The Warden* (1855)
		Dickens, *Little Dorrit* (1855–7)
Peace of Paris, 1856	Hugo, *Les Contemplations* (1856)	
	Champfleury, *Monsieur de Boisdhyver* (1856)	
	Flaubert, *Madame Bovary* (1857)	Borrow, *Romany Rye* (1857)
	Baudelaire, *Les Fleurs du mal* (1857)	C. Brontë, *The Professor* (1857)
	Banville, *Odes funambulesques* (1857)	Trollope, *Barchester Towers* (1857)
	Dumas *fils*, *La Question d'argent* (1857)	Elizabeth Barrett Browning, *Aurora Leigh* (1857)
		Thackeray, *The Virginians* (1857–9)
Unsuccessful attempt to assassinate Napoleon III, 1858 Meeting between Napoleon III and Cavour at Plombières, 1858	Augier, *Les Lionnes pauvres* (1858) Dumas *fils*, *Le Fils naturel* (1858)	Eliot, *Scenes of Clerical Life* (1858)
French win battles of Magenta and Solferino against Austrians, 1859 Peace of Villafranca, 1859	Dumas *fils*, *Un Père prodigue* (1859) Mistral, *Mireille* (1859) Hugo, *La Légende des siècles* (1859–83)	Meredith, *The Ordeal of Richard Feverel* (1859) Eliot, *Adam Bede* (1859) Dickens, *A Tale of Two Cities* (1859)
Plebiscites in Nice and Savoie favour union with France, 1860	Baudelaire, *Les Paradis artificiels* (1860) Sardou, *Les Pattes de mouche* (1860)	Hawthorne, *The Marble Faun* (1860) Collins, *The Woman in White* (1860) Eliot, *The Mill on the Floss* (1860) Dickens, *Great Expectations* (1860–1)

Painting and music	Criticism and aesthetic theory	Ideas and philosophy
Gounod, 1818–93 (*Faust*, 1859; *Mireille*, 1864; *Roméo et Juliette*, 1867)		
Courbet, 1819–77 ('L'Enterrement à Ornans', 1850)	Taine, *Essai sur Tite-Live* (1856)	Tocqueville, *L'Ancien Régime et la Révolution* (1856)
Offenbach, 1819–80 (*Orphée aux enfers*, 1858; *La Vie parisienne*, 1866)	Champfleury, *Le Réalisme* (1857) Pontmartin, *Causeries du samedi* (1857–80)	Buckle, *History of Civilization in England* (1857 and 1861)
Jongkind, 1819–91		
Harpignies, 1819–1916		
Ford Madox Brown, 1821–93		
	Taine, *Essais de critique et d'histoire* (1858)	
Franck, 1822–90 (*Les Béatitudes*, composed 1869–79; *Symphony*, 1889)		
Lalo, 1823–92 (*Symphonie espagnole*, 1873; *Le Roi d'Ys*, 1888)	Renan, *Essais de morale et de critique* (1859)	Marx, *Zur Kritik der politischen Ökonomie* (1859) Darwin, *On the Origin of Species* (1859) Mill, *On Liberty* (1859)
	Barbey d'Aurevilly, *Les Œuvres et les hommes* (1860–1906)	Burckhardt, *Die Kultur der Renaissance in Italien* (1860)
Smetana, 1824–84 (*The Bartered Bride*, 1866)		
Bruckner, 1824–96		

History	French literature	English literature
American Civil War, 1861–5 Napoleon III's Mexican 'adventure', 1861–7	Augier, *Les Effrontés* (1861)	Mrs. Henry Wood, *East Lynne* (1861) Reade, *The Cloister and the Hearth* (1861) Trollope, *Framley Parsonage* (1861) Eliot, *Silas Marner* (1861)
France acquires Mentone and Roquebrune, 1862	Augier, *Les Fils de Giboyer* (1862) Leconte de Lisle, *Poèmes barbares* (1862) Flaubert, *Salammbô* (1862) Hugo, *Les Misérables* (1862)	Borrow, *Wild Wales* (1862) Meredith, *Modern Love* (1862) Christina Rossetti, *Goblin Market and Other Poems* (1862)
Crédit Lyonnais founded as deposit bank, 1863	Fromentin, *Dominique* (1863) Gautier, *Le Capitaine Fracasse* (1863)	Eliot, *Romola* (1863)
French protectorate established over Cambodia, 1864	Goncourts, *Germinie Lacerteux* (1864) Dumas *fils*, *L'Ami des femmes* (1864) Vigny, *Les Destinées* (posth. publ. 1864)	Tennyson, *Enoch Arden* (1864 Dickens, *Our Mutual Friend* (1864–5) Mrs. Gaskell, *Wives and Daughters* (1864–6)
Napoleon III and Bismarck meet at Biarritz, 1865	Hugo, *Les Chansons des rues et des bois* (1865) Augier, *Maître Guérin* (1865) Sully-Prudhomme, *Stances et poèmes* (1865)	Swinburne, *Atlanta in Calydon* (1865) Kingsley, *Hereward the Wake* (1865) Carroll, *Alice's Adventures in Wonderland* (1865)
Austro-Prussian Seven Weeks' War, 1866	Augier, *La Contagion* (1866) Verlaine, *Poèmes saturniens* (1866) Hugo, *Les Travailleurs de la mer* (1866) Sully-Prudhomme, *Les Épreuves* (1866)	Eliot, *Felix Holt, the Radical* (1866) Swinburne, *Poems and Ballads* (1866)

Painting and music	Criticism and aesthetic theory	Ideas and philosophy
Puvis de Chavannes, 1824-98	Sainte-Beuve, *Chateaubriand et son groupe littéraire* (1861)	Spencer, *Education: Intellectual, Moral, Physical* (1861) Mill, *Considerations on Representative Government* (1861)
Boudin, 1824-98		
Johann Strauss, 1825-99 (*Die Fledermaus*, 1874)		Spencer, *First Principles* (1862)
Moreau, 1826-98	Freytag, *Technik des Dramas* (1863)	Lyell, *The Antiquity of Man* (1863)
Holman Hunt, 1827-1910	Scherer, *Études critiques sur la littérature contemporaine* (1863-95)	Mill, *Utilitarianism* (1863) Renan, *Vie de Jésus* (1863; vol. 1 of *Histoire des origines du christianisme*, 1863-83)
Rossetti, 1828-82	Taine, *Histoire de la littérature anglaise* (1864) Prévost-Paradol, *Études sur les moralistes français* (1864)	Michelet, *La Bible de l'humanité* (1864) Newman, *Apologia pro vita sua* (1864) Fustel de Coulanges, *La Cité antique* (1864)
Millais, 1829-96	Arnold, *Essays in Criticism* (1865 and 1888) Weiss, *Essais sur l'histoire de la littérature française* (1865)	Quinet, *La Révolution* (1865) Ruskin, *Sesame and Lilies* (1865)
Pissarro, 1830-1903		Bernard, *Introduction à l'étude de la médecine expérimentale* (1865)
Manet, 1832-83 ('Le Déjeuner sur l'herbe', 1865; 'Le Balcon', 1869)	First series of *Le Parnasse contemporain* (1866) Zola, *Mes Haines* (1866)	Ruskin, *The Crown of Wild Olive* (1866)
Brahms, 1833-97 (*Requiem*, 1869; *First Symphony*, 1876; *Violin Concerto*, 1878; *Fourth Symphony*, 1885)		

History	French literature	English literature
Last French troops evacuate Mexico and Emperor Maximilian shot, 1867	Zola, *Thérèse Raquin* (1867) Banville, *Les Exilés* (1867) Dumas *fils*, *Les Idées de Madame Aubray* (1867)	Trollope, *The Last Chronicle of Barset* (1867) Morris, *The Life and Death of Jason* (1867)
Freedom of press granted in France and parliamentary system adopted, 1868-9	Lautréamont, *Les Chants de Maldoror* (1868 and 1890) Daudet, *Lettres de mon moulin* (1868) Coppet, *Intimités* (1868)	Collins, *The Moonstone* (1868) Browning, *The Ring and the Book* (1868-9)
Opening of Suez Canal, the work of the French engineer De Lesseps, 1869	Sully-Prudhomme, *Les Solitudes* (1869) Baudelaire, *Le Spleen de Paris* (posth. publ. 1869) Verlaine, *Fêtes galantes* (1869) Flaubert, *L'Éducation sentimentale* (1869) Hugo, *L'Homme qui rit* (1869)	Trollope, *Phineas Finn* (1869) Blackmore, *Lorna Doone* (1869)
Franco-Prussian War, 1870-1	Verlaine, *La bonne chanson* (1870)	Dickens, *The Mystery of Edwin Drood* (1870) Rossetti, *Poems* (1870)
		Eliot, *Middlemarch* (1871-2)
Capitulation of Paris followed by the Paris Commune, March/May 1871 French loss of Alsace and Lorraine by Treaty of Frankfurt, 1871 Thiers elected French President, 1871		
	Coppet, *Les Humbles* (1872) Daudet, *Tartarin de Tarascon* (1872) Daudet, *L'Arlésienne* (1872)	Carroll, *Through the Looking Glass* (1872) Butler, *Erewhon* (1872) Hardy, *Under the Greenwood Tree* (1872)

Painting and music	Criticism and aesthetic theory	Ideas and philosophy
Burne-Jones, 1833–98		Bagehot, *The English Constitution* (1867)
Whistler, 1834–1903		Froude, *Short Studies on Great Subjects* (1867–83)
		Marx, *Das Kapital* (1867–94)
Degas, 1834–1917	Baudelaire, *Curiosités esthétique* (posth. publ. 1868)	
	Baudelaire, *L'Art romantique* (posth. publ. 1868)	
Saint-Saëns, 1835–1921 (*Le Rouet d'Omphale*, 1871)		Renouvier, *La Science de la morale* (1869)
		Mill, *The Subjection of Women* (1869)
Delibes, 1836–91 (*Coppélia*, 1870; *Lakmé*, 1883)		Arnold, *Culture and Anarchy* (1869)
Fantin-Latour, 1836–1904		
	Lowell, *Among my Books* (1870 and 1876)	Taine, *De l'Intelligence* (1870)
Bizet, 1838–75 (*La Jolie Fille de Perth*, 1867; *L'Arlésienne*, 1872; *Carmen*, 1875)	Haym, *Die romantische Schule* (1870)	
	De Sanctis, *Storia della letteratura italiana* (1870–1)	
		Tylor, *Primitive Culture* (1871)
Bruch, 1838–1920		Darwin, *The Descent of Man* (1871)
		Marx, *The Civil War in France* (in English, 1871)
Mussorgsky, 1839–81	Nietzsche, *Die Geburt der Tragödie* (1872)	
	Banville, *Petit traité de poésie française* (1872)	

History	French literature	English literature
	Zola, *La Curée* (1872)	
	Rimbaud, *Les Illuminations* (written *c.* 1872-4)	
Death of Napoleon III, 1873 Thiers replaced as President by MacMahon, 1873	Rimbaud, *Une Saison en enfer* (written 1873)	
	Zola, *Le Ventre de Paris* (1873)	
	Hugo, *Quatre-vingt-treize* (1873)	
	Cros, *Le Coffret de Santal* (1873)	
	Corbière, *Les Amours jaunes* (1873)	
	Daudet, *Contes du lundi* (1873)	
	Flaubert, *La Tentation de Saint Antoine* (1874)	Thomson, *The City of Dreadful Night* (1874)
	Verlaine, *Romances sans paroles* (1874)	Hardy, *Far from the Madding Crowd* (1874)
	Barbey, d'Aurevilly, *Les Diaboliques* (1874)	Eliot, *Daniel Deronda* (1874-6)
Republican constitution established in France, 1875	Zola, *La Faute de l'abbé Mouret* (1875)	
	Mallarmé, *L'Après-midi d'un faune* (1876)	Twain, *The Adventures of Tom Sawyer* (1876)
	Augier, *Madame Caverlet* (1876)	Meredith, *Beauchamp's Career* (1876)
	Gobineau, *Nouvelles asiatiques* (1876)	James, *Roderick Hudson* (1876)
Republicans defeat MacMahon's policy at the polls, 1877	Flaubert, *Trois Contes* (1877)	James, *The American* (1877)
	Zola, *L'Assommoir* (1877)	

Painting and music	Criticism and aesthetic theory	Ideas and philosophy
Cézanne, 1839–1906		
Tchaikovsky, 1840–93 (*Eugen Onegin*, 1879; *Nutcracker Suite*, 1892; *Piano Concerto*, 1892; *Sixth Symphony* ('*Pathétique*'), 1893)	Arnold, *Literature and Dogma* (1873) Pater, *Studies in the Renaissance* (1873)	Ribot, *L'Hérédité* (1873) Mill, *Autobiography* (1873)
Sisley, 1840–99		
Redon, 1840–1916	Gautier, *Histoire du romantisme* (1874) De Sanctis, *Saggi critici* (1874)	Sidgwick, *Methods of Ethics* (1874) Morley, *On Compromise* (1874) Quinet, *L'Esprit nouveau* (1874)
Rodin, 1840–1917 ('Les Bourgeois de Calais', 1884–9) Monet, 1840–1926 ('Les Nymphéas', 1898–1905)	Swinburne, *Essays and Studies* (1875)	Taine, *Les Origines de la France contemporaine* (1875–93)
Bazille, 1841–70		Ménard, *Rêveries d'un païen mystique* (1876)
Chabrier, 1841–94 (*España*, 1883)		Bagehot, *Physics and Politics* (1876)
Berthe Morisot, 1841–95		Renan, *Dialogues et fragments philosophiques* (1876)
		Spencer, *The Principles of Sociology* (1876–96)
		Engels, *Anti-Dühring* (1877)

History	French literature	English literature
	Coppet, *Les Récits et les élégies* (1878) Zola, *Une Page d'amour* (1878)	James, *Daisy Miller* (1878) Swinburne, *Poems and Ballads* (1878) Hardy, *The Return of the Native* (1878)
Grévy, a republican, elected French President, 1879 Amnesty granted to the Communists, 1879		Meredith, *The Egoist* (1879)
	Loti, *Le Mariage de Loti* (1880) Zola, *Nana* (1880)	Meredith, *The Tragic Comedians* (1880) Hardy, *The Trumpet Major* (1880)
Primary education in France made free and compulsory, 1881 Gambetta's Ministry, 1881	Hugo, *Les Quatre vents de l'esprit* (1881) Verlaine, *Sagesse* (1881) France, *Le Crime de Sylvestre Bonnard* (1881) Flaubert, *Bouvard et Pécuchet* (posth. publ. 1881) Maupassant, *La Maison Tellier* (1881)	James, *Washington Square* (1881) James, *Portrait of a Lady* (1881) Rossetti, *Ballads and Sonnets* (1881)
	Zola, *Pot-Bouille* (1882) Maupassant, *Mademoiselle Fifi* (1882) Becque, *Les Corbeaux* (1882)	Swinburne, *Tristram of Lyonesse* (1882)
French protectorate established over Annam and Tonkin, 1883	Verhaeren, *Les Flamandes* (1883) Zola, *Au Bonheur des dames* (1883) Loti, *Mon frère Yves* (1883) Maupassant, *Une Vie* (1883)	Stevenson, *Treasure Island* (1883)
	Zola, *La Joie de vivre* (1884) Huysmans, *A Rebours* (1884)	Twain, *The Adventures of Huckleberry Finn* (1884)

Painting and music	Criticism and aesthetic theory	Ideas and philosophy
Dvořák, 1841–1904 (*Stabat Mater*, 1880; *Slavonic Dances I & II*, 1878 and 1886; *Ninth Symphony* ('*From the New World*'), 1893)		Nietzsche, *Menschliches, Allzumenschliches* (1878)
Renoir, 1841–1919 ('Le Moulin de la Galette', 1876)	Bagehot, *Literary Studies* (1879)	
Sullivan, 1842–1900		
Grieg, 1843–1907 (*Piano Concerto*, 1869; *Holberg Suite*, 1884–5; *Peer Gynt Suites I and II*, 1888 and 1891)	Zola, *Le Roman expérimental* (1880)	
Douanier Rousseau, 1844–1910	Zola, *Le Naturalisme au théâtre* (1881)	Ribot, *Les Maladies de la mémoire* (1881)
Fauré, 1845–1924		
Gauguin, 1848–1903		Nietzsche, *Die fröhliche Wissenschaft* (1882)
Parry, 1848–1918		
D'Indy, 1851–1931	Brunetière, *Le Roman naturaliste* (1883)	Ribot, *Les Maladies de la volonté* (1883)
Stanford, 1852–1924	Bourget, *Essais de psychologie contemporaine* (1883)	Green, *Prolegomena to Ethics* (1883)
		Nietzsche, *Also sprach Zarathustra* (1883–92)
Van Gogh, 1853–90	James, *The Art of Fiction* (1884)	Seignobos, *Histoire de la civilisation* (1884–6)
	Verlaine, *Les Poètes maudits* (1884)	

History	French literature	English literature
	Daudet, *Sapho* (1884)	
	Leconte de Lisle, *Poèmes tragiques* (1884)	
	Moréas, *Les Syrtes* (1884)	
Re-election of Grévy as French President, 1885	Zola, *Germinal* (1885)	Meredith, *Diana of the Crossways* (1885)
	Laforgue, *Les Complaintes* (1885)	
	France, *Le Livre de mon ami* (1885)	
	Maupassant, *Bel-Ami* (1885)	
The Boulanger Affair, 1886-7	Vielé-Griffin, *Cueille d'avril* (1886)	James, *The Bostonians* (1886)
	Moréas, *Les Cantilènes* (1886)	Hardy, *The Mayor of Casterbridge* (1886)
	Loti, *Pêcheur d'Islande* (1886)	James, *The Princess Casamassima* (1886)
	Bloy, *Le Désespéré* (1886)	Stevenson, *The Strange Case of Dr. Jekyll and Mr. Hyde* (1886)
	Zola, *L'Œuvre* (1886)	
	Laforgue, *L'Imitation de Notre Dame la Lune* (1886)	
Sadi-Carnot French President, 1887	Mallarmé, *Poésies* (1887)	
	Zola, *La Terre* (1887)	
	Verhaeren, *Les Soirs* (1887)	
	Loti, *Madame Chrysanthème* (1887)	
	Sardou, *Tosca* (1887)	
	Barrès, *Sous l'œil des barbares* (1888)	Doughty, *Travels in Arabia Deserta* (1888)
	Zola, *Le Rêve* (1888)	James, *The Aspern Papers* (1888)
	Maupassant, *Pierre et Jean* (1888)	Henley, *A Book of Verses* (1888)
	Hugo, *Toute la lyre* (1888-93)	

Painting and music	Criticism and aesthetic theory	Ideas and philosophy
Chausson, 1855–99	Brunetière, *Histoire et littérature* (1884–6)	
Elgar, 1857–1934 (*Enigma Variations*, 1899; *Dream of Gerontius*, 1900; *Violin Concerto*, 1910)	Faguet, *Le XVIIe siècle* (1885) Montégut, *Écrivains modernes de l'Angleterre* (1885–92) Lemaître, *Les Contemporains* (1885–99)	
Leoncavallo, 1858–1919 (*Pagliacci*, 1892)	Bourget, *Nouveaux essais de psychologie contemporaine* (1886) Vogüé, *Le Roman russe* (1886) Ghil, *Traité du verbe* (1886)	Berthelot, *Science et philosophie* (1886) Huxley, *Science and Morals* (1886) Nietzsche, *Jenseits von Gut und Böse* (1886)
Puccini, 1858–1924 (*Manon Lescaut*, 1893; *La Bohème*, 1896; *Tosca*, 1900; *Madame Butterfly*, 1904)		
Seurat, 1859–90 ('La Grande Jatte', 1886)	Faguet, *Le XIXe siècle* (1887) Montégut, *Mélanges critiques* (1887) *Le Manifeste des Cinq* (1887)	Nietzsche, *Zur Genealogie der Moral* (1887)
Albéniz, 1860–1909	Leconte de Lisle, *Éloge de Victor Hugo* (1887)	
Mahler, 1860–1911	Maupassant's preface ('Le Roman') to *Pierre et Jean* (1888)	
Sickert, 1860–1942	Nietzsche, *Der Fall Wagner* (1888) Hennequin, *La Critique scientifique* (1888)	
Steer, 1860–1942	France, *La Vie littéraire* (1888–92) Lemaître, *Impressions de théâtre* (1888–1920)	

History	French literature	English literature
Construction of the Eiffel Tower, 1889	Barrès, *Un Homme libre* (1889) Bourget, *Le Disciple* (1889) Maeterlinck, *Serres chaudes* (1889)	Jerome, *Three Men in a Boat* (1889)
	Villiers de l'Isle Adam, *Axël* (1890) France, *Thaïs* (1890) Zola, *La Bête humaine* (1890) Verhaeren, *Les Flambeaux noirs* (1890) Claudel, *Tête d'Or* (1890)	Kipling, *Plain Tales from the Hills* (1890)
	Zola, *L'Argent* (1891) Barrès, *Le Jardin de Bérénice* (1891) Huysmans, *Là-bas* (1891) Gide, *Les Cahiers d'André Walter* (1891) Moréas, *Le Pèlerin passionné* (1891)	Wilde, *The Picture of Dorian Gray* (1891) Hardy, *Tess of the d'Urbervilles* (1891)
Pope Leo XIII orders French catholics to accept the Republic, 1892 The Panama Scandal, 1892	Maeterlinck, *Pelléas et Mélisande* (1892) Zola, *La Débâcle* (1892)	Kipling, *Barrack-room Ballads* (1892) Wilde, *Lady Windermere's Fan* (1892) Yeats, *The Countess Cathleen* (1892)
Franco-Russian Alliance, 1893	Samain, *Au jardin de l'infante* (1893) Heredia, *Les Trophées* (1893) Zola, *Le Docteur Pascal* (1893) Sardou, *Madame Sans-Gêne* (1893) France, *La Rôtisserie de la Reine Pédauque* (1893)	Wilde, *A Woman of No Importance* (1893) Pinero, *The Second Mrs. Tanqueray* (1893)
Casimir-Périer French President, 1894	France, *Le Lys rouge* (1894)	Kipling, *The Jungle Book* (1894)

Painting and music	Criticism and aesthetic theory	Ideas and philosophy
Ensor, 1860-1949	Pater, *Appreciations* (1889)	Nietzsche, *Die Götzendämmerung* (1889)
Charpentier, 1860-1956 (*Louise*, 1900)		
MacDowell, 1861-1908	Faguet, *Le XVIIIe siècle* (1890)	Renan, *L'Avenir de la science* (publ. 1890; written 1848)
Maillol, 1861-1944	Brunetière, *L'Évolution des genres dans l'histoire de la littérature* (1890)	
Debussy, 1862-1918 (*Prélude à l'après-midi d'un faune*, 1894)	Faguet, *Questions de théâtre* (1890-8)	
	Shaw, *The Quintessence of Ibsenism* (1891)	Morris, *News from Nowhere* (1891)
Delius, 1862-1934	Howells, *Criticism and Fiction* (1891)	Husserl, *Philosophie der Arithmetik* (1891)
German, 1862-1936		
Signac, 1863-1935		
Munch, 1863-1944		
Mascagni, 1863-1945 (*Cavalleria rusticana*, 1890)		Bradley, *Appearance and Reality* (1893)
Toulouse-Lautrec, 1864-1902		Stephen, *An Agnostic's Apology* (1893)
Sérusier, 1864-1927		Huxley, *Ethics and Evolution* (1893)
Vuillard, 1864-1940		
	Croce, *La Critica letteraria* (1894)	

History	French literature	English literature
Condemnation of Captain Dreyfus for treason (1894) and subsequent Dreyfus Affair, 1894–1906	Renard, *Poil de Carotte* (1894) Huysmans, *En Route* (1894) Feydeau, *L'Hôtel du libre échange* (1894) Zola, *Les Trois Villes* (1894–8)	Moore, *Esther Waters* (1894)
Founding of the Conféderation Générale du Travail, 1895 Félix Faure French President, 1895 Lumière brothers invent cinematograph, 1895	Gide, *Paludes* (1895) Verhaeren, *Les Villes tentaculaires* (1895) Leconte de Lisle, *Derniers poèmes* (posth. publ. 1895)	Crane, *The Red Badge of Courage* (1895) Wells, *The Time Machine* (1895) Kipling, *The Second Jungle Book* (1895) Wilde, *The Importance of being Earnest* (1895) Yeats, *Poems* (1895) Conrad, *Almayer's Folly* (1895)
France annexes Madagascar, 1896	Valéry, *La Soirée avec Monsieur Teste* (1896) Jarry, *Ubu Roi* (1896) Louÿs, *Aphrodite* (1896)	Hardy, *Jude the Obscure* (1896) Conrad, *An Outcast of the Islands* (1896)
Fire at the Bazar de la Charité, 1897	Rostand, *Cyrano de Bergerac* (1897) Barrès, *Les Déracinés* (1897) Vielé-Griffin, *La Clarté de vie* (1897) Bloy, *La Femme pauvre* (1897) Régnier, *Jeux rustiques et divins* (1897) Péguy, *Jeanne d'Arc* (1897) Gide, *Les Nourritures terrestres* (1897)	James, *The Spoils of Poynton* (1897) James, *What Maisie Knew* (1897)
Discovery of radium by the Curies, 1898 Fashoda incident, 1898	Samain, *Aux flancs du vase* (1898) Huysmans, *La Cathédrale* (1898)	Conrad, *The Nigger of the Narcissus* (1898) Wilde, *The Ballad of Reading Gaol* (1898)

Painting and music	Criticism and aesthetic theory	Ideas and philosophy
Richard Strauss, 1864–1949 (*Don Juan*, 1889; *Tod und Verklärung*, 1889; *Till Eulenspiegel*, 1895; *Ein Heldenleben*, 1899; *Salomé*, 1905; *Der Rosenkavalier*, 1911)	Lanson, *Histoire de la littérature française* (1894) Faguet, *Le XVIᵉ siècle* (1894)	
Sibelius, 1865–1957 (*First Symphony*, 1898; *Finlandia*, 1899; *Violin Concerto*, 1903)	Valéry, *Introduction à la méthode de Léonard de Vinci* (1895) Wyzewa, *Nos maîtres* (1895)	Tarde, *La Logique sociale* (1895) Durkheim, *Les Règles de la méthode sociologique* (1895) Nietzsche, *Der Antichrist* (1895)
Dukas, 1865–1935 (*L'Apprenti sorcier*, 1897)	Ricardou, *La Critique littéraire* (1896) Gourmont, *Le Livre des masques* (1896)	Bergson, *Matière et mémoire* (1896) Pareto, *Cours d'économie politique* (1896)
Busoni, 1866–1924 Satie, 1866–1925	Kahn's preface to *Premiers poèmes* (1897) Mallarmé, *Divagations* (1897)	Janet, *Principes de métaphysique et de psychologie* (1897) Durkheim, *Le Suicide* (1897) Berthelot, *Science et morale* (1897) Seignobos, *Introduction aux études historiques* (1897)
Kandinsky, 1866–1944	Brunetière, *L'Art et la morale* (1898) Gourmont, *Le Deuxième Livre des masques* (1898)	Tarde, *La Criminalité comparée* (1898)

History	French literature	English literature
	Van Lerberghe, *Entre-visions* (1898)	James, *The Turn of the Screw* (1898)
	Jammes, *De l'Angélus de l'aube à l'angélus du soir* (1898)	Wells, *The War of the Worlds* (1898)
		Shaw, *Plays: Pleasant and Unpleasant* (1898)
Loubet French President, 1899	Gide, *Le Prométhée mal enchaîné* (1899)	
Waldeck-Rousseau Ministry, 1899–1905	Moréas, *Les Stances* (1899–1901)	
	Zola, *Les Quatre Évangiles* (1899–1903)	

Painting and music	Criticism and aesthetic theory	Ideas and philosophy
	Tolstoy, *What is Art?* (1898)	
Granados, 1867–1916		
	Holz, *Die Revolution der Lyrik* (1899)	
Bonnard, 1867–1947		

Index

Action Française, 178; new nationalism institutionalized in, 176; Maurras leader of, 177.

Ampère, André-Marie (1775-1836), 2.

Anouilh, Jean, 78.

Art for Art's sake, and the English, 17; unsatisfactory, 18; Gautier protagonist of, 33; critical work on, 34; Flaubert and, 41; and poetry, 140.

Augier, Émile (1820-89), 78-82; his social comedies, 67; to be viewed in context of Second Empire, 75; critical works on, 83.

  Works: *Ceinture dorée*, 81; *La Contagion*, 82; *Les Effrontés*, 81, 82; *Le Fils de Giboyer*, 82; *Gabrielle*, 78; *Le Gendre de M. Poirier*, 79-80, 82; *Les Lionnes pauvres*, 82; *Madame Caverlet*, 82; *Le Mariage d'Olympe*, 80.

Ballad form, 28.

Balzac, Honoré de (1799-1850), and scientific progress, 3; permits subjective realism, 40; his programme compared with Zola's scientific aim, 155; Zola's *L'Assommoir* compared with *César Birotteau*, 158.

Banville, Théodore Faullain de (1823-91), 152 n.; and the official alexandrine, 139.

Barbey d'Aurevilly, Jules-Amédée (1808-89), Catholicism an aesthetic convention in fiction of, 179.

  Works: *Les Diaboliques*, 179; *Un Prêtre marié*, 179.

Barrès, Maurice (1862-1923), a *croyant non-croyant*, 12; and nationalism, 176, 177, 187; significance of Catholicism to, 179; Péguy and, 185; his early work, 186; a reactionary, 188; his prophylactic against fever of change, 189; France's patriotism and that of, 193; biographical note on, 195; editions of his works, 196; recommended works on, 197.

  Works: *L'Appel au soldat*, 187; *La Colline inspirée*, 187; *Les Déracinés*, 187; *Gréco ou le secret de Tolède*, 187; *Un Homme libre*, 186, 187; *Le Jardin de Bérénice*, 186; *Leurs Figures*, 187; *Sous l'œil des barbares*, 186.

Barrière, Théodore (1823-77), concentrates on surfaces of social life, 67.

Baudelaire, Charles (1821-67), 140; Gautier and, 19, 21, 22-3; and the 'scientific' in art, 40; subjective realism of, 42; understands Flaubert, 63; Verlaine's technique derived from, 86-7; Rimbaud and, 104; on woman, 119; symbolists and, 136; his tendency towards private language, 141; Mallarmé's early poems influenced by, 142.

  Works: *Les Fleurs du mal*, 19, 136, 142; *Le Spleen de Paris*, 108; 'Crépuscule du soir', 86; 'Voyage', 31.

Becque, Henri (1837-99), his studies of manners, 67; *Les Corbeaux*, 68.

Benda, Julien (1867-1956), 94, 95; *La France byzantine*, 100.

Bentham, Jeremy (1748-1832), 6.

Berger, John, *A Fortunate Man*, 48.

Bergson, Henri-Louis (1859-1941), Idealist, 1.

Bernanos, Georges (1888-1948), 182.

Bernard, Claude (1813-78), 2; and scientific physiology, 9; Zola and, 41.

Bert, Paul (1833-86), 192; educational reformer, 174; neo-Kantian ethical idealism animates work of, 192.

Bloy, Léon (1846-1917), and Catholic literary revival, 11, 12; his writings and Catholicism, 177-8; pillories the Republic, 178; importance of poverty in his view of Christian life, 179; and Huysmans's religious observance, 179-80; restores religious experience to fiction, 180-1; the mystique of poverty, 181; on the fire at the Bazar de la Charité, 181; his significance, 181-2; biographical note on, 194; editions of his works, 195; recommended biography and studies of, 197.

  Works: *Le Désespéré*, 180-1; *La Femme pauvre*, 181.

Blum, Léon (1872-1950), and Dreyfus Affair, 189.

Bouilhet, Louis (1821-69), critical of Flaubert's *Tentation de Saint Antoine*, 66; on women, 119; *Fossiles*, 3.

Bourget, Paul (1852-1935), Taine and, 9; and Catholic literary revival, 11, 178; and scientific progress and Catholicism, 12; and middle-class youth, 178; significance of Catholicism to, 179; his interest in the rational mind as foundation for morality, 190-1; biographical note on, 195; edition of his works, 196; recommended works on, 197.

Works: *Le Disciple*, 12, 191; *L'Étape*, 191.

Brecht, Bertholt Eugen Friedrich (1898-1956), 137.

Brieux, Eugène (1858-1932), his social drama, 68.

Brogan, Denis William, and Barrès, 188.

Brunetière, Ferdinand (1849-1906), and 'idealist reaction', 11; a *croyant non-croyant*, 12-13; and Maupassant, 117.

Camus, Albert (1913-60), Maupassant compared to, 121, 124.

Capote, Truman, *In Cold Blood*, 48.

Carlyle, Thomas (1795-1881), seen as an idealist, 11.

Carnot, Nicolas-Léonard-Sadi (1796-1832), 2.

Catholicism, Catholic revival, 1, 11, 12, 177-8; Renan's 'religion of the Ideal' and, 8; attitude of intellectuals to, 12-13; recommended works on Catholic revival, 16, 196; Verlaine converted to, 100, 111-12; Rimbaud's death-bed conversion to, 113, 114; and youth, 178; literature of Catholic revival, 178-83; Bloy and, 179-82; Claudel and, 182-3; Péguy and, 183, 184; and Freemasonry, 190.

Cézanne, Paul (1839-1906), 174.

Champfleury, *nom de plume* of Jules-François-Félix Husson (1821-89), and 'triumph' of Realism, 39; his idea of the novelist's duty, 40-1; prefers *roman réaliste*, 46; biographical note on, 49.

Chénier, André (1762-94), 98.

Christianity, nineteenth-century decline of, 2; Saint-Simon advocates 'new' Christianity, 4; nineteenth-century hopes of replacing by science, 10; Bourget's dilemma over, 12-13; Leconte de Lisle's attitude to, 25; collapse of, 37; Rimbaud's

attitude to, 102-3, 109; French nationalism and, 177; Péguy disclaims ties with, 184.

Claudel, Paul-Louis-Charles-Marie (1868-1955), and Catholic literary revival, 11; and Catholicism, 12, 14, 178; and the drama, 67; concerned with relationship of the human to the divine, 182-3; biographical note on, 194-5; editions of his works, 196; critical essays on, 197.

Works: *L'Annonce faite à Marie*, 182-3; *L'Échange*, 182; *Partage de midi*, 182; *Tête d'Or*, 182; *La Ville*, 182.

Clemenceau, Georges (1841-1929), 174.

Cocteau, Jean, 78.

Comte, Auguste (1798-1857), 1; his influence, 4-5; his *loi des trois états*, 5-6; and science of sociology, 6-7; moving towards 'scientism', 7; and science and Christianity, 10; his epistemological 'realism' questioned, 11; de Lisle and, 11; his ideas challenged by subjective idealism, 14; biographical note, 15; recommended works on, 15.

Works: *Catéchisme positiviste*, 15; *Cours de philosophie positive*, 5, 6, 7, 15; *Système de politique positive*, 15.

Courbet, Gustave (1819-77), and Realism, 39.

Cournot, Antoine-Augustin (1801-77), Neo-Criticist, 1.

Cousin, Victor (1792-1867), 2 and n.

Curel, François de (1854-1928), and 'idealist reaction', 11; and theatre of ideas, 68.

Curie, Pierre (1859-1906) and Marie (1867-1934), 173.

Cuvier, Georges (properly Léopold-Chrétien-Frédéric-Dagobert; 1769-1832), 2.

Dante Alighieri (1265-1321), Heredia's debt to, 31.

Debussy, Claude Achille (1862-1918), 'L'Après-midi d'un faune', 137, 173.

Decadents, the, and alexandrines, 139; decadent style of poetry, 139-40.

Degas, (Hilaire Germain) Edgar (1834-1917), 175.

Diaghilev, Sergei Pavlovich (1872-1929), 137.

Drama of nineteenth century, two conventions in, 67; social drama, 67-8.

Dreyfus, Alfred (c. 1859-1935), convicted of treason, 175.

Dreyfus Affair, the, significance of, 175-6;

class novels more symbolical, 164-6;
opts out of serious portrayal of politics,
166; effect of liaison with Jeanne Rozerot
on his work, 169; the working-class novels
the best, 169; his obsession with violence
and the sexual, 169-70; his pessimism,
170; and the nineteenth-century predicament, 170-1; biographical note on,
172; editions of his works, 172; critical
works on, 172; believes in Catholic plot
over Dreyfus Affair, 190.

Works: *L'Argent*, 168, 171; *L'Assommoir*, 155-60, 161; *La Bête humaine*,
166-7; *La Débâcle*, 155-6, 168; *Le
Docteur Pascal*, 168-9; *Germinal*, 155,
160-4, 166, 168, 170; *La Joie de vivre*,
167; *Nana*, 164-5; *Pot-Bouille*, 164, 165-
6; *Les Quatre Évangiles*, 169; *Les Rougon-
Macquart*, 41, 155, 169; *La Terre*, 156,
166, 168, 170; *Thérèse Raquin*, 39; *Les
Trois Villes*, 169; *Le Ventre de Paris*, 163,
166.